How to Be a Successful
COMPUTER
CONSULTANT

How to Be a Successful
COMPUTER
CONSULTANT

by
Alan R. Simon
Computer Education and Consulting

McGraw-Hill Book Company

*New York   St. Louis   San Francisco   Auckland   Bogotá   Hamburg
Johannesburg   London   Madrid   Mexico   Montreal   New Delhi
Panama   Paris   São Paulo   Singapore   Sydney   Tokyo   Toronto*

Library of Congress Cataloging in Publication Data
Simon, Alan R.
  How to be a successful computer consultant.

  (A Byte book)
  Bibliography: p.
  Includes index.
  1.Business consultants. 2.Electronic data
processing consultants. I.Title. II.Series: Byte
books.
HD69.C6S58 1985   001.64′068   84-25012
ISBN 0-07-057296-8 (pbk.)

1234567890   DOC/DOC   898765

ISBN 0-07-057296-8

The editors for this book were Tyler G. Hicks and Vivian Koenig,
the design supervisor was Mark E. Safran and the designer was
M.R.P. Design. The production supervisor was Teresa F. Leaden.
It was set in Century Schoolbook by University Graphics, Inc.

Printed and bound by R.R. Donnelley & Sons Company.

Part opening illustrations by Joanna Roy.

Contents

Preface

In November 1982, after reading several magazine articles extolling the potential rewards of computer consulting, I began investigating that profession as a supplement to my U.S. Air Force programming job. Chief among my reasons were (1) staying abreast of the microcomputer explosion, (2) supplementing my Air Force income, and (3) allowing for more flexible future employment options.

Over the next year I acquired a collection of books (as well as numerous periodicals), dealing with small businesses, consulting, and microcomputers, that supplemented my already bulging library. The lack of one comprehensive, concise reference source necessitated my massive search.

During the planning and growth stage of my business, Computer Education and Consulting, I often wished that just such a comprehensive guide existed for the computer consulting profession to aid the research process. This book is an outgrowth of that desire. I have attempted to combine in one volume all of the major topics that I found were critical in building a computer consulting practice.

Since, as I mentioned, information was gleaned from many sources (most of which are complete books themselves), it is impossible to cover every topic in exhaustive detail. Some subjects, such as the legal aspects of software writing, are merely summarized, with references to places where more detailed information can be obtained. If every topic had been covered to the degree they were in their original form, this book would probably have been titled *The Encyclopedia of Computer Consulting* and comprised several volumes!

Nevertheless, the subjects are covered in sufficient detail for this book to be both a tutorial and a comprehensive reference source for anyone considering a career in computer consulting. Since two chapters are devoted to contract and commercial software development, respectively, this book will also be useful to someone who doesn't wish to become a consultant but rather a software developer. Using the business and organizational material which is critical to building and managing a business, the reader can choose exactly what he or she wishes to provide to the public and pursue that avenue.

Much of the material is supplemented (either stated or implicitly) by personal knowledge learned through trial and error, especially the advantages and disadvantages of pursuing a consulting career on a part-time basis (and writing a book on top of that!).

Much time and effort has been devoted to making this book reflect the promise of its title. I sincerely believe that a computer professional, or anyone who possesses the skill and devotion and is willing to put forth the effort required to build a successful consulting practice, can do so by following the guidelines presented in the following chapters. Again, when I feel additional information is required for a more complete understanding of a topic, I have cited comprehensive references.

The book is divided into three major portions. Part 1 discusses the planning stages and early life of your consulting practice. Part 2 presents a detailed look at the major products and services your consulting firm will likely offer. Finally, Part 3 concludes with subjects of continuing concern after your practice is established, including management of your business operations and planning for the future.

No author's preface would be complete without the appropriate expressions of gratitude. Therefore, I would like to thank the following people: Sandy Davis, without whose typing and editing assistance you would not be reading these words now; my business partners, Ted Davis and Michael LaFollette, for reviewing portions of the manuscript and putting up with my preoccupation with this book; my brother, Jordan, for loaning his flexible name to my fictional consultant in the book; and finally, my parents, Bernie and Sandra (whose names have also been used in the text), for instilling in me the drive for success that was so critical in conceiving and finishing this book.

ALAN R. SIMON

How to Be a Successful
COMPUTER
CONSULTANT

PART 1

The Beginnings of Your Consulting Practice

CHAPTER 1

The Computer Consulting Profession

Since you are reading this book, you have probably entertained the idea of a career as a computer consultant, either on a part-time or on a full-time basis. The chapters of this book will address the many topics you need to be concerned with in starting and building a successful and profitable consulting career. First, however, we need to look at the characteristics of the computer consulting profession: why people use computer consultants, the consultant's role, what clients look for in a consultant, the characteristics and background a successful consultant should have, and what you should expect as a consultant.

Why Be a Consultant?

The first question you may be asking is, Why should I become a computer consultant? The best answer I can give is that as a consultant you will find yourself facing challenges and opportunities that would usually be unavailable to a person working in a large corporation, at least for a long while. Your income, growth, and reputation are dependent on a combination of your own business skills, technical expertise in your specialty field (in this case, computers), and dedication. You will see that your business skills will be nearly as important as your computer skills. As a consultant, you are your own boss; no one except you will determine the projects and contracts you work on. However, your computer work is accompanied by the added responsibility of managing and budgeting projects and interfacing with clients.

In other words, the computer consulting business offers you myriad opportunities that you probably wouldn't face until much later in a traditional computer career (i.e., one where you start as a programmer, advance to systems analyst or project leader, and eventually, if you are lucky, become an information systems director for a large corporation). Again, these opportunities are accompanied by increased responsibility.

Why People Use Computer Consultants

The importance of processing information in all areas of business, government, and the home has become increasingly evident in recent years. There has been much concern recently regarding the quality of education that students receive at all levels, from elementary school through college. Many schools are attempting to increase the accessibility of computer equipment to students. It will be several years, however, until the general population of the United States (or world, for that matter) is familiar and competent with computers.

In the meantime, the reliance of business and government on information processing increases. This has caused a shortage of qualified programmers, analysts, and other computer professionals in the business world. Periodic estimates of those occupations with the most job opportunities over the next decade or for the rest of the century usually include these professions. How are managers supposed to cope with this lack of qualified computer professionals in their organizations in the interim?

One way is to use a computer consultant. Consider for a moment the cost of employing one computer programmer on a full-time basis. Currently, the average entry-level programmer earns $15,000 as a minimum (most earn far more), and experienced programmers are compensated in the $30,000 to $40,000 range. Added to the employee's salary are paid vacations, unemployment insurance, social security (FICA) taxes, and benefits like health and life insurance.

Additionally, many programmers attend professional seminars, continuing-education classes, and other professional development courses, often at company expense. It is easy to see how *each* computer programmer or analyst on a company's staff may cost up to $50,000 per year.

An organization may be able to justify the expense of one or more full-time programmers through a cost-benefit analysis; there might be enough computer-related work providing tangible and intangible benefits to the firm that more than compensates for the salaries and benefits.

However, assume we are dealing with a small employment agency, staffed by eight employees in addition to the owner, Mr. Johnson. Facing both an increase in clients and a backlog in processing clients' requests, Mr. Johnson decides to purchase a computer to assist in matching up hiring companies with job seekers. Since no one in the company has a good working knowledge of computer system selection and implementation, Mr. Johnson is faced with having to hire a programmer or systems analyst to analyze the company's information needs, select hardware and software, and implement the system (which includes training the employees).

Once these tasks are completed, which may be from 1 to 6 months from the start of the computerization effort, Mr. Johnson is then faced with maintaining a relatively expensive employee on the firm's payroll, even though it may be several months or years before any further efforts are required from the programmer. It is normally considered a bad business practice to hire someone as a full-time employee for a short period of time and then fire him or her once the required task is completed.

Mr. Johnson's most desirable option is to hire a programmer or analyst on a *temporary* basis until the computerized employment system is implemented. The most common type of temporary computer professional is the consultant. In addition to paying for professional computer services only when they are needed, Mr. Johnson (or any other person utilizing a computer consultant's services) realizes several other important financial benefits. Since the consultant is not a full-time employee of the hiring firm, no unemployment insurance, social security taxes, or vacation pay needs to be spent by the contracting organization. In addition, it is the consultant's own responsibility to stay current with computer topics by attending seminars and courses. Therefore, hiring a consultant is often advantageous to a company with short-term or sporadic needs for professional computer services.

Another reason for a client to use computer consulting services is that the computer industry is rapidly evolving into a number of subspecialties, in a manner reminiscent of the legal and medical fields. There are still generalists, but a growing number of programmers, consultants, and analysts are choosing to specialize in areas like local-area networks, database management systems, microcomputer operating systems, or another of the many possible alternatives. A client may employ several general-applications programmers, but the implementation of a local-area network might require additional expertise from someone specializing in communications. As we will discuss later in this chapter, the ever-increasing complexity of these subspecialties and the computer industry as a whole preclude true expertise in many different areas.

What Clients Look for in a Computer Consultant

When a person hires a computer consultant, he or she is looking for more than just technical expertise. If an individual or business representative is to commit funds to you in exchange for your services, you should possess the traits that make someone feel comfortable in what is likely a strange and foreboding world of computers. These traits include:

1. *Someone who understands the general principles of a client's business:* In order to propose a solution to a business's problem or opportunity, you need to understand the intricacies of a client's business. If you are hired to design a realtor's property management computer system, you must understand the unique characteristics of property management: what types of information are stored, how often this information is updated, and what reports are important to a property manager.

This is not to say that prior to your first meeting with your client you must know his or her business intimately; many businesses conduct their operations in a nonstandard manner or consider certain information more important than do similar businesses. You should, though, know generally what a "standard" business in that industry does and be able to discuss that business intelligently. Only when you understand these features can you successfully evaluate commercial software or design a new computer system for that industry.

2. *Someone who speaks the language of the business:* Your client will likely question your capabilities if you require a translation of every industry-specific acronym or term used. You probably won't know every such term, but you should be able to discuss business operations without saying "What does that mean?" every 5 minutes.

3. *Someone who doesn't use technical computer jargon:* Your client should not have to ask *you* for a translation every time you describe a computer topic related to his or her business. Your vocabulary should be purged of terms such as "reentrant," "coprocessor," "subroutine," "instruction set," and "virtual memory" when talking to your client.

If you must explain some of these computer concepts to your client, describe what you are talking about in English without delivering a 45-minute lecture about, for example, the miracles of virtual memory. Don't elaborate just to impress your clients with your technical knowledge; they are impressed by results, not jargon. Explain these subjects in terms of the benefit they provide for your client's particular business.

If it seems that you are making the effort to learn your client's business language *and* translate your computer jargon into a middle ground, you're right. Remember your client is paying you to perform several functions, one of which is to make computers more understandable and less threatening.

4. *Someone who proposes sensible, cost-effective solutions:* If a customer requires an application system to manage large data files and access the information quickly, a cassette-based computer system would obviously not be a sensible solution because of the relatively slow access time. Similarly, a client who needs a computer to manage several mailing lists and simplified accounting applications probably doesn't need a $15,000, 32-bit multiuser system with five workstations.

Remember that what is appropriate for one client may not necessarily be appropriate for another, even in similar circumstances. Two clients with a need for file and database management may require totally different levels of complexity in the database software, based on projected uses and access patterns of the data.

5. *Someone who appears to be a business person:* This doesn't mean that every meeting should be conducted in a three-piece suit. You should dress according to the "dress code" of your respective clients because they will feel more comfortable talking to someone who is similarly attired. A three-piece suit would probably be appropriate for a meeting with the branch manager of a large bank, but a sport coat and tie may be more in line for a meeting with a record store manager. The key is to be flexible but look professional. No matter how adept you may be in computer design and programming, blue jeans and a T-shirt will not draw the professional clientele that a successful consultant desires. You are not just locked in your den doing computer programming; you are representing your business to the public.

Characteristics and Background of a Successful Computer Consultant

As stated earlier, a successful computer consultant needs an appropriate mix of computer and business skills to build and manage a consulting firm. Additionally, certain personality traits and general skills tend to be characteristic of a successful consultant. In his book *Consulting: The Complete Guide to a Profitable Career,* Robert Kelley cites an Association of Management Consultants (AMC) study that lists essential attributes of successful consultants.[1] The most important appear to be

Ability to deal with people	Professional etiquette
Integrity	Self-confidence
Objectivity	Creativity
Problem-solving skills	Ambition
Written and verbal communications skills	

Other studies have cited variations of these characteristics, but these could be considered the minimum set of traits a consultant should possess.

A consultant must also be able to operate successfully in an environment of uncertainty. Since you are not a cog in the wheel of a giant corporation, you must be able to sleep at night knowing that your current project ends next week but a subsequent job has not been contracted for yet.

Another important attribute is learning from your mistakes. People working their way up through a large corporation are likely to have a mentor show them how to "play the game." Since your business is your own, your knowledge will come primarily from research and practical experience.

Not every idea you try will be a success; you must be able to analyze your actions and their results objectively and unemotionally to prevent repetition of errors.

A computer consultant's primary assets are his or her computer knowledge, of course. You are being hired as an expert in your field to analyze problems and opportunities for a client. Unless you can propose commonsense solutions to solve problems or exploit opportunities, you may quickly find yourself with a failing practice. The essential computer skills you should possess are:

1. *Demonstrated ability:* You must have the ability to analyze a company's business operations and successfully implement a computer-based solution to problems or opportunities. You need more than classroom theory in systems analysis and design; you should have initiated, developed, and completed a computer system design project.

2. *In-depth knowledge:* You should possess an in-depth knowledge of your segment of the computer industry and a fairly complete understanding of the computer industry as a whole. If you specialize in single-user microcomputers you must stay up to date about new products, peripheral devices, and new technology. You should also know what is going on in other segments of the computer industry in order to provide a frame of reference for new products and services.

3. *Knowing where to find the answers:* I would be *very* skeptical of anyone claiming to know everything about database management, communications, operating systems, hardware, and software (among other topics). The technical aspects of computing are so complex and numerous that it's impossible to be an expert in everything. Additionally, you will need to learn much about the industries you'll be designing for.

The next chapter discusses how to specialize your consulting practice to maximize its success (and avoid driving yourself crazy!). Even with specialization you will often find yourself facing a question or problem and not immediately knowing the answer.

The key is not to try and know everything, but know where to find the answers. Chapter 14 discusses books and periodicals with which you should be familiar. As long as you know what direction to begin an information search you are halfway to solving problems facing you.

4. *Familiarity with hardware requirements:* You must know about the different classes of hardware available (single-user, single-function; single-user, multitasking; multiuser, multitasking, etc.) and their relative advantages and disadvantages in different implementations. You should be able to conduct a capacity analysis to analyze a client's prospective user requirements (number of terminals or workstations), internal memory capacity required for all applications, and secondary storage requirements—floppy disk, hard disk, how much storage. Chapter 9 discusses the world of hardware.

5. *Familiarity with software:* You should know what software is currently available (or is being developed) commercially for both the general computer user in your industry segment (for example, new microcomputer operating systems or new releases of existing operating systems) and for any industry you are specializing in (real estate, medical, legal, etc.).

You should be able to analyze existing software for ease of use, freedom from bugs, reliability, expandability, and execution speed. It is also helpful to have an understanding of the relative trade-offs among the computer languages used to develop software (assembler, BASIC, PASCAL, etc.) to help analyze existing software or contract for developing new programs.

6. *Programming:* While technically not required among a consultant's skills, a good programming background is helpful in understanding the design philosophy behind the software and systems you evaluate. More importantly, you won't be forced to either refuse or subcontract projects requiring new programming or maintenance of existing software.

As has been stressed, your business knowledge and skills are critical for the growth and survival of your business. Unlike a large corporation, a single-member consulting firm doesn't have a marketing director, chief financial officer, accounting staff, personnel director, and legal officer. *You* accomplish these tasks.

Obviously, you may find yourself contracting for outside assistance in certain areas; your accountant will probably prepare your tax return, and your attorney may handle incorporation or other complicated tasks. However, you don't want to have to run to your outside advisers every time a business decision needs to be made; they are professionals just as you are, and command compensation that is forbidding for a beginning business on a regular basis. Therefore your business skills should include:

1. *Marketing:*   This is probably the most crucial. Without the ability to determine and analyze a target market, develop products and services to meet the market's known and projected needs, choose a competitive and profitable price, and make your market aware of the availability of these services, the best computer analysis skills, business background, and personality traits won't make you successful in your consulting venture. You must find the most appropriate and cost-effective means of advertising and distribution.

2. *Finance and accounting:*   You should have a basic understanding of different types of costs, budgeting and forecasting, and projecting capital requirements, and you should be able to manage at least a simplified set of income and expense books. As your business grows, you should know the relative trade-offs of financing sources such as banks and venture or seed capital firms. And of course, you must determine an appropriate fee structure for your services.

3. *Business law:*   As a consultant you will be party to many types of contracts. You should know how to protect both yourself and your products (software, books, etc.) from liability and infringement, as well as how to develop contracts that are fair to your client.

4. *Personnel:*   When your practice expands you may find yourself hiring other consultants to meet the increasing workload and administrative help (office manager, secretarial, and clerical workers). You need to know how to manage and motivate people to achieve maximum performance (which doesn't mean working everyone 80 hours per week, either), what compensation strategies to provide (salaries, stock options, partnerships, bonuses), and, if necessary, how to fire someone.

5. *General management:*   Finance, marketing, accounting, law, and personnel functions don't operate in isolated environments; they all interact very closely with one another. For example, as you prepare your business plan (Chapter 6), your financial projections must be supported by your marketing analysis and your available resources.

Who Should Not Be a Consultant

So far, I've pointed out many of the attractions of the consulting profession along with the associated responsibilities, skills, etc. You should now examine your own attributes to see if you should seriously consider a consulting career. Everyone's situation is different, of course. The guidelines presented in the previous section are not set in concrete; you should, however, give serious thought to waiting on your consulting career if you:

1. *Have little experience:*   If you have just a basic "textbook" understanding of computers with little practical experience in system design and implementation, you should probably spend some time working as a programmer or systems analyst to gain more practical experience prior to trying it on your own. You might work as a subcontract programmer for a local consultant's major project, learning the business from observation and questions.

The real world is full of considerations that are covered lightly or not at all in an educational environment, such as catastrophe management (What happens if a fire destroys the computer? Where should backup data be stored? How often should data be backed up?) and user acceptance (the so-called computerphobiacs need to be assured of the ease of use and nonthreat of a new computer system).

As you gain experience, try to handle a couple of contract programming or design jobs part-time for friends, family, or business acquaintances. This may give you a clue as to how competent you would be consulting on a regular basis.

2. *Have insufficient business knowledge or aptitude:*   Many graduates of computer science departments associated with engineering colleges or independent programs filled their electives and core courses with engineering, liberal arts, or other general-studies classes. A person who graduated from a business college computer program likely attended courses in marketing, finance, accounting, and other business topics. While the computer science major may arguably be more technically adept at the intricacies of hardware operating systems, and similar topics, the information systems graduate may have a stronger combination of the business and computer skills required of a successful consultant.

Additionally, some people just don't have the aptitude or desire to manage a business, which, again, is what a consulting firm is. Though the lack of aptitude may just be a lack of knowledge, even the most technically qualified person should possess the minimum skills listed earlier in this chapter before venturing out on his or her own.

Someone who desperately desires to try consulting but doesn't feel qualified to manage the business end of the profession may consider joining an existing firm in a nonmanagerial capacity prior to (if ever) setting out on his or her own. The computer science undergraduate (or hobbyist who has become very technically adept) might consider pursuing a Master of Business Administration (MBA) degree to acquire the necessary skills.

3. *Feel uncomfortable with a lack of job security:* Someone who does not like to take risks may only feel secure working 8 hours per day, 5 days per week with a regular biweekly paycheck. As a consultant you will likely face periods where no matter what you do or how much you advertise, no one seeks your services. Unless you have the commitment and dedication to stay with it until things turn around and can put up with living or past revenue on your savings, your discomfort is likely to make your life miserable.

4. *Take setbacks as personal defeats:* I've seen many "sure" contracts suddenly cancelled. You must be able to shrug off each setback and look ahead, learning from any mistakes you may have made. Don't view each bad turn of events as a personal loss.

Summary

This chapter has presented an overview of the consulting business. While it is a profession with virtually unlimited opportunities and rewards for the person willing to extend the effort and make the sacrifices, many additional responsibilities that the ordinary computer professional doesn't face now become major concerns. Attributes and backgrounds of successful consultants were viewed, along with an overview of client-customer relations. After reading this chapter, you should have a clear understanding of the computer consulting profession and whether or not you should seriously consider entering the business. Succeeding chapters will discuss many of these topics in further detail.

Let's now meet someone who will travel through the subsequent chapters with us. Bernie Jordan is a computer programmer-analyst with the local city attorney's office. He began his current job after receiving his master's degree in information systems from the State University College of Business.

During his first 3 years with the city attorney's office he was involved in a number of projects, including membership in the City Automation Task Force, a group whose assignment was to modernize data entry and information access needs of city offices through a personal computer network.

Upon completion of the project, Bernie expected to be promoted to a project manager position. However, due to legislature-imposed budget cuts, a projected system which would have connected the local personal computer network with the state attorney general's system (as well as with other nearby cities' computer systems) was postponed indefinitely, and Bernie has spent the last 2 years primarily performing systems maintenance on the network and other city systems. Increasingly frustrated by the lack of challenge in his job despite the rather comfortable salary, he gave serious thought to leaving his job and joining the computer division of a large consumer goods manufacturer.

Two features in a popular business magazine caused Bernie to reconsider. The first dealt with the growing need for organizations' personal computers to be able to communicate with each other and with the company mainframes and minis. The second mentioned the growing role of computer consultants in helping businesses stay informed about the quickly changing world of small business computers; even experienced data processing professionals were confused by the growing number of different personal computers and the relative trade-offs.

Thinking about his own experience, Bernie contemplated entering the computer consulting profession. Since both his undergraduate and master's degrees had been in information systems programs from business colleges, he had a strong background in the financial, accounting, marketing, and general business principles necessary to start and operate a business. With 5 years in the computer industry plus two university degrees, Bernie felt that he had sufficient experience in many areas of computing, particularly in the field of small business computers and communications networks.

Bernie had always been very self-motivated, having held several part-time jobs while in college despite a heavy course load. He also enjoyed a challenge, and starting his own consulting business would be the greatest challenge he had faced.

End Notes

1. Robert E. Kelley, *Consulting: The Complete Guide to a Profitable Career*, Scribner's, New York, 1981, pp. 15–16.

CHAPTER 2

Planning Your Services

Once you have decided to try the consulting profession, your next task is determining what products and services you will offer. This is extremely important, since you must have an idea of what your business is based on before you can market your services and attract clients. You need to consider your areas of expertise, your own business connections that can lead to your first contracts, the competition you will face, and on what scale your services will be offered.

Choosing Your Services

As a computer consultant you can base your business on one or more product or service offerings. You may analyze the information system needs of your clients and recommend complete computer systems, both hardware and software, to meet these needs. You may also specialize in recommending software for clients' existing computer systems. If your programming skills are particularly sharp, you can emphasize contract programming for clients who want customized software.

These services are what could be considered the traditional computer consulting services. Additionally, you could build your business around seminar and training offerings, specializing in educating users about specific hardware and/or software.

A good computer consultant should be adept at as many of the afore-mentioned services as possible; the more services you offer, the greater your potential client base (and revenues) will be. As a beginning consultant, especially when starting alone, you should choose one or two areas and stress them as your primary product offering. You need to build your expertise in whatever services you offer; as mentioned in the last chapter, a dynamic field like computers requires continual learning and reeducation on the part of anyone who wishes to stay on top of the underlying technology, as well as the products in the marketplace.

Your goal should be to choose one or two closely related services and build your business around them. For example, you may provide software advice and write programs for customers if no suitable packages can be found. Or you may build a series of educational computer seminars coupled with in-house training for client companies.

This is not to say that you shouldn't accept any contracts outside of your beginning specialty area; you may find that after several profitable jobs in a side area you switch your service and marketing emphasis to a potentially more profitable area.

Later chapters in this book cover commercial software development, books, and magazine articles. As with all of the previously mentioned services, a good consultant who wishes to be respected in the computer field should consider writing (and software writing, if qualified). However, these are "supplemental features" to your consulting business.

If the majority of your revenue comes from commercial software, you really can't be considered a consultant, since you are not providing services for clients (at least in the traditional consulting sense); you are now more of a software developer. Similarly, if most of your earnings come from books and magazine articles, you are really an author rather than a consultant.

Again, this is not to say that a consultant should not be a writer (either publications or software); I stated that a well-rounded consultant offers a wide range of expert services, and spreading your knowledge either through written materials or useful software provides services to your customers (or readers) just as the more traditional services do.

Additionally, the royalties from a book or published software package can provide the revenue streams (see Chapter 4) that balance the peaks and valleys in earnings that you may face with contract-based services.

How do you choose your mix of products and services? As stated earlier, one of your considerations should be your own areas of expertise.

If you have been primarily a programmer or systems analyst during your career in the computer field, you may want to work with analyzing information needs and designing computer systems to meet these needs. However, an instructor (college, university, or corporate) with little or no programming and design background might consider developing an educational seminar program coupled with sizable training contracts from independent businesses.

Finally, you should have a contingency plan available. You may design a seminar series based on training clients to use spreadsheet software. Two weeks before your first class is scheduled the local computer store offers a free spreadsheet–word processing class, with weekly meetings for the next 3 months.

Should you continue with your series and risk low attendance that is unable to cover your costs? Probably not. Should you give up your hopes of an independent consulting career? You won't have to if you have prepared for problems such as this. You may have a second series covering database software that could use much of the same material you have prepared (advertising copy, handouts, etc.) without too much revision. Your spreadsheet software program could be offered at a later date. The main point here is that you should always be prepared for the impossible, the unthinkable, and the unexpected, because *nothing* is impossible, unthinkable, or unexpected.

Choosing Your Applications Specialties

Just as you should concentrate on a manageable product and service line, you need to narrow the range of applications in which you will be an expert. One look at the *PC Clearinghouse,* a comprehensive software list, will convince you that it would be extremely difficult to know all the names of available software for more than a few applications areas, let alone be able to evaluate and recommend the same software. Also, each edition of most computer periodicals contains lists of new software, so the number of available packages increases each day.

While you may eventually expand into different applications areas (especially as your business grows and you subcontract work or hire employees) it is critical that your clients and you speak the same language when discussing their businesses. We saw in Chapter 1 that as a consultant, your role is to provide advice and expertise to help your clients solve their business problems and exploit their opportunities. If you don't thoroughly understand their businesses and the current software available, you won't be as helpful to them as you should be.

As with choosing your services, you should start your applications specialties with areas you know. For example, if you have spent several years working as a programmer in a large hospital you may specialize in medical software, encompassing billing, hospital management, nutritional analysis, diagnosis, and other subspecialties.

Choosing Your Hardware Specialty

Also important is choosing a class of hardware in which you will specialize. While this book is aimed toward microcomputer consultants, you should narrow your specialty even further. Just as specializing in more than a few services and applications is difficult, so is being an expert in more than one or two hardware classes.

Chapter 9 discusses the classes of hardware in more detail, but basically you should decide if you will specialize in single-user, single-tasking systems, single-user, multitasking machines, or larger multiuser, multitasking systems.

Be cautioned that even if most of your experience has been with minicomputers (DEC VAX, Data General Eclipse, Prime), many of the sites that would utilize machines of this price and power range are likely to have their own in-house programmers and analysts. In order to provide a successful market niche, you would have to specialize even further—for example, micro-mini communications between IBM PC and VAX. Your jobs in that case would likely be of longer duration and for larger sums due to the increased level of expertise (now you are providing consulting to computer people as opposed to noncomputer business people), but you will likely have fewer of them. The same is true, perhaps even more so, of mainframe computers. You would then probably find yourself working as more of a subcontractor, as with government systems.

Most small businesses employ fewer than 20 people and are more likely to have one or more microcomputers than a minicomputer.

Making the Decisions

As mentioned earlier, you should base your decisions about products and services, applications, and hardware on what you are familiar and experienced with. Chapter 5 will further discuss developing and analyzing target markets; however, you should realize that in addition to your experience there must be a need for your expertise in your chosen areas in order for you to be successful as a computer consultant.

If you are entering the consulting business with one or more partners, your experience in different areas will allow you more flexibility in choosing applications areas, a wider range of products and services, and more varied hardware expertise. The same principles we discussed still apply, however; stay with what you are familiar with or can learn quickly and do not spread yourself too thin among these areas.

An important point to realize is that once you determine the above specialties, you are not limited to or locked into them. Any opportunities for consulting business that arise should at least be considered; if you feel competent to complete the task successfully and if it doesn't conflict with existing business obligations, you shouldn't turn down the job just because it is, for example, designing a medical accounts payable and receivable system while your expertise is in legal systems. Again, the key word here is "competent"; you should be able to learn quickly (if you do not already know) both the application and the hardware class involved. *Don't* get in over your head.

Competition

Assume that you decide to develop a seminar series for local accountants, demonstrating commercial accounting software. You perform a market analysis of accountants you know and speak with the local chapter of the CPA association, projecting a turnout of 25 to 30 attendees based on your sample survey. Since you are charging $125 per attendee, your revenues should be at least $3125. You plan for a 5-hour seminar at a local hotel conference room and arrange with a local computer store to loan hardware and software in exchange for an announcement of acknowledgement.

The day your first advertisement appears in the Sunday business section of the local newspaper, the facing page features an advertisement by another local computer retailer offering a *free* 4-hour accounting computer systems seminar in their education center. Despite the fact that you are an independent consultant as opposed to a computer store pushing its own products, is that worth $125 to an accountant? Probably not.

The point is that you may have selected your areas of expertise, your products and services, and your hardware specialties, but it might be a crowded field. Chapter 5 deals more with choosing a target market and reading the competition. Be aware, though, that you are not operating in isolation; factors such as your potential competition must be considered. Remember also the principle mentioned earlier in this chapter; because nothing is impossible, have a contingency plan available.

Summary

While you are considering what your consulting business will offer, you need to determine (1) your product and service line, (2) your applications specialties, and (3) your hardware specialties. The key is to choose these specialties in such a way that they maximize your potential earnings and business contacts within the scope of your own expertise and the potential markets.

Let's look in on Bernie Jordan, hard at work in his den. Since he was familiar with the special problems involved in the legal profession, Bernie decided to specialize in computerized legal systems, particularly litigation management. Several assistant city attorneys who had since entered private practice told Bernie casually one day that they were interested in having a litigation system developed for their practice, coupled with an office management and legal billing system. They offered to assist Bernie with the latter applications, since he had not worked with any type of legal billing system before. They also knew several other lawyers with the same information system needs.

Bernie had spent most of his tenure at the city attorney's office defining information system requirements and writing computer programs to handle legal data. He had also conducted several training sessions for the clerical and management personnel in the office, teaching them how to use their personal computer network workstations.

With this background, Bernie also decided to emphasize the systems analysis and programming aspects, since the first leads were in that area and he had spent most of his career performing these functions. However, in case the proposed contracts didn't become a reality (or after they were completed), Bernie decided to develop a seminar in legal computer systems both to bring in revenue and to stimulate new business.

He checked the local newspapers daily for several weeks, scanned the Computer Systems Designers and Consultants section of the *Yellow Pages,* investigated the local computer stores, and concluded that no one seemed to be addressing the computer systems needs of the legal community.

The local chapter of the American Bar Association had a computer committee, and the chairman told Bernie that they hadn't received much support from local computer stores in providing general and specific information about legal computer systems. After reviewing and analyzing the information he had collected, Bernie Jordan felt he had found a specialty for his new consulting profession.

CHAPTER 3

Planning and Organizing Your Consulting Business

Now that your firm's products and services have been determined, your next step is building a business organization around them. As you will see, unless you have a strong business organization to support these services, success in the consulting arena becomes difficult or unlikely. This chapter will cover the preliminary organizational requirements such as choosing a business name, planning your first expenditures (and keeping your costs to a minimum), building a computer system for your own use, making the "full-time versus part-time" decision, and finding a business location.

Choosing a Business Name

By what name should your consulting firm be known? The first decision is whether or not your own name should appear as part of the business name (this doesn't mean Al's Consulting and Garage). Many consultants operate under their own name, such as Mary Jones Consulting Service or simply Mary Jones, Consultant. This follows the practice of the majority of accountants, lawyers, and physicians: no gimmicky names, just a statement of the person or people involved and possibly the service offered.

Other consultants prefer a simple name such as Computerized Medical Consultants.

When should you use your name and when should you choose a fictitious name? If you have strong name recognition in your geographic consulting area (local, state, or national, whichever you choose to market your services in), your own name serves as a marketing and advertising tool as much as or more than any descriptive title. Of course, a combination name, such as Mary Jones Computerized Accounting Consultants, provides a description of services provided for those currently unfamiliar with your name.

My own choice when I began consulting was Computer Education and Consulting because of a lack of name recognition in the Colorado Springs area. The name was a simple statement of the services provided by my firm: general computer consulting and educational (computer literacy and training) services. In retrospect, however, the name may be descriptive in print but is a mouthful to say when answering phone calls or otherwise speaking the name because of the number of syllables.

Another consideration when selecting a descriptive name is *not* to inadvertently limit your potential business by your chosen name. Computerized Accounting Consultants may have a hard time convincing a client legal firm that they do indeed know the legal-applications area as well as accounting ones and aren't just moonlighting to gain additional business. If the firm evolves into specialties different from the original target markets, as was mentioned in Chapter 2, a name change may be necessary to realign the business specialties. Business Microcomputer Consultants still defines a target market (small business computers, as opposed to home systems or mainframes) but allows for a wide evolution of service lines within the range implied by the firm's name. Your advertising could then be targeted toward the specific applications areas for which you are aiming.

Once you choose your name, how do you keep someone else from using it? Similarly, how do you make sure that you are not treading on someone else's territorial rights? This depends on your form of business organization (discussed later in the chapter). The business name of a sole proprietorship or partnership is usually registered at the local, county, or state level by the appropriate recorder (see Figure 3-1). The name must be registered for each geographical area in which you will be operating (multiple cities or counties). If your business is incorporated, you can choose a name that will be registered with your state's corporation commission at incorporation time. If you plan to be incorporated in more than one state, you must register that name in each state.

Once you decide on a name, your next trip should be to the local or county recorder or corporation commission. They have a list of all regis-

```
STATE OF ARIZONA
COUNTY OF MARICOPA

Bernard Jordan              of the County of Maricopa
in the State of Arizona, being first duly sworn upon oath deposes and says that
Jordan Business Computer Systems
is the name under which a business or trade is being carried on at
7300 N. 27th Ave. Phoenix, AZ 85021
in the County of Maricopa, State of Arizona.
That the full name and address of all the persons who are represented by the
said name of Jordan Business Computer Systems is as follows,
to wit: Bernard Jordan 7300 N.27th Ave.Phoenix, AZ 85021
                                         Bernard Jordan
                      Subscribed and sworn before me this 30th day of November,
   NOTARY           1984. My commission expires January 31, 1985.
   PUBLIC                         Joan Anderson
```

Figure 3-1 County name registration form.

tered business names that are in effect in the covered area. Occasionally you may need to do a little searching, since they might have an alphabetized computer printout effective through the beginning of the month, for example, and a handwritten, unalphabetized, temporary log for all registrations since the printout and prior to the next update. Others may have an online system that is continually updated. Normally a small fee is required for registration and notarization; $5 is typical. Incorporation, of course, is more expensive.

What happens if you arrive at the recorder's office and your chosen name is already on file? You should have several alternatives. *ISO World* (now known as *Micro Marketworld*) reported in November 1983 that because of the proliferation of businesses, products, and magazines in the microcomputer world unique names for trademarks and business registrations were becoming extremely difficult to generate; one company even christened itself SOLFAN Corporation, an acronym for "Sick of Looking For A Name."

If you are using your own name you are less likely to find a conflict. You may if you have chosen John Smith Consultants, but you are highly unlikely to find too many Stanislaw Fontanez Consulting Groups. If you do find a business name conflict, don't go to your lawyer and change your own name; change the business name slightly—for example, John Smith Consulting Group.

If you should find subsequently that another group is using the same name that you have registered, contact the individuals involved and inform them that you have registered that business name; they may simply be unaware of the registration rights. If they don't cease operating under your name, legal action may be necessary.

Minimum Business Needs

When viewing a lucrative contract prior to officially beginning practice, new consultants may be tempted to purchase full-page advertisements in the *Yellow Pages,* buy 2000 business cards and 10,000 letterhead-envelope sets, and run weekly display ads in the Sunday newspaper's business section. Before they know it, the profits from the first contract have been converted into fixed overhead costs and the next contract is nowhere in sight. The rule to remember is to provide for your minimum business needs without spending your life savings or mortgaging the next 3 years' profits. The absolute minimum you should consider includes:

1. *Business cards:* While they may be cheaper in lots of 2000, 500 business cards will go a long way. Remember that every time your business location, phone number, or anything else changes the cards become outdated and it's reordering time. Old business cards may be great for writing phone messages on, but scrap paper is cheaper: Don't be stuck with a lot of unused cards.

Shop around, also, as prices and quality vary widely among printers. Find high-quality cards that reflect favorably on your business and professionalism and are reasonably priced. You may or may not choose to include a business logo on your cards, but *don't* spend several hundred dollars at the beginning to have a logo designed. If you insist on one, do it yourself or let the printer design it or find a starving art student to do it for you.

2. *Letterhead and envelopes:* The above rules also apply to your business stationery. Shop around, don't buy extraordinary amounts, and get good-quality paper (20-pound bond, for example).

3. *Advertising:* You should be listed in the *Yellow Pages* under Computer Systems Designers and Consultants or a similar title; when people "let their fingers do the walking," you don't want them to walk right by you. You should not, however, spend $75 per month for a display ad when you have little or no business; a bold-faced entry with a surrounding box could serve the same purpose for less money. A sample box listing is illustrated in Figure 3-2.

Be cautioned if you choose to work out of your home and don't have separate phones for business and personal use: you may have to convert your residential phone to a business one and pay the higher business rate in order to be listed in the *Yellow Pages.* You can keep your personal

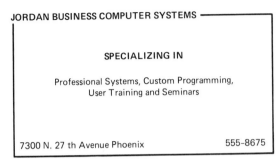

Figure 3-2   Yellow Pages box advertisement.

listing in the white pages for a monthly "additional listing" charge. The advertising as well as the difference between a business and residential listing is tax-deductible as a business expense, of course. Check with your local phone company for their business and residential policies.

4. *Office supplies:* You will need file folders, paper, pens, paper clips, and other office material. You should wait to purchase expensive material such as file cabinets, bookshelves, and others until you have enough revenue to cover the expenses.

5. *Post office box:* If you base your consulting business in your home, you may want to rent a post office box for business mail. This is especially useful if you have several partners in the business, all working from their own residences. Rather than designate one location as the principle business location you may choose a post office box. This is helpful when one or more partners are out of town for long periods of time; all mail will still be accessible to the remaining partners. It could also prevent reprinting business cards and stationery when addresses change or a partner leaves the firm (if his or her address had been the one used). Small post office boxes cost around $15 for 6 months.

6. *Checking account:* Even if you are starting your consulting business on a part-time basis you should still establish a separate checking account for business expenses and revenue deposits. This will prevent the mixing of business funds with personal ones and help establish in your mind that your business is a separate financial entity with separate funds flow, regardless of whether it is a separate legal one. Banks, savings and loans, and even many credit unions will allow you to establish a business checking account.

Shop around for an interest-bearing account with little or no minimum balance or service charge. Business accounts that pay no interest or require a large minimum balance but offer interstate network access are of little use unless you will be conducting business over a wide geographical area and plan to either travel a lot or establish business locations in many of these areas.

7. *Invoice forms:* Since you are not in an industry with large daily volume, simple letterhead with a typed statement of services performed and associated fees is usually sufficient; there is no need to purchase several hundred preprinted invoice forms. This will also save on overhead expenses.

8. *IRS registration:* If your business is operated as a sole proprietorship, no Internal Revenue Service registration is required; your business tax identification number is just your social security number, which appears on the rest of your tax forms. A partnership, however, needs to register a separate tax identification number to be used with any tax information returns (since more than one person is involved in a partnership, one partner's social security number would be insufficient).

9. *Answering machine or answering service:* A beginning consultant probably doesn't need an expensive answering service, especially if consulting is being done on a part-time basis. A telephone answering machine can be purchased for under $100. Advanced models that let you call from a remote phone for your messages are a little more expensive but still more cost-effective than an answering service. Additionally, the machine would be eligible for both a tax deduction as a business expense and an investment tax credit (see Chapter 13).

10. *Computer system:* It would probably not seem appropriate to your clients if their computer consultant didn't have a computer system of his or her own. Additionally, you will probably need a computer for evaluating software and possibly developing your own, for internal use or commercial sale.

A minimum system that you could use for your own business operations should have (*a*) word processing software, for typing business letters and reports, (*b*) a spreadsheet program, for conducting financial analysis of your own and your clients' operations, and (*c*) a database or file manager, for maintaining mailing lists, organizing your reference material, and other data management needs. As your practice expands an accounting program will help save you valuable time in organizing your receivables and payables and present an accurate picture of how business operations are doing.

Full-Time or Part-Time Consulting?

One of the most crucial decisions you must make is determining whether you should enter the consulting profession on a full-time or part-time basis. There are many trade-offs that you must consider. While it may be tempting to quit your present job, make a relatively small investment for overhead expenses, and then watch the money roll in (or so the scenario goes), you need to consider your present and projected situation, financially and otherwise.

Bureau of Labor statistics show that approximately 4 million people work at two jobs, with half of them being managers, executives, professionals, and technicians.[1] Why would you want to begin your consulting career on a part-time basis? There are several reasons.

1. *Security:*   If you maintain your present employment until your consulting business is *very* established, you gain a chance to test the waters—to see if your market analysis, business projections, and computer skills meet the requirements of the consulting marketplace. Rather than forfeit the security and steady income of your current job, you can begin your business organization and early contracts as supplementary income.

2. *Infeasibility of quitting your present job:*   Sometimes it is difficult or impossible to terminate your present employment prior to embarking on your consulting career. If, for example, you have another 3 years until you are vested in your company's retirement plan, it may not be desirable to leave their employment at this time. You may not want to postpone beginning your consulting career, though, because of extremely promising market niches that you wish to exploit. Part-time consulting may be the answer, at least on an interim basis.

The same principle applies to someone who cannot leave his or her present job because of contractual agreements; a military officer with 2 years left until separation from the service can't walk into the commander's office and say, "Sorry, sir, I'm resigning to become a consultant." Because I was an Air Force officer when I founded Computer Education and Consulting, I am especially familiar with this situation.

3. *Growth:*   Until you gain more experience and confidence in all of the business and computer topics we've discussed, you can use part-time consulting as a learning forum.

4. *Burnout:*   A consultant is likely to be dealing with many new situations and responsibilities not previously faced. Many hours will be spent mastering the "consulting learning curve." At periodic intervals you may feel burned out. A part-time consultant can take a break from consulting responsibilities and still have regular income from a full-time job.

Of course, there are disadvantages to coupling your consulting tasks with another job. The major one is time. Your consulting activities are likely to cut deeply into your leisure time. This problem is compounded if you have a spouse and family. There are many times that a part-time consultant may spend 8 to 10 hours working at a regular job during the day and then have to spend 5 more hours in the evening working on a design project or software task. It's because of these situations that burnout can result. You must determine if you're willing to make the extra sacrifice required for this type of lifestyle.

Another potential problem is conflicts of interest with your present job. As a military officer you cannot maintain any off-duty employment with a company (your own or otherwise) that conducts business with the defense department; therefore, an Air Force computer officer is forbidden by law from providing third-party contract software to another Air Force agency.

You need to check with your present employer to determine what restrictions, if any, exist for outside consulting activities. Many employers consider legal action if you leave a firm and clients follow you to your new employment; you must be aware of any contracts that are binding upon you.

Inconveniences can result if you are currently employed in an 8-to-5, Monday-through-Friday job. Not only will you be doing almost all of your consulting work in the evenings and during weekends and holidays, but many of the management functions you need to do, such as visiting your accountant, going to the bank, and arranging for printing must be accomplished during lunch hours. Many of your potential clients may not desire to meet with you during weekends and evenings, and this can cost you business opportunities. If your current job is one with flexible hours, this problem can be alleviated, of course.

Another problem may occur when you are suddenly flooded with many opportunities that you can't possibly handle yourself during the limited time you have available. You might then find yourself forced to refuse certain contracts (though we will see later that subcontracting these opportunities provides an opportunity to alleviate this predicament).

Finally, some clients may view a part-time consultant as less professional than a full-time one; they may feel that if you were worth the fees that you charge you would be consulting full-time. Others may not see you this way, especially if you are consulting part-time because of contractual agreements. I've had clients take both stands; most seem to understand that as an Air Force officer I must consult part-time. Even they, however, sometimes have doubts about the time, though not the capabilities, I will have to complete a contract.

If you decide that the time involved and other deficiencies of starting part-time are too great and therefore wish to take the plunge into full-time consulting, you should ensure the following:

1. You have at least one *guaranteed contract* that will provide enough income for living expenses, early business growth, etc. While this contract is underway you can begin or continue marketing efforts for subsequent business.

2. In case the first contract falls through or additional business doesn't follow as quickly as you had planned, you should have *sufficient savings* to provide you with living and business expenses. How much is sufficient depends on how long you are willing to stick it out and what your actual living and business expenses are.

If you have an office with a $1500 per month lease, your business expenses are obviously greater than if you are working in your home. Living expenses will be greater in a city like San Francisco than a smaller city like Tucson or Colorado Springs.

3. You *limit your initial expenses* just in case things don't work out as planned. That's why a limited purchase of business cards and letterhead is a wise decision until you see what directions your business takes you.

A major advantage that a venture into full-time computer consulting has over many other types of consulting is that if you fail for any one of many reasons (lack of business, customer dissatisfaction, the desire to discontinue practice) you can usually find new employment rather easily because of the current and projected demand for qualified computer programmers and analysts.

Work at Home or Lease an Office?

Thought you were done with the difficult decisions, didn't you? It is highly recommended that a beginning computer consultant base operations out of his or her home. The added expense of a monthly office lease could absorb business capital and revenue at a quick enough pace to force you to give up consulting. Many of your meetings will take place at your clients' business locations; an office is basically an expensive prestige item.

There are several things that you should be aware of regarding working out of your home, however. You must separate your "work time" from your "home time." Just because you don't get into your car and drive to a business location every morning doesn't mean that you aren't working; you must avoid household distractions (including your spouse and children).

Also be sure to check your local zoning laws. If you are just basing your operations in your home rather than having clients constantly trooping through, you shouldn't face any problems. Some neighborhoods, though, may have covenants providing some restrictions; be sure of what you sign and know your own zoning laws.

When meeting clients at your home, you must present a businesslike appearance. Your office or den should reflect the professional nature of your consulting profession. Interruptions and distractions are a wonderful way to lose a client.

You must also check with your local or county zoning commission to learn exactly what zoning laws are in effect for your neighborhood. Some neighborhoods have covenants that prohibit a business from being operated in a residence; usually this refers to a retail operation. Others restrict the number of clients you can meet with at one time. If this is the case, you may not be able to hold a large seminar at your residence.

If you are operating your practice from your home, you are most likely eligible for tax deductions of a percentage of your home mortgage or rent for business use of the home. This will be discussed further in Chapter 13.

If you *must* rent an office because of the infeasibility of working at home, investigate leasing a small one-person office or desk space within an office suite. Your costs will be much less and often copying, telephone answering, and secretarial services are included with your rental fee.

Form of Business Organization

You will probably begin your consulting business in the simplest of the three legal business forms, the *sole proprietorship,* meaning you are running your business as a solo effort. You and your business are the same legal entity; this is business talk for "You are personally responsible for your firm's financial and business obligations." If your sole proprietorship tallies up $100,000 in business debts or is successfully sued, your personal assets are open game to meet these obligations.

The second major form of business organization is the *partnership.* As you might suspect, you need at least one partner to be considered a partnership. You are still considered responsible for the financial and legal obligations of your firm, but not by yourself. Partnerships are discussed in more detail in Chapter 15.

Finally, there is the *corporation.* The primary benefit a corporation offers you is the legal separation of your business from you (and your partners, if applicable). Bankruptcy or legal liability by the business will only affect you to the extent of your stated investment in the business; only those assets are subject to loss. Corporations are also discussed in Chapter 15.

Which business form should your practice have? If you will be designing and marketing much software, either for a limited number of users or for the commercial market, incorporation may provide protection from potential lawsuits by competitors, software publishers, or customers.

Remember, ours is a litigious society, and successful businesses are often targets of lawsuits.

Bear in mind that incorporating just for prestige is probably not worth the incorporation and legal fees; you should have a legitimate need for the protection. If your primary services are seminars, training, and writing, your lawsuit potential is less than if you actually provide operational software, either by recommending its purchase or actually developing it.

Additional Considerations

When you register your business (usually when you apply for your business name), check with your local, county, and state business governing

---

Checklist of Initial Concerns

_____ Business cards	_____ Stationery
_____ Advertising	_____ Office supplies
_____ Postal box	_____ Business location
_____ Checking account	_____ Invoice forms
_____ Business name registration	_____ IRS registration
_____ Answering machine or service	_____ Computer system

Figure 3-3 Checklist of initial concerns.

agencies for any regional regulations that may apply to you. You shouldn't have to worry about collecting and remitting sales tax, since you most likely won't be selling any taxable goods, but rather services.

Be sure to review Chapters 4, 5, and 13 for additional operational concerns such as bookkeeping, tax filing, and advertising. A checklist of preliminary business considerations is provided for your use in Figure 3-3.

Summary

Well, what is Bernie Jordan up to? He is more convinced than ever that he can enjoy a successful career as a computer consultant. He begins planning for business operations, first choosing the name Jordan Business Computer Systems to provide both name recognition for himself and define his area of expertise. Though he will begin by emphasizing legal systems, he does plan to expand his applications base as business grows and doesn't wish to change the firm's name as new specialty areas develop.

Bernie contracts with a local printer for 250 business cards and 500 letterhead-envelope sets. He also begins a business checking account at his current bank. Bernie already owns a personal computer that he uses for investment management; he feels it is sufficient to use for his consulting practice. He currently has word processing, spreadsheet, and database software. He has decided against spending $1000 for an accounting system because early business volume is expected to be light enough to manage accounting data manually, assisted by his spreadsheet and database programs. After business volume increases he can then write or purchase an accounting system.

Bernie has 2 years until he qualifies for benefits from the city retirement plan to which he has been contributing since he began working with them. If he resigns now he will receive a refund consisting only of his contributed funds and 5 percent accrued interest. After his 10-year employment anniversary he will receive matching funds ($.50 for every $1 he has contributed) beginning at age 45. For this reason, as well as still being unsure of his future consulting revenues, he decides to begin consulting on a part-time basis rather than quit his job now. His first legal computer system development contract can be completed during evening and weekend hours, his clients assure him.

Bernie's wife Sandra, an accountant, just started an evening MBA program at a nearby university and will be spending many of her own evening and weekend hours studying. Together, the Jordans decide that the additional time Bernie will be devoting to his consulting activities will not present any personal problems.

Finally, Bernie decides that leasing an office would be a waste of money that could be better utilized for personal and other business expenses. His programming for the first contract will be done at his client's legal office and the design and development work can be completed in his den at home, which will become his office.

End Notes

1. William C. Banks, "You're Not Alone in the Moonlight," *Money*, April 1984, p. 219.

CHAPTER 4

Financial Considerations of Consulting

Regardless of whether you or your accountant does your firm's books, you must still understand some important financial and accounting principles. We saw before that your business skills are as important as your computer skills in building and maintaining a successful consulting practice. This knowledge is also useful in understanding many of your clients' business problems.

In this chapter we will discuss some financial topics of concern to you as you begin your business. We will review revenue patterns and their effects on your business operations. We will look at cash flow analysis and budgeting as a tool to aid in your financial planning.

We will also discuss the basics of financial statements and their importance, as well as ways to obtain further information from their numbers. We'll look at how an understanding of different categories of business costs is essential to business analysis and planning. We'll talk about different ways to obtain initial business capital. Of course, you need to know how to compute your consulting fee. Finally, we'll see how scenarios can be used to try to predict the future status of your business.

Revenue Patterns and Cash Budgeting

Your revenue patterns will depend on the types of products and services you will be offering. *Revenue spurts* will occur when you depend primarily on single-service, short-term contracts such as designing specific computer systems or contract programming. Your contracts are not likely to come at regular intervals, and dead times, with little or no revenue, can happen. *Revenue streams,* however, tend to result when you depend primarily on royalties from commercial software or books, or long-term contracts for business earnings. One example of a long-term contract would be a 2-year weekly seminar series about various computer legal topics for the American Bar Association at many locations around the country. Another is a long-term system development contract where your client is billed monthly for services rendered.

If you rely primarily on services that provide spurts of revenue, you should try to balance the active and inactive billing periods with some royalties or other revenue streams. This will provide capital for business and living expenses when other revenue producers temporarily slow down. By devoting your early inactive periods to developing commercial software or writing a book (as I did), the deferred income will hopefully provide you with enough business and personal capital to prevent cannibalization of your personal and business assets.

An important tool to help you plan your income and expense timing is the *cash budget,* illustrated in Figure 4-1. The cash budget's purpose is to help you recognize and plan for your cash needs and determine if sufficient cash will have been collected to meet these needs. For example, it is unlikely for any business to earn and collect $1.50 for every $1 that it spends, in perfect synchronization. Revenue could have been earned but if it is not collected yet, you may be forced to borrow or dip into your personal and business savings to cover the expenses. Peter Drucker, a well-known business and management professor, stated in a recent interview that the "whole secret of financial management [is to] know when you'll need money and make sure of it before you need it."[1]

A cash budget covers a number of periods, usually monthly, and examines known and projected cash inflows and outflows for each period. The projected revenues and expenses must be estimated as closely as possible. If revenue doesn't meet expectations for a particular month, the future periods being examined must be adjusted to reflect the lack of cash carrying over into the next period. This is where an electronic spreadsheet on your own computer system will come in very handy; changes can be made and the results can be shown instantly.

The cash budget displayed in Figure 4-1 is a simple one; basic projections of revenues and expenses are made. The first section shows the esti-

Cash Budget
Jordan Business Computer Systems

	JANUARY	FEBRUARY	MARCH	APRIL
Projected revenue collections	3000.00	500.00	1000.00	500.00
1st month (70%)	2100.00	350.00	700.00	350.00
2nd month (30%)		900.00	150.00	300.00
Total	2100.00	1250.00	850.00	650.00
Receipts				
Total collections	2100.00	1250.00	850.00	650.00
Bank loan	1000.00			
Total	3100.00	1250.00	850.00	650.00
Payments				
Letterhead	75.00			
Business cards	25.00			
Post office box	15.00			
Accounting services		50.00		
Answering machine	150.00			
Office supplies	25.00	10.00	5.00	7.50
Phone (business)	10.00	10.00	10.00	10.00
Yellow Pages ad		12.50	12.50	12.50
Miscellaneous advertising			75.00	60.00
Total	300.00	82.50	102.50	90.00
Beginning cash balance	—	2800.00	3967.50	4715.00
Net cash gain loss for current month	2800.00	1167.50	747.50	560.00
Ending cash balance	2800.00	3967.50	4715.00	5275.00

Figure 4-1   Cash budget.

mated revenues for each of 4 months, as well as the time period in which these amounts will be collected. An assumption is made that 70 percent of all revenues are collected in the month earned, while 30 percent is collected in the subsequent month. An existing business could make this determination from sales and collection histories, while a new firm would have to rely on estimates and research.

Also note that receipts for January include a $1000 bank loan; even though this amount is not considered revenue, it is still cash inflow, which is what we are concerned with.

The bottom section contains the beginning cash balance, net cash flow, and calculated ending cash balance for each month. Jordan Business Computer Systems should not have any cash flow problems if actual revenues and collections are on target with the estimates; each month shows a positive ending cash balance. If any ending cash balance were negative (including insufficient cash to meet the month's obligations), borrowing or other financing would need to be arranged. If Bernie were planning to purchase a $6000 computer system in March, additional capital would be required. For further information about cash budgets, consult one of the finance texts referred to in Chapter 14.

Financial Statements

If you have studied accounting or finance while in school, you know that financial statements can present a useful picture of your firm's financial health. An *income statement* displays the income, expenses, and net earnings (or net loss) for a particular period of time, such as a 3-month interval (fiscal quarter) or an annual period. Income statements can become extremely detailed and complicated as the information reporting requirements increase, but a simple one (as illustrated in Figure 4-2) will probably serve your own needs.

An income statement contains three sections: (1) the *revenue section,* which lists a summary of income and adjustments to income (such as refunds and allowances for uncollectable accounts); (2) the *expense section,* showing the business expenses incurred for that period divided into various categories; and (3) the *net income section,* a summary of the total adjusted revenues less total expenses. Income taxes are included in this section.

A *balance sheet* provides a "snapshot" of a firm's assets, liabilities, and net worth at a given instance. When the amount of a firm's *assets* (what it owns) is greater than its *liabilities* (what it owes), the firm has a positive net worth; the company could be dissolved today and if all assets could be sold for *book value* (the stated value on the balance sheet) all debts could be paid off and there would be money left over for the owner.

Similarly, a negative net worth (liabilities greater than assets) could cause problems; for example, the owners would not be able to recoup their initial and subsequent investments following business dissolution or they might face possible bankruptcy for not being able to pay debt installments. A sample balance sheet is shown in Figure 4-3.

Both assets and liabilities are divided into two categories: current and long-term. *Current assets* are (1) cash and (2) other assets that are expected to be converted into cash within 1 year from the date of the

---

Jordan Business Computer Systems

Income Statement for Year Ended
December 31, 1984

Revenues			
Consulting revenues	$15,350.00		
Less: Uncollectable accounts	2,000.00		
Net consulting revenue		$13,350.00	
Interest revenue		55.00	
Total revenues			$13,405.00
Less expenses			
Office and postage		175.00	
Miscellaneous supplies		125.00	
Depreciation		300.00	
Insurance		125.00	
Advertising		350.00	
Telephone		150.00	
Total expenses			1,225.00
Pretax income			12,180.00
Less income taxes			1,500.00
Net income			$10,680.00

Figure 4-2 Income statement.

balance sheet. *Current liabilities* are debts that will be paid within 1 year from the balance sheet date. *Long-term assets,* such as land, buildings, and equipment are those that will be on the books past the next year. Similarly, *long-term liabilities* are those that will not be paid off within the next year.

If you operate your business under the *accrual basis* of accounting (discussed further in Chapter 13), you recognize revenues on your books at the time earned rather than when cash is collected. It is possible that a large contract completed at the end of the year would show a large amount of revenue that hasn't been collected. Anyone reviewing your company's financial statements may see a year with high net earnings and substantial net worth; if your client were to default on payment and it couldn't be collected, the revenue then would not really exist (barring successful recovery through a collection agency or lawsuit). At some future

Jordan Business Computer Systems

Balance Sheet as of
December 31, 1984

	ASSETS			LIABILITIES	
Current assets			Current liabilities		
Cash	$12,750.00		Loan	$1,000.00	
Accounts receivable	500.00		Taxes payable	1,500.00	
Total		$13,250.00	Total		$2,500.00
Fixed assets			Long-term liabilities		
Equipment	2,000.00		None		
Less: Accumulated					
Depreciation	(300.00)		Owner's equity		
Total		$1,700.00	Contributed capital		1,770.00
			Retained earnings		10,680.00
			Total liability plus		
Total assets		$14,950.00	owner's equity		$14,950.00

Figure 4-3   Balance sheet.

Jordan Business Computer Systems

Statement of Changes in Financial Position
Year ended December 31, 1984

SOURCES AND USES OF WORKING CAPITAL

Sources

Net income	$10,680.00	
Add back noncash expenses		
Depreciation	300.00	
Total operational cash sources		$10,980.00
Proceeds from long-term debt		—
Total sources of working capital		$10,980.00

Uses

Acquisition of equipment		—
Net increase in working capital		$10,980.00

Figure 4-4   Statement of changes in financial position.

time the revenue will be subtracted from that future year's revenue as uncollectable.

The *statement of changes in financial position* helps you and anyone studying your firm's finances recognize these situations by showing changes in your company's individual accounts and the overall effect on either your cash balance or your *working capital,* the amount of assets you have at your disposal to meet expenses. Working capital is defined as the difference between current assets and current liabilities. Figure 4-4 shows this statement.

Bernie's statement of changes is an extremely simple one to prepare and understand. Since his business has not undergone many financial transactions during the past year, he has not had to use his working capital to purchase equipment (he already owned his computer), retire long-term debt, or increase inventory (since he doesn't have any inventory). For a more detailed explanation of the statement of changes, as well as more complex examples, consult a financial accounting text such as one of those mentioned in Chapter 14.

Naturally, if you are operating on a part-time basis, only maintain a few clients, and don't have many business expenses, you should instinctively know how well your firm is doing financially. As your operations expand and more contracts are handled, however, the financial statements take on added importance in helping you comprehend your firm's financial health.

Ratio Analysis

Large operations often need financial analysis over and above that which could be determined from the financial statements we have seen. This is to isolate problem areas that otherwise may remain hidden. Most finance textbooks devote a chapter to ratio analysis; several are listed in Chapter 14. If you feel additional financial information is required, ratio analysis of your firm may be necessary.

Initial Capital

Once your initial expenses are defined, as we saw in the previous chapter, you must determine how much capital is initially required and where this money will come from.

The most common capital sources for a consulting business are savings withdrawals, loans, and capital investment. Loans may assume many forms: bank loans, home-equity loans, borrowing from friends or relatives, or Small Business Administration loans. Capital investment may also be from many sources, such as friends, relatives, or venture capital firms.

The primary difference between a loan and capital investment is that you are legally obligated to repay a loan but do not give up partial ownership of your business, while investors are "subordinated" to creditors but gain partial ownership of their investment target (i.e., they are purchasing stock in the firm).

Most consultants, if they follow the guidelines for starting slowly, should have minimal capital needs, easily met from savings or minor bank loans. During your firm's conception stage, at least, there should be minimal need for venture capital or other forms of equity investment.

Of course, you may have a particular product or service that does require a large amount of financing. In this case, refer to Chapter 15 for a detailed discussion of various forms of business capital.

Costs

An understanding of the various types of costs involved in a business's expenses is important. You must distinguish between *fixed costs* (those that exist whether revenue is earned or not) and *variable costs* (those that are a product of the revenue-earning activity). Your goal should be to earn enough income to reach the break-even point.

The *break-even point* for a financial period is when all costs have been covered by revenue earned and no net loss will occur. For every income-producing activity, the difference between the revenue earned and the associated expenses is known as the *contribution margin,* or profit resulting from that activity.

When the sum of the contributing margins for all activities is equal to the total fixed costs for the period, your net earnings will be zero and the break-even point will be reached. Any revenue after the break-even point will contribute toward the firm's net profits. This assumes, of course, that each activity will contribute more revenue than the associated variable costs. It would be a rare job you would accept that produces a net loss from that contract.

Examples of fixed costs are *Yellow Page* advertising (a yearly contract), annual business licenses, post office box rental, answering service, and, if you don't work at home, office rent, phone, and utilities. Any salaries you pay to employees other than on a "when-used" basis will also be fixed costs.

Variable costs may include subcontractor payments for specific jobs, photocopying services for seminar materials, and seminar room rental. These variable costs would not be incurred if the contract weren't accepted.

For example, Bernie Jordan has calculated the following fixed costs for the upcoming year:

Yellow Page advertising	$180
Business cards, 1-year supply	30
Business stationery, 1-year supply	40
Answering machine, 1st year's depreciation*	20
Post office box rental	30
Total	$300

*See Chapter 13 for details on depreciation.

Bernie's goal is to ensure that over the next year his contracts provide enough net income (i.e., total contribution margin) to pay for these fixed costs. If every contract were to fall through, he still would incur these minimum expenses.

Another way to classify your business costs is as either direct or indirect. *Direct costs* can be defined as those that can be allocated to a specific contract, while *indirect costs* could be defined as "supporting expenses."

If Bernie signs a contract with a brokerage firm to conduct a seminar about investment software, the costs of printing workbooks would be considered a direct cost of that assignment. His *Yellow Pages* advertisement that attracted that contract is an indirect cost; it can't be directly allocated to the seminar in any identifiable portion.

At the end of the year, he could allocate a portion of his total indirect costs to each contract in proportion to the relative revenue of each job. Such allocation, however, is similar to an allocation of a portion of fixed expenses to each contract.

Speaking of fixed costs, it seems that the distinction between direct and indirect costs is similar to that of variable versus fixed expenses. An indirect cost could be variable one, though, just as a direct cost could be fixed. Variable costs are not synonymous with direct costs, nor do fixed costs always imply indirect expenses.

In our seminar example, Bernie has calculated the following data:

Revenue per attendee	$100
Cost of handouts per attendee	10
Conference room rental and coffee service	75

The contribution margin per attendee, again defined as revenue minus variable costs, is $90 ($100 − $10); the only variable cost involved is the expense of handouts.

The conference room rental, however, is both a direct and a fixed cost; it can be identified as an expense of this particular seminar, and is fixed in the sense that once the seminar is held, the $75 will be paid whether 1 or 30 people attend.

Finally, the advertising, postal box rental, and other items listed previously are both indirect and fixed costs; they can't be designated to any specific assignment and are incurred despite the number of contracts undertaken or revenue earned.

General newspaper advertising (as opposed to that for a particular seminar offering) would be considered an indirect and variable cost. Unless you have contracted for a minimum number of column inches per year, you can vary this advertising expense as you see fit; it can't, however, be allocated to any particular contract as a direct cost would.

The key is to be able to identify any expense you face as either a variable or fixed cost, as well as direct or indirect. In order to intelligently manage the financial operations of your consulting firm, a close hold should be kept on any costs. Knowing how to calculate contribution margins, break-even points, and contract profit potential is extremely important. Your financial statements, as mentioned before, present a picture of your firm's financial health, but only after the fact; fading "vital signs" on a balance sheet or income statement may appear too late for you to salvage your practice. Closely controlled costs help prevent problems from occurring in the first place.

A final type of business cost, though different from the above ones, is the *opportunity cost* you face with every decision you make. If you decide to conduct the brokerage firm seminar we just examined, your opportunity cost is the revenue (if any) you pass up from *not* conducting some other seminar or accepting a client contract.

Determining opportunity cost can often be tricky. It is easy to see that if you refuse a contract in order to work on your 6-month commercial software project, the opportunity cost is the revenue you would have earned from the contract. But what about the reverse situation? If you take time away from your software project (or book project, as I did while writing this volume) to conduct a seminar, how do you determine what your opportunity cost is? If the time away just means submitting your software or book to the publisher 2 weeks later than anticipated, you don't really have any opportunity cost (assuming you don't go over a submission deadline and lose a portion of your advance or incur some other financial penalty). The best approach is to determine approximately what revenue you will lose, if any, and use that figure as your opportunity cost.

Often, you may choose to accept one contract at the expense of losing another even though the refused contract would provide more revenue. This may be because the first job will lead to a series of subsequent contracts that, over the long term, provide much more revenue than the second one. In this case, you are choosing the project that has the least opportunity cost over the long term, rather than looking at just short-term projections. The lesson: Be sure to look at both current and future revenues when making any opportunity cost decisions.

Scenarios and Planning

If you could exactly forecast all future revenues and expenses you should consider a career in fortune-telling rather than computer consulting. The rest of us need to make predictions based on market research, knowledge of business capabilities, and similar managerial tools.

Since the future is obviously uncertain, you should establish various scenarios (situations) to estimate various outcomes. What will happen if a "sure" job falls through at one of several points during the contract's duration? How will actual seminar attendance that is half (or double) the planned registration affect revenues (both from the seminar itself and potential future clients)? How do you determine what your future revenue will be for opportunity cost decision making, as we saw in the preceding section?

The important point here is that you should be prepared for the unexpected. Any business operation must always have contingency plans to invoke when situations change or don't develop as planned. The more complete your scenario planning is the more likely you will be able to adapt to unexpected situations.

The scenarios developed form the basis of *pro forma* financial statements. A pro forma income statement is a projection of revenue and expenses over the scenario's period, while a pro forma balance sheet projects a snapshot of the firm at a future point. By analyzing the financial outcomes of the scenarios a realistic picture of the likelihood of success as a business operation can be determined.

Your own computer again comes in handy here. By using a spreadsheet analysis program, just as with your cash budget, pro forma statements can be automatically adjusted to reflect the outcome of different business strategies and situations.

Determining Your Consulting Fees

The fee you charge your customers for consulting services represents a combination of three items: (1) your income, in the form of a salary equivalent; (2) a means to pay your business's financial obligations; and (3) business profit.[2] The main component of your fee is your billing rate, or the amount charged for your services for a specified period of time (normally by the hour or business day).

You *must* be able to justify your billing rate to your customers, though you may not do so verbally. Often, consultants' fees, like those of physicians and attorneys, are viewed as almost pure profit; obviously, this is not the case. We'll see in a moment various ways to calculate the billing rate, but you must allow for coverage of both business expenses and your own living costs (assuming your practice is your primary source of income). Also, the next chapter discusses how marketing interacts with your fee determination.

If you are consulting on a part-time basis and your major source of living income lies elsewhere, the salary portion of the fee structure is not as important as if you had no other income; you can afford to lower your salary requirements without hindering your standard of living. Of course, the profit portion is still important unless you just like working with computers and people and don't care if you make any money from your practice.

As a general rule, though, a part-time consultant's hourly compensation after expenses and reinvested profits should be roughly equal to his or her full-time job's hourly rate or that of an alternative job. For example, you may have the opportunity to teach computer classes at a local community college and be paid $10 per hour. Unless your net consulting earnings are equivalent, the opportunity cost decision would determine that you can receive more compensation for your time if you choose the teaching position.

Even if you are consulting full-time, it is unlikely that you will be paid your hourly rate for 40 hours of work per week. Therefore, don't let the dollar signs fly up thinking that $40 per hour will provide business earnings of $1600 each and every week. You will likely have some dead time due to client inactivity, seminar preparation, commercial software development, management responsibilities, and personal affairs, to name a few.

However, deferred revenue from commercial software development or book writing can distort the hourly rate compensation. You need to have a clear understanding of what portion of your total revenue comes from hourly earnings and what part from revenue streams. Even a reliance on seminars for revenue can provide a variety of earning rates, contingent upon attendance.

The first step in determining a consulting fee is to determine estimated billing hours. Assume that Bernie Jordan will devote 25 hours per week to consulting activities, including 10 hours of necessary management overhead (billing, correspondence, marketing, etc.). This leaves 15 billable hours per week, or 750 for a 50-week business year (assuming 2 weeks of well-deserved vacation).

His utilization rate, therefore, is 60 percent (750 billable hours divided by 1250 total consulting hours). This means that, on the average, 60 percent of the time he spends on consulting-related activities can be billed to customers. This number serves as a reference point for further revenue, cost, or other financial analysis.

Robert Kelley discusses various means to determine the actual billing rate.[3] The most commonly used method is the Rule of Three, or the assumption that total consulting revenues can be allocated equally to meet salary requirements, overhead, and business profit.

The starting point is the salary requirement. Let's assume that Bernie wants to earn $10,000 from consulting, exclusive of "profits" (which he will reinvest in business expansion). Therefore, total revenues must be $30,000, computed as follows:

Salary	$10,000
Overhead	10,000
Profit	10,000
Required revenue	$30,000

With 750 annual billable hours, simple mathematics will determine a billing rate of $40 per hour ($30,000 divided by 750 hours).

Dr. Kelley points out that this formula could be varied according to the relative percentages of salary, overhead, and profit. Since Bernie is starting his practice on a part-time basis, based from his home, the respective weights may be 50 percent salary and 25 percent for overhead and profit. Following the same method of starting with salary requirements, the following figures result:

Salary	$10,000
Overhead	5,000
Profit	5,000
Required revenue	$20,000

Dividing the $20,000 figure by the same 750 billable hours yields an hourly billing rate of approximately $27.

Once you calculate your billing rate, you then need to determine in what manner you will charge your clients. The simplest method is on an *hourly basis,* using your hourly billing rate multiplied by the actual number of hours worked for a client.

In practice, though, your billing rate will become the basis of other fee arrangements as well. You may consult on a *fixed-rate basis;* based on a project's time estimate (which hopefully is accurate) you quote a fixed dollar amount in exchange for your services. Under this arrangement, you bear most of the risk, since any hours over those you have built into your fixed rate can't be billed for.

You should only agree to fixed-rate contracts when you have substantial experience with projects of the type given (the application, hardware, developmental language, etc.) and can effectively control the task's costs. If you are using subcontractor assistance on a fixed-rate project, be sure your arrangements with your subcontractors are also fixed-rate.

The advantage of a fixed-rate contract to a consultant is that if the project is finished in less time than had been estimated and built into the fee, the excess is retained rather than refunded to a client. Though it may appear tempting to overbid any fixed-rate contract and pocket the overage, remember that your client must first accept the estimate and contract for your services. If your bid is ridiculously high, the chances of acceptance are probably not very good (assuming the client competitively bids or has a good idea of what the project should generally cost).

A combination of the hourly and fixed-rate methods is to contract on an hourly basis with a *cost ceiling.* That is, you quote a client a rate of $40 per hour with an estimate of 40 hours. To ease your client's fears that you will run way over budgeted cost you place a ceiling of 50 hours, or $2000, as the maximum cost. If the project becomes more complicated than you had estimated, the client is protected against cost overruns and you assume the risk. Unlike a fixed-rate contract, however, you will receive payment for the actual time spent on the project up to the maximum rate.

This is probably the least advantageous billing method to consultants, but someone just entering practice without a strong record of successfully completed projects may need to employ such a method in order to win contracts from some clients. As with a fixed-rate contract, you should be familiar enough with the task at hand to confidently place a ceiling on the project.

Another fee arrangement is the *retainer.* The primary purpose of a retainer is to guarantee your services to a client for a specified number of hours per month. Any consulting performed in excess of the retainer hours will be billed separately. The ethical considerations of retainers, including possible conflicts of interest, are discussed in Chapter 13.

There are several other fee arrangements (see Kelley's book for details), but those discussed here are the most common arrangements for computer consultants. Again, part of your earnings, such as those from magazine articles, books, seminars, and commercial software, will be covered by different compensation methods. A thorough analysis of respective earnings percentages will provide assistance in determining billing rates and fee arrangements.

Summary

In this chapter, we saw how important the financial aspects of a consulting business are. We looked at many types of financial statements, analyzed the different types of costs a consultant can incur, and saw how to determine your consulting fees. In the next chapter we will see how your financial projections integrate with your marketing decisions. Later, in Chapters 13 and 15, we will look at other financial topics, such as bookkeeping, accounting, taxes, and raising capital for business expansion.

Now, back to Bernie Jordan. Based on his projected concentration of services, Bernie expects to receive most of his income in spurts as various contracts are negotiated and executed. His proposed series of legal software seminars will, once in full swing, provide some steady income (revenue streams) to balance the revenue flow.

After determining his initial expenditures, Bernie developed the cash budget shown in Figure 4-1. Since his expenditures will be modest and he will be working from his home, no borrowing is projected; modest withdrawals from savings and future paychecks will cover the initial year's expenses.

Bernie is familiar with accounting and financial statements because of his business degrees. Since his consulting operations haven't begun yet, there is no data from which meaningful financial statements can be developed. However, he develops several scenarios for the upcoming year's business, with various levels of business activity. This way, he can see the effect on the bottom line of different situations. After studying the pro forma statements Bernie is further convinced of the likelihood of success as a computer consultant.

End Notes

1. "How New Entrepreneurs Are Changing U.S. Business," *U.S. News & World Report,* March 26, 1984, p. 68.
2. Robert E. Kelley, *Consulting: The Complete Guide to a Profitable Career,* Scribner's, New York, 1981, p. 72.
3. Ibid., pp. 80–88.

CHAPTER 5

Marketing Your Consulting Business

It was stated back in Chapter 1 that of all the business skills you will utilize in your consulting practice, marketing may very well be the most important. Marketing is where many of your independent decisions intersect and you determine if you can potentially be successful in your new venture. More specifically, your *product* (what services will you be providing, and to whom?), *price* (what is your pricing strategy for these services?), *promotion* (how will you make it known that these services are available?), and *place* (through what channels will the services reach your clients?) are joined into an integrated marketing plan. These are the so-called 4 P's that form the basis of most marketing plans and efforts.

Chapter 2 already dealt with the product decision. You determined what products and services you would concentrate on. This chapter will more thoroughly discuss the techniques of marketing. We discussed how to calculate your fee structure in the last chapter; we will now see how to determine if the market will support this price. We will also review the other two P's—promotion and place.

We'll start by discussing the benefits of marketing, then techniques for analyzing your target market. We'll see ways to promote your business, including (but not limited to) advertising. We will discuss how to allocate time between consulting and marketing activities. Finally, we'll look at some selling techniques, particularly those to use during face-to-face client meetings.

The Benefits of Marketing

Consultant Robert Kelley outlined four major benefits the marketing effort provides to your practice[1]:

1. *Marketing focuses your business and your efforts:* By determining the answers to your marketing-mix questions of product, price, promotion, and distribution, your resources can be directed toward your chosen services and marketing methods, rather than scattered among a haphazard range of ideas. Remember that since you are performing a variety of business functions, the fewer wasted or misdirected resources the better off you will be.

A *marketing orientation,* consisting of two critical functions, is essential for a consulting practice. You must first determine the needs and wants of your target market (as we'll see shortly), followed by an adaptation of your organizational efforts toward meeting these needs and wants. You are not the only person in the world offering computer consulting advice, so don't expect everyone to beat a path to your door begging you to help them.

2. *Marketing makes you do today what is required to secure next year's business:* By continually reevaluating your marketing mix, you can keep your efforts on track. As your marketing efforts attract new clients, your practice can survive and grow from the additional revenue.

3. *Marketing makes you visible:* You will become very familiar to your potential clients through your marketing efforts. They will become aware of the services you offer, your prices, and your expertise.

4. *Marketing improves your organization:* As you and your practice become well known, you can command higher fees for your services. The incremental revenue earned provides capital for additional employees, advertising, and general business expansion. Your business reputation will improve, as will the long-term survival prospects of your business.

Analyzing Your Target Market

By now you should have a general idea of your target market, based on what services you will be offering. The general public is not a specific target, and a target of "current nonusers of computers" isn't limited enough. "Local real estate agencies with little or no computerization" is narrow enough to allow you to concentrate both your product and service development and your marketing efforts.

Your target should state (1) the geographic range, (2) types of businesses, and (3) computer expertise of your intended client base. Your marketing efforts will differ if, for example, you were targeting (1) accountants with installed computer systems wishing to expand usage or (2) nonautomated accounting firms.

Because you don't have unlimited resources (time, money, and knowledge) it is important that your target market be within the capabilities of your existing resources. Again, as we saw in Chapter 2, don't eliminate the possibility of adjusting or overhauling your targeting efforts as situations change; the key to survival, especially in an industry as dynamic as computer services, is flexibility and adaptability.

If revenue or the number of clients begins to decrease (or never grows), you must try to determine the reason. If it is because of inadequate advertising, a poor pricing structure, or another controllable factor, you obviously need to adjust the business strategy that is inhibiting your firm's growth. If, however, you determine that there is no longer a widespread need for your particular products and services, it is time to reassess what products and services should be marketed.

One way of analyzing your intended market is through a marketing survey. If you are targeting local legal offices, a one-page survey mailed to all local legal firms may confirm your preliminary research, as well as provide exceptional insight into special problems and opportunities of which you may not be aware.

Another important benefit of a survey is providing name recognition for your firm and notifying your (hopefully) future clients that you are available for computer consulting services; in other words, you are advertising your services as well as conducting market research. Mailing letters announcing your entry into business may not evoke much response, but a survey indicating insight into your clients' business operations and presenting a forum for them to express their problems and wishes provides substantial benefit for the cost. A sample survey and cover letter are illustrated in Figure 5-1.

Assuming that your city has 250 legal firms, the survey would cost about $162.50 (see below) and, unlike newspaper or other forms of advertising, it provides you with feedback (through responses).

$$250 \times .40 \text{ postage } = \$100.00 \text{ (2 stamps each)}$$
$$250 \times .15 \text{ copying } = 37.50 \text{ (3 sheets each)}$$
$$250 \times .10 \text{ envelope } = \underline{25.00} \text{ (2 envelopes each)}$$
$$\text{Total cost } = \$162.50$$

JORDAN BUSINESS COMPUTER SYSTEMS
7300 North 27th Avenue
Phoenix, AZ 85021

November 12, 1984

Ms. Jane Sanders
1234 N. Mill Avenue
Tempe, AZ 85281

Dear Ms. Sanders,

Jordan Business Computer Systems is a Phoenix metropolitan-area
consulting firm specializing in computerized applications for the
legal profession. In order to better serve the needs of our clientele,
we could appreciate it if you could take several minutes to respond to
the attached survey.

We feel that computerization will soon be a way of life for legal firms
of all sizes, and Jordan Business Computer Systems has extensively
analyzed the major legal applications systems commercially available
today: correspondence management, legal research assistance, billing,
and office management. Additionally, we have developed several custom
software packages for our legal clients. Your assistance with this
survey will ensure that we continue to understand the special
opportunities and problems of computerization in the legal profession.

For your convenience, we have enclosed a stamped envelope addressed
to us. Again, our sincerest gratitude for your assistance.

Sincerely,

Bernie Jordan

Bernie Jordan

Figure 5-1 Marketing survey and accompanying cover letter.

Be sure to do the following things in your survey:

1. Explain the reason for your survey: you are beginning to offer consulting services to members of the specified industry and would like to
conduct additional research to determine what problems appear most frequently among industry members.

Jordan Business Computer Systems

Questionnaire: Use of Computer Systems among Phoenix Metropolitan Area Legal Firms and Attorneys

Section I. *Current Computer Resources*

1. Does your firm currently use computers to assist with any tasks?

   Yes _____   No _____

   If you answered Yes, please skip to question number 3.
   If you answered No, please answer question number 2.

2. Does your firm have plans to utilize computerization during the next 2 years?

   Yes _____   No _____

   If you answered Yes, please answer the rest of the questions (number 3 on) in the perspective of your future plans.
   If you answered No what is the primary reason?

   _____ Not enough work to justify the cost of a computer.

   _____ Not sure what a computer can do for a legal firm.

   _____ We had one once and it didn't help our firm's operations.

   _____ Other. (Please explain.)

   _____

   _____

   _____

   If you answered No to question number 2, we thank you for your time.

3. What type of computer support does your firm utilize? (Please check all applicable items.)

	Current	Planned during the next two years
Microcomputer		
Timesharing		
Terminal access to legal database		
Other (please explain)		

Figure 5-1 Marketing survey and accompanying cover letter (*continued*).

If your firm currently has one or more microcomputers, please complete this section:

4. How many microcomputers does your firm have? _____

   What models are included? _____

   _____

   _____

5. Please rate each model computer listed above as excellent, good, fair, or poor.

   Computer Model   *Rating*   *Comments*

   _____   _____   _____

   _____   _____   _____

   _____   _____   _____

6. What commercial software packages do you use and how would you rate their performances—excellent, good, fair, or poor?

   Software   *Rating*   *Comments*

   _____   _____   _____

   _____   _____   _____

   _____   _____   _____

7. Do you use any custom-developed software?

   Yes _____   No _____

   If you answered Yes, for what applications (such as billing, payroll, litigation support, etc.)?

   _____

   _____

   _____

   _____

8. How satisfied are you with the overall performance of your custom software? (Please note if packages are excellent, good, fair, or poor.)

   _____

   _____

   _____

   _____

Figure 5-1   Marketing survey and accompanying cover letter (*continued*).

9. If any of the above areas (hardware, commercial software, or custom software) are unsatisfactory, what do you feel the major problems are?

_____

_____

_____

_____

10. What is the major benefit computerization provides your firm?

_____

_____

_____

_____

11. What is the major problem (if any) you have found with computerization?

_____

_____

_____

_____

12. Please note any other comments.

_____

_____

_____

_____

Section II.   Your Legal Firm

1. How many people are members of your firm, in the following categories?

	Total	Those who use one or more computers
Attorneys		
Paralegal assistants		
Clerical assistants		
Other (Please list job title)		

Figure 5-1   Marketing survey and accompanying cover letter (*continued*).

2. Over the next 2 years, the number of people in your firm is expected to:

    _____Increase   (If yes, which categories will increase the most?)

    _____

    _____

    _____Stay the same

    _____Decrease   (If yes, which categories will decrease the most?)

    _____

    _____

3. Who has the primary responsibility for any computerization decisions? What is
    your usual source of computer hardware and software (retail store,
    manufacturer's sales representative, wholesaler)?

    _____

    _____

    _____

    _____

We thank you very much for taking the time to complete this survey. We hope
to continue serving the legal community of Phoenix as best we can, and your
assistance has helped us enhance our understanding of the legal profession's
computerization efforts.

Figure 5-1   Marketing survey and accompanying cover letter (*continued*).

2. Mention a little bit about your projected services (consulting, contract software, informative seminars, and whatever else you are offering).

3. Make the survey short enough so the addressee is less likely to toss it in the In basket (to be lost in oblivion) or throw it away. A marketing research specialist could probably add many more questions to the survey in Figure 5-1, hoping to obtain more information, but the larger and more complicated the survey gets the less likely you are to receive a response. The questions presented will give an overall picture of computerization in the legal profession.

4. Enclose a self-addressed stamped envelope to increase potential response.

What should you expect to learn from your marketing research? Most importantly, you must try to determine if your planned products and services can be sold to your prospective clients. Without a potentially receptive audience, your efforts may very well fall on deaf ears. You can also find out what percentage of your market can be eliminated for various reasons, such as already having a computer system or not considering one for whatever reasons.

As stated several paragraphs ago, you may become aware of special problems and opportunities. A group of attorneys, for example, may express a strong desire to access legal databases and download the data into a word processing system to produce legal opinions. If enough respondents desire this capability, you may investigate the feasibility of including these systems and software among your offerings.

Additionally, you can learn what specific buying patterns exist among your future customers. Members of the consumer goods retail industry, for example, may not do much systems purchasing between mid-October and mid-January because of the heavy holiday season workload. A certain target market may be particularly cautious when purchasing computer equipment and take several months to make affirmative or negative decisions. Armed with this knowledge, you can adjust your marketing efforts to take advantage of certain features of your market segment.

You should also try to determine what may motivate your potential clients. Several times I have mentioned that you and your services should help your customers solve problems or exploit opportunities.

These two benefits you provide can be defined as dealing with negative and positive motivators, respectively.[2] A client's *negative motivator* could be falling behind on order processing, causing customers to cancel orders rather than wait for delivery. Another would be a backlog of correspondence, also resulting in lost customers. Negative motivators imply that a problem exists.

A *positive motivator,* however, is a potential incremental benefit to the client rather than the solution to a problem. His or her current procedures may be able to process all customer orders with minimal delay, but a computer system could allow a doubling of orders without a corresponding increase in clerical workers. Similarly, a word processing system could provide mass mailing capability with minimal effort, increasing that company's advertising and promotion efforts.

It is important that you know what motivates your potential clients because this provides directions for your marketing and advertising. A client base strongly motivated by solutions to critical problems will not likely be stirred by advertisements catering to positive motivators.

I also mentioned in Chapter 2 that you may find your mix of products and services changing over time. In addition to finding new opportunities, this may also be due to changing markets. All markets, those you target as well as others, are unlikely to remain static. Because of changing demographics and other factors you may find your own clients losing interest or formerly unprofitable markets becoming attractive. Through a perpetual marketing effort, including periodic market analysis, you can be forewarned of these shifts and react accordingly in a timely manner.

Marketing and Your Fees

In Chapter 4 we looked at various methods to calculate your consulting fees, based on salary and expense requirements, utilization rates, etc. This financial analysis, however, must be accompanied by an indication that your future clients are willing to pay these rates.

You may determine that your billing rate should be $60 per hour, based upon your minimum requirements. However, there may be several reasons why you will be unable to command these fees on a regular basis. First, your geographical area may preclude fees that wouldn't raise an eyebrow in New York City, Los Angeles, or Pittsburgh. A smaller city with a low cost of living accompanied by traditionally low compensation for services probably doesn't have too many consultants, computer or otherwise, charging $60 per hour.

Additionally, your chosen target market, even in a medium to large city, may not support a high billing rate even though another industry in the same city would. You may foresee a large demand for computer systems among local retailers, but the local chamber of commerce's Small Business Committee provides free computer advice to members, primarily through the volunteered time of computer-experienced members. Your other target market, real estate agents, has assistance from the area Data Processing Management Association (DPMA) chapter through a special Board of Realtors contract; they receive advice at $10 per hour. Think you can charge $60 per hour and have customers ringing your phone off the hook?

Your marketing research should provide information about any possible obstacles facing your projected fees; if competition or other factors loom menacingly, your fee structure may require recalculation. Think seriously about pursuing any market if a recalculated fee, supportable by that audience, requires tremendous sacrifices on your part in terms of business profitability. You're not a charitable organization, after all.

Promoting Your Business

There are three principal ways to attract clients for your business. These include (1) using friends or associates as your first customers, (2) explicitly advertising the products and services you offer, and (3) establishing a reputation for excellence in your field. All play an important role in developing a comprehensive market plan.

Bernie Jordan entered the consulting profession with his first client almost contracted; many consultants are not that fortunate. Your immediate operational goals (as contrasted to the support goals of planning your product, financial, and service strategies) should be directed toward attracting clients and establishing your business reputation.

One of the most important assets any business can have is name recognition. When you think of fast-food hamburgers, automobile rental agencies, or television sets, one or two companies usually come immediately to mind. When legal offices desire advice about computerization options, Bernie Jordan would like Jordan Business Computer Systems to be the first consulting firm to come to mind.

Because a consultant is a professional (akin to a doctor, dentist, lawyer, or accountant), certain media may not be suitable for advertising. Television and radio, for example, tend to detract from the professional reputation you are trying to develop and brand you a "mass marketer." Even though some physicians and lawyers choose to advertise their practices, the majority don't, relying instead on references and walk-in business.

Newspaper advertisements tend to be more appropriate for your intended clientele. A firm specializing in real estate applications could advertise periodically in the local newspaper's real estate section. The type of advertisement is also important. Boldfaced headlines screaming **"SPECIAL: THIS WEEK ONLY"** are also inappropriate for a professional firm.

You do, however, want to follow the basic rules of advertising: attract the customer's attention, explain the product and how it will be of benefit, and provide a point of contact (address or phone number). Newspaper advertisement rates are usually based on the number of column inches involved. One word of caution: at the beginning, stay away from "special" rates with a lower per-inch charge but a high minimum number of inches per year. These special rates are more appropriate for larger firms employing several consultants with a substantial advertising and promotion budget.

Another forum for advertising is trade publications of your targeted industry. The local or state board of realtors, for example, may have a monthly newsletter that would provide an excellent advertising medium.

Many national magazines also offer regional advertising instead of or in addition to their national advertising. You could, for example, place an advertisement in the west coast edition of a magazine that research has shown members of your target market read frequently. This may be a bit much when you are just starting out, but as your business expands (and with it your geographical target) you may consider this option.

A final medium you should consider is the local *Yellow Pages*. Mentioned in Chapter 3 as a minimum starting business expense, this form of advertising informs anyone with a phone book of your business services. As with regional magazine advertising and bulk newspaper advertising, you should shy away from quarter-page display ads during your firm's early growth period. A bold-faced business name and a two- or three-line statement of services surrounded by a ¼-inch box (see Figure 3-2) will serve nicely for the first year or two at far less expense while still providing you with visibility in the *Yellow Pages*. Monthly costs average between $10 and $20, depending on location.

Once every month or two you may consider inserting an ad in the newspaper just stating the availability of your services. These serve to provide the name recognition your business needs. The more frequently you advertise, the more your reputation is likely to be built up. Frequent advertisements convey an image of a successful business; since these ads cost money, the public assumes you are earning money to pay for the notices.

The primary problem with advertising is the cost involved. While your practice is in its early growth stages, you don't want to be pouring both your savings and your initial revenue into advertising costs. There are other ways to build your practice, starting with your very first customer.

Word of mouth (i.e., references) may be the most important means of building a client base. One satisfied customer often leads to referrals for several more, who in turn refer your services to several more; before long your customer database on your business's computer system requires a hard disk because one floppy disk can't store all of your customers (or so you hope!). In all seriousness, referrals by satisfied clients are an important way to build your business. A realtor is more likely to take note when another realtor tells him or her about this wonderful computer system that is increasing efficiency and revenues than by reading an advertisement in a newspaper or trade journal. Be warned, however, that the inverse is also true; one dissatisfied customer can spell disaster for your business.

There are other ways to make yourself known to your market. Speaking at trade association breakfasts, luncheons, banquets, or other meetings to discuss computerization topics of interest to the audience can produce the spark that could lead to clients. It provides you with visibility; people see you and, hopefully, will be impressed by your insight into both their business and the computerized tools available to increase their productivity and solve their problems. You can also demonstrate your communication skills. (But try not to talk with your mouth full; this tends to detract from your professionalism!)

Another tool to use in promoting your business is the press notice. When something occurs that will be of interest to your public, you can develop a notice for publication in the local newspapers. The event may be introducing a new product, hiring new personnel, or opening a new business location. Check with your local papers to determine their policies regarding press notices. Don't overlook the power of free advertising!

Finally, after your business has grown a bit, you may print promotional brochures that describe your services and products. A folded, glossy-paper, color brochure can add sophistication to your business promotion, but make sure that the resulting brochure is a professional product. You could arrange for computer retailers or professional organizations to distribute the brochures to interested individuals and companies, or you could mail them to members of your target market (perhaps enclosed with your marketing survey).

The important point is that a successful marketing effort doesn't consist of just newspaper advertising or referrals. An integrated plan must be developed to reach your intended clients at a reasonable cost within your budgeted expenses and establish your reputation as an expert in your field.

Symbiotic Relationships

Often a joint effort with another institution can provide you with a means of gaining customers. If you have demonstrated to a local computer store your expertise in certain areas on prior contracts, you may be referred to their customers who need custom programming, general consulting, or training that the retailer doesn't provide.

It is important to build your reputation and contacts with as many local computer stores as possible; as your reputation grows they may want to impress their customers by consulting with you, the expert, on particularly difficult problems. This provides you with future clients as well as another important feature; someone else is assisting you with marketing your services. For every other person, store, or organization who recommends you as a successful implementor of computer solutions, the pyramiding effect of referrals is that much more powerful.

Another joint effort that can assist you with both marketing and producing revenue is working with (and eventually receiving endorsements from) a professional organization. The local board of realtors, for example, might have a computer committee to assist members with their automation efforts. Providing consulting services to this committee may lead to myriad contracts as individual members attempt to computerize their operations. Educational and informative seminars for board members are another possibility.

Again, this symbiotic relationship is of great benefit to your practice: you are providing expert advice to your clients, and they are providing you with highly reputable marketing services.

Another relationship that can benefit you is working with a national or regional main office, such as a national realty organization. Under contract to the organization as a whole, you can be recommended to the member branch offices by the main office when computer services are needed. As with professional organizations, you are utilizing the reputation and credibility of the sponsoring agency to assist you with your marketing.

How Much Time Do You Spend Marketing?

As soon as you begin your first contract it is likely that you will spend almost all of the time devoted to your consulting activities (whether full- or part-time) completing this task. You may not have the time to perform the marketing functions we have discussed in this chapter: speaking, advertising, meeting with prospective clients, and generally building your reputation. Once your first contract is completed, however, you may find yourself with no following assignment. The first rule of consulting is "No job, no income" (with the exception of royalty cash flow, which most beginning consultants don't have). You then begin your marketing efforts to find a client. That assignment ends, you have no future contract, and the cycle repeats.

A better plan is to allocate a certain percentage of your time and effort to executing a comprehensive marketing plan, simultaneously working on your contracts. Remember that as an independent consultant, you have no marketing department (as in a large organization) to attract future clients while you concentrate on business operations; that is another one of the many functions that you must perform simultaneously.

For example, a 1-month project (based on 8 hours per day, 5 days per week) could be extended by just over 1 week if an average of 2 hours per day is spent on marketing and related functions. The type of job a beginning consultant would work on is unlikely to be of such a critical nature that a 5½-week completion time frame rather than 4 weeks would be disastrous for your client and cause you to lose the project. Naturally, when planning a project you wouldn't tell your client, "Well, this will take 5½

weeks rather than 4 because I want to spend time marketing my services";
that is a quick way to turn a prospective client into a former prospective
client.

This also doesn't mean that you will spend exactly 2 hours each day
on marketing efforts; you may attend a ½-day meeting with the computer
services subcommittee of a local accountant's group one day and perform
no marketing functions the next day. You should just allocate your time
appropriately to meet your tasks.

You may even find yourself involved in a long-term contract on a flat-
fee basis. In this case, the sooner the contract is concluded, the sooner
other projects may be started. Under these circumstances, you may
decrease your marketing efforts to maybe 3 to 5 hours per week to speed
up completion of the current job. The key is to be flexible in your
approach to marketing (and all business) functions.

The Personal Selling Touch

Just as any well-designed plan must actually be implemented in order to
achieve desired results, your total marketing effort must be capped off
with successful personal selling. The main focus of your advertising and
personal contracts is to attract potential clients' interest in your services;
once they do show interest, it is up to you to successfully close the sale.

Sounds a bit more like a retail salesperson than a professional consultant, doesn't it? If you were working in a large corporation as a computer programmer or systems analyst, you wouldn't need to be concerned
with any type of selling; the organization's marketing department or sales
division has that responsibility. However, it is up to you as a consultant
to take a client's interest in what you have to offer and cement those ideas
by convincing him or her of exactly what benefits you can provide.

Most people have a natural fear of rejection, and this brings on great
amounts of stress in a selling situation. You *must* get over this phobia in
order to succeed as an independent consultant. If a client ultimately
rejects your proposed services, it is normally not a dismissal of you as a
person but rather of the services themselves. As long as your behavior has
been businesslike and you don't do anything to obviously cause any personal distaste, your personal characteristics shouldn't be the deciding
factor.

The fear of rejection can sometimes be associated with the fear of failure; failing to win a client contract becomes a personal defeat. Consider
this: if you were a baseball player, you could fail to hit safely two-thirds
of the time and still be considered very successful with your .333 batting

average. The same principle is true of consultants; not every meeting you attend will result in a contract, but your goal is to obtain sufficient projects to make your practice successful.

How then do you go about selling your services to your prospective clients? The most critical portion of this plan is your initial interview. Both you and the prospective client should have "creative tension" at this first meeting; he or she is assessing your understanding of the immediate needs as well as your professional competence, while you are determining if you can help solve the problems as well as the probability of winning that contract. You should also be assessing any possible competition you may have.

You should attempt to put the customer at ease, and at the same time demonstrate your competence. Don't brag about your skills, your "infinite, instinctive understanding of the problem," and your "fantastic solution," or anything else; if you've worked on a similar project in the past, mention that project and that client's name (if reference permission had been granted). Perhaps the prospective client knows your former one and a good reference will be the sales clincher.

Another goal is to assess the other person's readiness to award the contract. Naturally, he or she should have the authority to do so; if you are speaking with a store manager but a division director is necessary to approve any computerization contracts, little subsequent time should be devoted to meeting with the store manager *in the capacity of project approval,* especially if your first meeting is to assess the project at hand and isn't being paid for (more on this later). Naturally you should not rudely dismiss any further conversation with the store manager, especially if assessing project requirements, but don't waste valuable time attempting to sell the contract if you determine that he or she possesses little influence in the purchasing decision.

If you receive a verbal commitment at the first meeting that is contingent upon some other action by you, such as submission of a written proposal, you should complete this action as soon as possible; a prolonged delay may cause a decision reversal by the client.

If your verbal commitment is contingent upon some action by the client, such as obtaining either permission from a regional manager to proceed or sufficient funds, you may find yourself in limbo. That may have merely been a ploy to avoid giving you a direct no, or the prospect may simply be unconvinced at the present. You should, by all means, continue selling your services through subsequent phone calls or other means—not three times each day, but at whatever interval you feel is appropriate. If a long series of unreturned calls or "We're still waiting for the main office's go-ahead" speeches convince you that the likelihood of putting the contract into action is remote, a generic letter or noncommittal proposal stating your availability for X, Y, and Z services at a given rate may be submitted, followed perhaps by one more phone call. If no decision is in sight, it may be better to file any paperwork for future reference and redirect your efforts. The contract may eventually come through, but you shouldn't divert scarce resources from viable and promising projects toward dead ones.

In short, then, you need to be a persistent and confident salesperson without being a pushy one. Your final task prior to actually beginning work on a contract is to convince prospective clients that they actually want to become clients.

Summary

As you can see, the key to most of your business decisions—product and service lines, fee determination, and reaching prospective clients—lies with your marketing plan. A well-run marketing effort will direct your energies toward prospects through the most efficient and cost-effective means.

Depending on whom you are trying to reach, your advertising methods and channels will vary. Again, perhaps the most important tool you can utilize is word-of-mouth references, which can be practice-builders or practice-destroyers. Realize also that as a consultant, you will be doing some personal selling to your prospects.

Let's see what marketing Bernie Jordan has developed. In order to better gauge the possibility of doing concentrated work with the local legal community he designed the marketing questionnaire shown in Figure 5-1. Hoping for sufficient response to determine if there is indeed a demand for computer services in this market, he will then decide whether to further pursue the marketing of legal systems.

Assuming that he will find sufficient demand, Bernie decides to place a small but distinguished-looking advertisement in the monthly *Phoenix Law Review,* the most commonly read publication among local attorneys. He has also spoken with acquaintances in the legal profession about speaking at the Arizona Bar Association monthly breakfast in the near future. He will eventually prepare a brochure of services available and has already prepared a "business brief" notice for local newspapers discussing his firm and its services.

Feeling that this effort will be sufficient and very cost-effective for the near term, especially since he is still consulting part-time, Bernie will review the marketing plan periodically to see what changes must be made to meet shifts in target markets, increasing competition, or other situations.

End Notes

1. Robert E. Kelley, *Consulting: The Complete Guide to a Profitable Career,* Scribner's, New York, 1981, p. 105.

2. Herman Holtz, *How to Succeed As an Independent Consultant,* Wiley, New York, 1983, p. 84.

CHAPTER 6

Putting It All Together: The Business Plan

So far we've looked at a variety of financial, product and service, managerial, and marketing decisions, mostly as individual entities. Just as we discussed the relationship between the financial and marketing aspects of setting your fees, though, all of your business decisions must fit together as though they were pieces of a jigsaw puzzle. No decisions should be made in isolation from one another.

The *business plan* is a document that contains the specifics of what products and services you will offer, to whom and through what channels they will be directed, how the operations will be financed, and innumerable other decisions; in short, an overall plan for your business.

It is arguable what the most important use of the business plan is. It would be extremely difficult, if not impossible, to obtain financing for your business without presenting a business plan; anyone investing in or loaning funds to a firm wants a realistic projection of that business's chances of success.

Perhaps more important, though, is that a business plan forces the consultant to think through all aspects of his or her strategic plans, including conducting any necessary further research. It is one thing to have the brilliant idea to conduct hands-on training for small groups of accountants. You must know, however, exactly what hardware and software is required to conduct these services, how to finance this equipment, and whether a market even exists for your divinely inspired plan. It is much better to discover during the planning stages that your ideas aren't feasible than to invest time and money in an ill-fated business operation. At the very least, you should be able to avoid unpleasant surprises like unexpected competition and unforeseen expenses.

Many books and magazine articles have discussed business plans, presenting several different formats. A typical business plan might include the following[1]:

1. A *cover page* containing your company's name, address, phone number, and date

2. An *introductory summary* explaining the major points presented

3. A *table of contents* for lengthy documents, including page numbers

4. *Information* about your company, describing your industry classification and what products and services you intend to provide

5. Information about your company's *industry classification,* including its history, current factors, and estimated future prospects

6. *Market research,* including estimated market size, trends, and competition

7. A *market analysis* covering your customers and estimated market share and sales you hope to capture

8. A *marketing plan* discussing marketing strategies, pricing decisions, advertising methods, and other promotional means

9. What *professional assistance* you will use, such as attorneys, accountants, bankers, financiers, and other help

10. A *general operations plan,* including geographical business location and strategy

11. Any applicable *research and development programs,* which especially concerns those consultants developing commercial software

12. The *time schedule* for implementing your plans

13. Any *critical risks and problems* you may face, such as competitive responses, unfavorable industry trends, and failure to achieve revenue projections

14. A *financial plan,* including forecasting profits and losses, a pro forma balance sheet, applicable cash flow analysis, and break-even charts

15. Plans for *financing* your firm's operations

16. Your firm's *legal organization* (sole proprietorship, partnership, or corporation)

A business plan prepared by an entrepreneur seeking $5 million in second-round financing is likely to be more comprehensive than one completed by a potential part-time consultant. The business plan presented later in this chapter was prepared from the latter viewpoint, with less emphasis on external financing and financial projections than would be required by a potential investor. Bernie Jordan, our traveling consultant and the plan's preparer, is more concerned with integrating his random thoughts and chicken scratchings into an organized blueprint.

Finally, before we present our business plan, let's look at some general guidelines for preparing and presenting business plans[2]:

1. A business plan should be no more than ¼- to ½-inch thick and loosely bound in a clear plastic cover. Some venture capitalists receive 500 to 1500 business plans each year; in order to have your submission seriously considered, it should be concise and readable. If your plan is primarily for internal use, why prepare a 3000-page document?

2. A business plan submitted for financing should be preceded by a phone call or, better yet, a referral from a respected friend or business contact. If you don't have much business experience prior to submission, your accountant, attorney, or a satisfied (and influential) client may pave the way for serious consideration of your plan.

3. Venture capitalists tend to fund only certain types of businesses, sometimes limited to certain geographic areas, and at certain business life-cycle stages (start-up, operating at a loss, operating at break-even, etc.). By consulting *Venture* magazine's annual *Venture Capital Directory* or a similar listing you can select prospective investors suitable for your project, location, and stage of operations.

4. While small business consultants and others can professionally prepare a business plan for you, investors are less interested in a highly polished, computer-generated document than one which is well thought out and contains essential information. Of course, your plan should contain correct grammar and spelling, be neat and well organized, and reflect your professionalism. Your business plan is a reflection of your own organizational ability and skill at expressing ideas.

5. Your competition, both current and projected, should be detailed and realistically evaluated. If you are proposing a nonproprietary product or service, such as educational seminars, how quickly could a local retailer cut into your market share? What are your relative strengths and weaknesses as compared with those of your competition?

Now that we've discussed business plans in a general manner, let's look at the one Bernie Jordan has prepared, based on his preliminary research and analysis (see Figure 6-1). Many items have been discussed

JORDAN BUSINESS COMPUTER SYSTEMS

7300 N. 27th Avenue
Phoenix, AZ 85021
(602) 555-8675

December 20, 1984

Introduction

This business plan has been prepared by Mr. Bernard Jordan for the strategic direction of Jordan Business Computer Systems. Information presented here is primarily for internal company use in the area of strategic planning. This plan will be updated as necessary to reflect changes in the strategies or organizational features of the consulting firm.

Background Information

Jordan Business Computer Systems is a computer consulting firm specializing in consulting and software services. Currently, marketing efforts are directed toward the Phoenix metropolitan-area legal profession. At appropriate future times, product and service lines will be expanded and new markets, including expanded geographic areas, will be targeted. Detailed descriptions of product and service lines and the target market will be presented in the Operations Plan section.

Industry Background

Traditionally, consulting firms have provided services to businesses of all sizes in many operational areas: general management, marketing, personnel, and computerization, to name a few. The explosive growth of the microcomputer industry has been accompanied by a growth of computer support services, including consulting for small businesses. Many businesses have computerized their operations and, rather than hire programmers or other computer professionals either for a short duration or for long-term employment, seek short-term assistance from computer consultants to analyze automation needs, select hardware and software, install systems, and train users.

Estimates of microcomputer growth have been revised downward recently from the lofty predictions of several years ago. Nevertheless, continued technological advances should provide sufficient opportunities for software designers, consultants, and other support segments as new hardware replaces old systems.

Market Research

As stated previously, the current primary target of Jordan Business Computer Systems is Phoenix metropolitan-area attorneys. Currently, this geographical area has an estimated 3000 attorneys. A market research survey, answered by 60 percent of those polled (1808 respondents), indicates potential growth for com-

Figure 6-1 Sample business plan.

puter consulting services to that profession. Allowing for the fact that many legal firms were represented in the survey by more than one attorney, analysis determined that only 10 percent of local law firms currently featured any computerization. However, 25 percent of all firms (including those who already utilized automation) had definite plans to purchase at least one computer by December 31, 1985. An additional 30 percent were considering computerization but had no definite plans.

It can be stated, therefore, that the trend among Phoenix legal firms is toward automation of several administrative and operational functions. The most desired applications are:

1. *Word processing,* emphasizing "boilerplate" (fill-in-the-blanks) legal correspondence management.

2. *Litigation support,* tracking due dates and associated documents for client cases.

3. *Automated filing and retrieval* of client records and other documents.

4. *Remote database access,* providing retrieval of information from legal databases.

Finally, attorneys interviewed by this plan's author have expressed great interest in expert consulting services. The prevailing opinion is that they are willing to spend a bit of extra money prior to system selection to ensure a usable and expandable computer system that supports their business operations.

Market Analysis

Jordan Business Computer Systems currently has a contract to develop a litigation-support computer system, including custom software, for a local legal firm. Several other legal offices have expressed interest in the subsequent purchase of a customized version of this system.

Based on market research results that indicate legal firms are willing to pay for consulting services, an estimated 50 percent of the organizations considering computerization (approximately 600 firms) are candidates for consulting services.

Market research has also revealed that no Phoenix metropolitan-area consultants or system designers specifically target the legal profession. There are two local software companies that produce commercial software for attorneys and law firms, but to date they have refused all requests for contract software development or customizing of their software for individual clients. Several consulting organizations are retained by legal firms, among other clients. Therefore, a concerted marketing effort, outlined in the next section, should provide a large market share.

Marketing Plan

The prevailing theme of Jordan Business Computer Systems' marketing efforts is *specialization.* As mentioned in the previous section, no firms currently

Figure 6-1 Sample business plan (*continued*).

target the legal profession as their primary clients for either total system or applications software development.

The legal profession is unique among industry groups in that it is one of very few (such as the medical profession) in which extreme specialization is a common form of operation. Attorneys tend to specialize in narrow areas such as tax law, divorce, contracts, or real estate, among many other possibilities. In most cases, a tax attorney doesn't have enough experience with the complexities of divorce law to represent a client to the best of his or her ability.

Specialization is the key to this firm's strategy. All marketing and strategy will stress the extreme competence of Jordan Business Computer Systems and its familiarity with systems and software for the legal profession; e.g., advertisements could proclaim, "You specialize in what you know best; so do we!" Since the applications mentioned in the Market Research section cross boundaries among legal specialties (a real estate attorney would use different boilerplate word processing forms than a corporate lawyer, but the basics of the word processing systems would be the same), the same basic skills will serve all clients.

Jordan Business Computer Systems will concentrate most marketing effort on means other than paid advertising in order to spare capital for internal expansion. The primary paid advertising will be a ¼-inch box in the Phoenix *Yellow Pages* under the Computer System Designers and Consultants section. This will cost $11.75 per month; there is an extra $15 per month charge for conversion of a residential phone to a business one.

The total marketing effort will consist primarily of the following areas:

1. The *Yellow Pages,* as mentioned in the previous paragraph

2. Speaking occasionally at the monthly Arizona Bar Association luncheon, stressing the benefits of computerization to a legal firm (with inference to the firm's assistance with these efforts)

3. Notices sent to the local newspapers of any noteworthy events, including formal commencement of business operations

4. Heavy emphasis on word-of-mouth recommendations from satisfied clients

Eventually, brochures will be printed for promotional use. Since most attorneys themselves rely on recommendations rather than formal advertising, establishing a marketing and promotion strategy similar to their own is a marketing strategy in itself.

Professional Assistance

Legal assistance will be provided by the firm of Jones, Smith, Jackson, and Johnson, specialists in small business needs and problems. They were recommended by several other attorneys, including this firm's first client.

Accounting services will be provided by Wilson, Williams, and Whittier, who also specialize in services for small businesses. Initial accounting functions will include tax form preparation and tax advice; journals and ledgers will be managed by Jordan Business Computer Systems itself, since a low and manageable transaction volume is expected.

Figure 6-1 Sample business plan (*continued*).

For the early stages of the company, this outside assistance should be sufficient.

General Operations Plan

Jordan Business Computer Systems will conduct operations in the Phoenix metropolitan area, including suburban cities. Geographic expansion will be considered at an appropriate time in a manageable manner.

The firm's product and service line will initially consist of:

1. *General computer consulting* to legal firms, including advice and assistance with choosing computer hardware and software.

2. *Contract programming,* either accompanying system selection or for clients with existing hardware.

3. *Information seminars* conducted at novice experience levels. Topics will include basics of computer systems, hardware and software evaluation criteria, reviews of legal applications software, and cost-benefit analysis of computerization. Every effort will be made to utilize hands-on computer experience (in some sessions). The seminars will be utilized as both a profit center and a marketing tool.

4. *Commercial software development* during periods when no contracts are being completed. A search of existing programs and their features, ease of use, etc., will hopefully determine several niches where commercial software is lacking.

Since Bernie Jordan, the firm's owner and preparer of this business plan, will be conducting business part-time, the previous list of services includes those that can be accomplished in evenings or during weekends. The part-time working situation will be discussed later under Critical Risks and Problems.

Research and Development

Most research will be conducted in the course of investigating hardware and software for clients. This research, as mentioned previously, should yield several areas where commercially available software is inadequate or nonexistent.

These results will lead to development of commercial software, to be marketed in a manner determined later (self-publishing, license agreements, etc.).

Occasionally, general research of commercial programs will commence, even if the firm doesn't have a client investigating particular applications. This will keep Jordan Business Computer Systems apprised of the new software being published, as well as its relative quality.

Time Schedule

Jordan Business Computer Systems is currently developing a contract litigation system, with supporting integrated office management functions. This project is estimated to take 100 hours of development time and be completed by

Figure 6-1 Sample business plan (*continued*).

February 15, 1985. Several other legal firms have expressed an interest in a similar system, and negotiations are currently underway.

The overhead involved in setting up the consulting practice (checking account, letterhead, etc.) has already been completed. Bernie Jordan is scheduled to speak before the Arizona Bar Association's monthly luncheon 1 week prior to the estimated completion date of the currently active project.

At this time, a detailed time schedule for 1985 cannot be determined because of the uncertainty of future client contracts. Highlights of the schedule for 1985 include:

First contract: January 1–February 15
ABA luncheon speech: February 8
First seminar: April 15
Midyear operations review: June 30
Commercial software development: Begin in September
1986 Operations plan development: October–November
Year-end operations review: December 30

Subsequent seminars will be scheduled in response to demand for the first one and projected future interest. Contract programming and systems development projects will be scheduled as they become available.

Critical Risks and Problems

The major critical success factor for Jordan Business Computer Systems will be available time. The firm's owner has 2 years until retirement qualification from his current job with the city of Phoenix; therefore, operations will be conducted on a part-time basis for at least 2 years.

Any periods of excessive work load or outstanding opportunities will be managed with subcontractor assistance, if necessary. The major problem with time availability will be for business-hours meetings with clients and others. The use of vacation days is anticipated if alternative meeting times cannot be scheduled.

There should be minimal financial risk, as little initial capital expenditure is expected. A personal computer system will be converted to business use, and initial operating expenses were financed primarily from personal savings. The sole exception was the purchase of a letter-quality printer, financed by a short-term credit union loan. This loan will be repaid when the first contract is completed and revenue is collected. All subsequent expenditures will be financed from cash flow, excluding any major future expansion.

Competitive response is not expected to harm operations; the firm's marketing strategy is designed to gain the confidence and support of the legal community, and by the time any potential competition becomes aware of operational strategy the firm should be firmly entrenched as a legal computer system specialist. While operating part-time could prove to be somewhat detrimental, the computer profession is known as a cottage industry, with many qualified part-timers and moonlighters. Most clients will recognize this fact and judge the consulting services by their quality and references from others.

Figure 6-1 Sample business plan (*continued*).

Financial Analysis

The following financial statements and cash budget were developed as a projection of the financial requirements and results for the upcoming business year.

(Author's note: Bernie's documents appear in Figures 4-1, 4-2, and 4-3; rather than repeat them here, please consult the appropriate reference points.)

Financial Strategy

As mentioned previously, Jordan Business Computer Systems has financed its initial start-up expenses from the owner's savings and a short-term loan, which should be repaid by March 1, 1985. The business strategy being pursued by the firm can be categorized as low capital-intensive; there is no inventory to supply and maintain, no office or other business location, and no employee salaries. Nearly all expenses incurred during the next few years can be financed from cash flow; therefore, no subsequent debt financing is anticipated.

This may change at the time the owner decides to pursue consulting full-time, expand operations geographically, hire employees, or otherwise undertake a major operational expansion. Every attempt will be made to anticipate expenditures and finance them from cash flow, but major expansion that will require financing will also be anticipated far enough in advance to determine the most appropriate forms and sources of capital.

Legal Organization

Jordan Business Computer Systems is organized as a sole proprietorship; the owner is Mr. Bernard Jordan. As the need dictates, incorporation may be desirable to provide legal protection of personal assets. This will probably occur as commercial software developed by the firm is marketed.

Figure 6-1   Sample business plan (*continued*).

in some detail in the summary case studies at the end of the preceding five chapters and are repeated here. After all, as we stated several paragraphs ago, the purpose of the business plan is to take general ideas and random thoughts, couple them with necessary research, and produce a workable business strategy that can help guide the consultant to a successful full-time or part-time business.

Please note that the business plan contains fictionalized data; the intent is not to present an analysis of the Phoenix legal market but rather to illustrate a sample business plan. Therefore, let's take a look.

Summary

The business plan is where you tie all of your independent decisions together, ensuring they mesh with one another. Your operations, financial, and marketing plans should come together as a well-researched business plan, acting as a blueprint from which you can build and manage your consulting firm.

The complexity and size of the plan will vary with the intended readership; one meant to convince a venture capitalist to invest $750,000 in your firm will be more complex than one meant as a guide for the preparer alone—a part-time consultant. Regardless of the user, the plan should be detailed enough to be of use to that reader.

End Notes

1. Robert E. Kelley, *Consulting: The Complete Guide to a Profitable Career,* Scribner's, New York, 1981, pp. 45–46.
2. Sabin Russell, "What Investors Hate Most about Business Plans," *Venture,* June 1984, pp. 52–53.

Jordan Business
Computer Systems

founded 1984

PART 2

Your Products and Services

CHAPTER 7

Conducting Seminars

Financial planners, stockbrokers, realtors, and other professionals have long used seminars as a means to create and build a client base. Offered at little or no cost, these seminars have provided a means for professionals to demonstrate their skills in various areas of business. Additional sessions between the client and the professional can be scheduled to arrange a working relationship.

Seminars have also been a way for people in all businesses to learn the latest methods and technology in their areas in a short period of time. In the computer field programmers, analysts, and others have been able to stay current in a rapidly changing environment.

The explosive growth of microcomputer use has been accompanied by a growing pool of computer owners and operators with little or no previous experience with hardware or software. Many of these people are categorized as "technophobiacs," or those afraid of the new technology. With the mass media's increasing coverage of computer-related topics, however, the general population is being inundated with the idea that the information age revolution currently underway will rival the industrial revolution in changing our business and personal lives. The desire for computer literacy is and will continue to be a strong motivator for business people.

The computer training market, handled both through computer stores' training courses and independently conducted seminars, is expected to capture $3 billion of the $14 billion personal computer market by 1986.[1] Many consultants are earning substantial revenues by concentrating on educating a willing public in the ways of the computer. This chapter will discuss how to target your market and choose your seminar topics, whether or not you should offer your seminar in conjunction with another party (such as a local computer store), the logistics and pricing strategy involved, preparation, and general seminar techniques.

Seminar Goals

Before you begin planning a series of seminar offerings, you should determine exactly what your goals are. Are you planning on using the seminars primarily as a revenue producer, with little expectation of gaining future clients from the attendees? Or are you using the sessions mainly as a marketing tool, with little substantial resulting revenue?

Your own objectives will determine your marketing and pricing strategies. A seminar meant to be a profit center will have to provide enough revenue to justify your efforts and costs of producing the class, while the objective of attracting future clients for individual consulting services can provide less earnings. Be sure that you have clear objectives in mind when planning the course contents, pricing, and marketing means.

Targeting Your Market

The rule presented in the first section of this book applies here as in all other areas of your consulting business; choose a target market and concentrate your efforts there. You could conceivably conduct seminars in the following areas:

1. *General computer knowledge for both business and home applications:* These seminars have been extremely successful and have proliferated in number. However, many universities, colleges, community or junior colleges, and technical schools have been adding classes of this type to meet the increased public demand. In order to compete, your seminar should be differentiated somehow from the multitude of offerings. Follow-on clients may be somewhat sparse unless you gear your advertising toward businesses rather than home and general use.

2. *Specific applications area:* Many owners or managers of businesses studying computerization of their transaction processing and other business functions consider attending an introductory-level computer seminar that specifically discusses their business area prior to purchasing a system. They often consider this a small investment in the front end of the computerization process. Many realtors, insurers, and other business operators become increasingly frustrated and confused as they journey among the many retail computer outlets in their region only to hear every salesperson recommend a different computer and software package as "the ultimate solution." A seminar conducted by an independent consultant, with no affiliation to any hardware or software brand or a specific computer store, might be seen as a forum for objective information.

3. *Intermediate topics:* These may include general computer knowledge for the experienced user (such as latest developments in certain applications software areas), computer language instruction (BASIC, PASCAL, etc.), or crash courses in microcomputers for the mainframe computer professional. One word of caution: Many attendees of intermediate-level courses often like to demonstrate how much they know, so you must thoroughly understand your topic. (This is also true of all seminars and classes you conduct, of course.)

4. *Teaching specific software packages:* A large seminar market in the personal computer field has been instruction in specific software bestsellers such as VisiCalc, WordStar, dBASE II, and Lotus 1-2-3. The virtues of word processing, spreadsheets, and database managers have been extolled in the computing and general media and people would like to learn how to use these systems. The novice user usually seems more comfortable learning from an "expert" rather than from self-paced instruction (including on-line interactive tutorials).

5. *Computers for children:* These sessions could cover elementary programming (including instruction in LOGO, an educational language that is gaining wide acceptance), graphics techniques utilizing videogames, or general principles. This area is increasingly being emphasized in computer camps and elementary, junior high, and high schools as a result of the emphasis on improved state-of-the-art education, so potential growth in this area is uncertain.

Cosponsoring a Seminar

Several options exist for planning, organizing, and conducting a seminar. Many consultants prefer to work alone; that is, the seminar is sponsored and conducted by the consultant and the firm's partners, if any exist. When you want to stress your independence and nonpartisanship to your potential audience this is normally the desired route.

When your business is in the early stages, however, communicating your competence to your potential clients may be difficult. Over time, a satisfied client base coupled with strategic advertising can establish your reputation. In the seminar business, however, you need credibility from the beginning. Why should someone pay $50 or more to hear you speak about or teach computer topics if you are an unknown entity? Endorsement from a local, well-established computer store, hardware vendor, or software publisher may be the key to making your first gains in this area. You should be careful not to become too dependent upon or intertwined with you cosponsor. Your clients deserve the open mind and wide search range that an independent consultant provides, and you should do nothing to tarnish that reputation. However, the initial endorsement and sponsorship may be beneficial to the success of your business.

You will be sharing the revenues from the seminars, of course, but you will also be sharing the expenses and are likely to attract a larger attendance than if you attempted to start on your own. It is possible, therefore, that in addition to the increased potential clientele, your net income will also be greater than from a solo effort.

Why, then, should a retail computer store cosponsor a seminar with you or any other consultant? After all, they are supplying the legitimacy to the overall seminar package. Presumably, their reputation as a solid community business will attract customers.

The answer is simple: Computer stores often do not have the expertise that you offer. Many store owners, managers, and sales personnel have a limited knowledge of computer hardware and software. They are primarily sales people with a lack of experience in such critical applications areas as real estate, insurance, and accounting. Some associates are extremely knowledgeable about computers, of course, but may not understand the business applications. You can provide them with a service, just as they provide you with one. A store conducting a seminar in conjunction with a computer consultant is less likely to be perceived by the public as conducting the seminar solely to sell attendees on a specific computer system. They are now providing an educational service to a target market and are one step closer to being a full-service store rather than just a retail outlet.

Additionally, many computer stores that are just beginning operations have limited resources. You are providing them with publicity and professional services just as they are performing the same function for you. By working closely with you, they are building their resources of local consultants who may bring customers to them.

Another advantage that you enjoy from working with a computer store is access to hardware and software, particularly if your seminar will involve hands-on experience (seminar techniques will be discussed later in the chapter). When your consulting operation is in the early stages of its life you are usually constrained by a somewhat limited budget. Even if you have a large capital pool from which to spend, making the substantial investment in hardware and software necessary to support hands-on seminars, or even those with demonstrations of different software packages, is a questionable action given the volatility of the computer industry. Why purchase hardware and software for demonstration purposes when it will probably be obsolete within 6 months? By then new stars of the computer world will have appeared. Computer stores usually can provide enough hardware and software to provide hands-on training for 10 to 20 attendees, increasing your maximum supportable audience.

As stated earlier, you must be careful not to become labeled a front person for your cosponsor. One of the simplest ways to avoid this is to work with several cosponsors. You may start with one computer store and conduct a seminar in general computer principles, and then you might hold the same session with a second computer store along with a real estate seminar. A third store could cosponsor a BASIC language class and a medical system seminar.

You need to be honest with all parties in this relationship. The computer stores or other cosponsors should be aware that you intend to maintain your independence when dealing with any clients on a postseminar basis. Ethics are discussed further in Chapter 13. Briefly, though, you should not be expected to favor your cosponsor over other stores just because they worked with you on a particular seminar. For those clients you do recommend to a particular cosponsor, you should not be relied on to recommend a high-priced system just to boost the store's revenues. Any cosponsors expecting such treatment should be avoided.

Sponsorship and Endorsement

In addition to possibly working with a partisan store or vendor, you should strive for another form of sponsorship, especially for seminars covering specific applications. Few things will attract a computer-shy realtor to a real estate computer system seminar more than endorsement by the local board of realtors. Similarly, the state bar association or local chapter of the American Medical Association lends an image of reputability to your presentation. Just as with any seminar when you are starting out, gaining this sponsorship may be difficult. You do have an advantage over advertising a general computing seminar in the local newspaper and hoping for a large turnout. You can submit an agenda and proposed list of demonstrated software to the governing organization and sell the idea. You have the opportunity to hold a demonstration session to prove your competence and knowledge of their industry. You should stress to your contact on the committee or board that you are interested primarily in endorsement to stress to members of that profession that you can fill a valuable role for them. Monetary sponsorship is not your primary goal (but you should think twice before turning away any funds!).

You should initiate contact with the sponsoring organization (let's use the local board of realtors as an example) through a contact you have in that profession: the realtor who sold your last house, for example. If you don't know anyone personally in that profession, ask a business acquaintance or friend of a friend. Eventually you will be in contact with someone who serves on a subcommittee of the board of realtors and can connect you with the president of the board or someone else of influence. Some organizations have a computer resources or education subcommittee that would be your first official contact. Once you gain subcommittee endorsement your program may then be voted upon by the full board of directors.

After gaining board endorsement you should attempt to get publicity for the seminar in any local newsletters or other professional publications. For example, a real estate seminar may be publicized in the beginning advertising pages of the local multiple listing service.

Another potential cosponsor is a "free university" or similar continuing-education program. These groups offer a wide range of classes and meetings to the general public in athletics, arts and crafts, health, business, and personal finance. Many also offer beginning computer-education classes. In exchange for their share of the registration fees these organizations offer wide distribution of class schedules (and thus a large potential audience at little or no advertising cost to you) and the umbrella of endorsement, which again can be valuable if you are just beginning your seminar programs. An advantage over working with a computer store is not having to worry about conflicts of interest, but you are less likely to attract a high-paying professional clientele from these classes.

Finally, seminar companies with national audiences such as the American Management Association offer seminars around the country. It is possible that you could arrange to work with them on a seminar in your geographical area or, if your schedule allows it, become part of their traveling instructor group.

Location

The location of your seminar can be critical to successfully attracting the desired target market. If you are conducting a seminar to discuss computer systems with members of the legal, medical, or similar profession, a session conducted in a hotel conference room is more likely to be perceived as a professional offering than one held in an unused elementary school classroom on Saturday morning. A class teaching children elementary programming, though, would be better suited to that classroom than a conference room. Be flexible in your locations. No two seminars are exactly the same and location should be carefully considered for each offering.

A third alternative is to hold the session in your office (assuming you have one). The major problem here is that space often limits you to a certain number of attendees (assuming you don't have an on-site educational facility). The advantage, of course, is lower fixed costs for room rental and miscellaneous services.

Seminars offered in conjunction with a computer store can be held at the store's educational facility if access to a wide range of computer equipment is needed. Otherwise, your impartiality will be enhanced by a conference room or other site offering.

When you decide to schedule a seminar in a hotel conference room, you should look for:

1. *Price:* Wide variation exists in the price of hotel conference services, sometimes depending on the time and date chosen. Be sure to shop around. Prices also vary among major cities.

2. *Services:* Are coffee, water, and other beverage services available? Will your room be configured as you desire?

3. *Advertising and publicity:* Does the conference have a publicity service listing their upcoming classes and seminars? If so, what charges, if any, are added to your bill?

4. *Rooms:* If your seminar will be lasting longer than 1 day and will be attracting clients from other cities, they will need sleeping arrangements, preferably at the same hotel where the conference is located. You should obtain information about guaranteed reservations and group discounts, if any exist.

5. *Flexibility:* Can an alternative room be scheduled if attendance will be greater or less than anticipated? If so, what are the additional charges?

Time and Duration

The time, season, and weekday can affect the success of your seminar. The session should be scheduled for a time when most members of your target market are likely to be free to attend. A seminar for retail merchants conducted between Thanksgiving and Christmas, regardless of the weekday and time, will likely be unsuccessful because of inconvenient scheduling. Saturday mornings may be convenient times for children's sessions, while evenings may be better for members of certain professions.

The duration of the seminar is also important. Some people like to "take a big gulp" and attend an all-day session (6 to 8 hours), while others prefer short meetings (1 or 2 hours) for several consecutive weeks. The best guideline here is to try one method, and if your attendance is low you may want to switch tactics for your next offering. Certain seminar topics are better suited to one form than the other, of course. A class teaching BASIC to beginning students is better suited to several hours per week for 8 to 10 weeks, while "Advanced Features of System X Database System" for current users may be better received as a 1-day session.

Scope of Marketing

When entering the seminar circuit, at least during the beginning of your offerings, you should limit your marketing efforts to local businesses and public. Advertising costs and other expenses will be reasonable and you are at a stage when your main goal (aside from producing revenue, of course) is to build both your client base and your reputation. As you become an acknowledged expert in your specialty areas you can then begin targeting markets on a regional or national basis.

Price

The big question every consultant must ask is "How much should I charge?" The answer is an unshakable "It depends." A seminar dealing with general computer knowledge readily available in the mass media (if someone wants to look for it) should be less expensive than a narrowly targeted topic, such as property management applications.

You can pursue one of two different strategies in determining your price: *price penetration* or *price skimming*. Price penetration means setting your fee low enough to attract many customers; the high volume will offset the relatively low margin. Price skimming is when you set a high price, hoping to attract the select few able and willing to pay for your services and knowledge. Which strategy you choose is dependent on your target market *and* your available resources.

For example, you specialize in medical and dental applications and operate your consulting business alone. Therefore, each client who hires you should contribute enough revenue to cover your expenses and provide enough net income to compensate for your entire resources being concentrated on his or her project. In other words, you need to make every dollar count. Assuming that you want to attract new clients through a medical system seminar, you should probably pursue a price-skimming strategy because doctors can be perceived as willing to pay more for your services than grade school children attending an elementary programming class. While you could offer a relatively low-cost seminar with follow-on consulting services priced at $60 per hour, you might then be perceived as baiting your clients with a low-cost enticement, rather than as a professional consultant—not exactly the reputation you hope to convey.

A class discussing general computer knowledge, however, would probably not be too successful with a price-skimming strategy. Many of the attendees who become later clients will be looking for simple computer systems or general advice. These services will require relatively little of your time and resources while still producing enough revenue to make the effort spent with the client worthwhile. As mentioned earlier, general computer knowledge is available through many sources, so a high price tag is not likely to attract a large audience; you are just throwing away potential revenue.

Please note that price skimming does not mean robbing your customer: $5000 for a 5-hour session can be considered somewhat extreme! A *general* guideline is charging between $10 and $25 per hour of seminar time depending on geographic location, seminar topic, competition, and similar factors.

These pricing strategies also apply to other aspects of your practice; you can mathematically calculate an hourly rate (Chapter 4) and analyze whether your market can support this price (Chapter 5), but the skim-versus-penetrate strategy pervades your overall business and marketing goals.

You should also offer group discounts for several people from the same office, family, or organization enrolling at the same time. This is likely to increase attendance. Early registration discounts, such as a $100 seminar being reduced to $90 if registration is received prior to 1 week before the seminar, encourage people to commit themselves to attending. If a potential attendee hasn't paid and the seminar day brings 2 feet of snow (or 85° temperatures and bright sunshine) your class may fall victim to environmental factors. Once someone has already paid a fee of $125, however, the snow suddenly becomes surmountable and the sunshine less attractive than if the fee had not been committed.

Break-Even Analysis

Each seminar arrangement should be preceded by a break-even analysis. You should know how many attendees are necessary for you to meet all of your costs. The concept we introduced in Chapter 4 of variable and fixed costs will be reexamined.

Assume that you plan a seminar to introduce local dentists and physicians to the medical office billing systems commercially available. You will be conducting the seminar by yourself at a local hotel's conference room. Based on your research and past seminar experience, you arrive at the following revenue and cost figures:

Fixed costs	
Conference room rental (20–30 attendees)	$ 75
Coffee/water service	25
Newspaper advertising	300
Direct mail advertising (300 mailings)	
Postage (20 cents each)	60
Letter photocopies (5 cents each)	15
Envelopes	3
Total fixed costs	$478
Contribution margin per attendee	
Seminar price	$ 75
Less: Handout materials	2
(40 pages per person, 5 cents per copy)	2
Total margin	$ 73

The following assumptions have been made here:

1. The attendees must preregister; no at-the-door registration will be allowed. Therefore, the exact number of handout packages can be printed. If preregistration were not required, a handout reserve for last-minute registrants would be included under fixed costs.

2. One price is applicable to everyone; if mutiple-pricing strategies were used, an average price per attendee must be estimated and used in your calculations.

3. No calculations are made for future revenue from registrants who become clients; the seminar will be viewed as a stand-alone profit center.

Based on the previous figures, 6.5 people must attend for you to break even and cover all fixed costs ($478 divided by $73 net earnings per registrant). Since one-half of a person seldom attends a seminar, you would round up and your break-even registration is seven people.

What do you do if registration is not sufficient to meet your fixed costs? Some costs may be recoverable, such as room rental (possibly after subtracting a small charge). Advertising costs, however, cannot be recovered and you will be faced with a loss whether or not you cancel the seminar.

Even though your time involved in seminar preparation may be substantial, no allowance for that cost has been included, since you don't pay yourself. However, the opportunity cost (Chapter 4) should be considered in your decision making; if you spend 50 hours preparing a seminar that doesn't have enough registrants and therefore is canceled, those 50 hours could have been spent on software development, magazine article writing, or some other revenue-producing activity. Naturally, the number of preparation hours will depend on whether this is the first time you have developed this seminar. If you are using a seminar package that you have presented before, most of your time will be spent on revision and updating, substantially reducing the preparation time over that of initial development. When considering opportunity cost, determine if your *projected* attendance will cover both the actual fixed costs and the revenue that likely (not wishfully) could be otherwise earned.

Advertising

There are many ways to advertise a seminar. The key to choosing your method is what will attract your target market. A real estate systems seminar should be advertised in the real estate section of your local Sunday newspaper, while a general computer information course would be out of place in the same location. You should consider the following media:

1. *Newspaper:*   This is the preferred choice for most locally marketed seminars. The business section of the Sunday newspaper is excellent for business applications and other sections may be used for narrowly targeted applications (for example, the sports section for "Use of Computers in Coaching"). Many newspapers also have free columns such as calendars of upcoming business events, local business news, or general-interest classes open to the public. Check your local newspapers to see if they contain similar features and contact the appropriate editor.

2. *Direct mail:*   You should only use direct mail for a narrowly defined target market, such as local accountants. Mailing lists can often be obtained from the professional organizations discussed earlier; if not, the *Yellow Pages* provides a convenient reference to your market. Letters should be professionally written on your letterhead and contain pertinent information regarding price, date, time, location, and most importantly, how the addressee will benefit from attending.

3. *Professional journals:* For specific applications seminars, especially those endorsed by a professional organization, you may be able to promote your session in the local or regional (or even national) newsletter or journal publication. If your seminar carries the endorsement of the local board of realtors, for example, your notice should state that fact, as it is a *strong* selling point.

4. *Speaking engagements:* Organizations often have periodic breakfasts, brunches, or other social-business events. Speakers are sometimes desired for these occasions. While you probably won't earn much revenue, if any, from these speaking engagements, a well-delivered and appropriate speech may promote your seminar (and your firm) to your audience more than all other advertising combined. You should check with the endorsing organization and watch the appropriate events calendar in your newspapers to learn which events frequently occur.

Timing is a critical factor in your advertising. An initial newspaper advertisement appearing 3 days before a seminar will be of limited use in attracting clientele who must preplan a busy schedule. Generally, initial newspaper advertising should appear 3 weeks to 1 month before your seminar date, with following announcements at periodic intervals continuing until the seminar. If direct mail is used the letters should also arrive with 3 to 4 weeks of lead time. The letter will coincide with the newspaper advertising and the lead time will give busy managers time to read the letter.

Preparation

Few events are as embarrassing as a presentation where everything goes wrong, especially when presented to an audience of clients offering potentially lucrative business. All spoken material should be rehearsed and criticized by a sample audience. *Do not* read your material, but don't expect to speak from memory during the entire session. You should be comfortable enough with your subject to use simple note cards or an outline.

All software demonstrations should be tested for correct operation and results. If sample data files are needed they should be created before the actual seminar. You may want to demonstrate data-entering techniques of several software packages, but don't force your audience to watch while you enter large amounts of data.

You should also verify arrangements with your seminar location contact (such as hotel conference staff) several days prior to your seminar. It is difficult to convince an audience of your competence when you and they are standing outside a locked conference room door waiting for the janitor to bring the key.

Supplies

You should arrive early on the seminar day to configure all hardware and software and make at least one more trial run of any demonstrations. You should also ensure that beverages (coffee, tea, water), condiments (sugar, artificial sweetener), and supplies (glasses, cups, saucers, spoons, stirrers) are set up by the hotel staff or whomever has that responsibility. For a small group (20 or less) doughnuts or sweet rolls may be offered for a morning session, or snacks (nuts, coffee cake) for an evening class.

Name cards (large index cards bent in half work nicely) should be supplied for all attendees along with markers. Extra pens, pencils, and paper can be furnished. Receipts for the amount paid should be already prepared for prepaid attendees and created for same-day audience members.

All visual aids should be set up before any clients arrive. This allows time for you to meet informally with your audience. Visual aids could include a slide projector, chalkboard (don't forget chalk!), easel, and flip-charts, or overhead projector.

A reference material packet should be given to each member of the audience; it should contain (1) an outline, (2) appropriate textual material, (3) copies of important slides or other visual aids, (4) references for further information, (5) a critique sheet to provide you with feedback, (6)

Seminar Checklist

_____ Verify your arrangements	_____ Be there early
_____ Prepare your materials	_____ Name cards
_____ Visual aids	_____ Reference material packet
_____ Refreshments	Outline
Condiments	Text and slides
Utensils	Reference material
Beverages	Critique sheet and response form
	Business card

Figure 7-1   Seminar checklist.

a form for the attendee to fill in name, business, address, phone number, and current computer equipment for you to arrange possible follow-on services, and (7) your business card clipped to the front.

Lecture Techniques

One short section of this book cannot teach you how to speak to an audience, but you should be aware of several important points.

1. *Give your audience what they want:* At the beginning of the presentation goals should be established to provide you with guidelines. By asking the audience what they expect to learn from the seminar, you are establishing an interactive dialogue between you and them and at the same time narrowing your range of topics. If you have prepared a general real estate seminar equally covering finance, investment, and property management but the audience appears to be heavily interested in property management to the exclusion of the other two topics, you may be able to adjust the emphasis of your topics more in the direction of property management subjects.

2. *Don't talk down to your audience:* You obviously need to communicate your competence and knowledge to the assembled group, but using highly technical computer-specific terms that the audience is not likely to understand is *not* the way to impress your audience. As a consultant, you are the interface between the technical world of computers and the prospective users. You need to explain many complicated and confusing technological factors to an audience not skilled in these areas and at the same time understand their own industry-specific applications and problems. The attendee is probably confused enough already; the moment you start speaking a strange language you have lost your communications link to that person, and probably that person's business.

Occasionally you may find yourself lapsing into computer jargon. Tell the audience at the beginning of the session to ask you to clarify anything that they do not understand. Refer back to Chapter 1 for more information.

3. *Encourage questions and interaction:* When your audience feels comfortable enough to ask many questions and propose scenarios you are able to communicate more easily than if you speak nonstop for several hours on end. By the type of questions asked you will be able to determine how much of your material is being successfully transmitted to the audience.

4. *Offer hands-on experience where possible:* It will probably be difficult to provide hands-on activity for an audience of 45 people because of the probable imbalance of your computer hardware and software resources and the number of clients. If you have approximately the same amount of resources and attendees, you should allow them to use several software packages and proceed through several sample problems.

Many audience members may be touching a computer for the first time. Under close supervision and by proceeding slowly they can quickly gain confidence in their ability to operate a computer. For larger audiences that will be using machines, you should have several assistants to provide close supervision over a portion of the group. By dividing up the supervisory work you can proceed more quickly than if you must resolve all questions and problems that arise.

5. *Use visual aids:* Even if hands-on experience will not be provided, you can rent or borrow a machine that projects your terminal image on a large screen. This will allow the audience to see exactly what happens during the operation of various software packages. Other visual aids should be used, including appropriate graphs, charts, and outlines.

Following Up Client Leads

The response forms included in the reference material package provide you with a convenient means to build your prospective client database. During any session breaks and after the seminar is concluded, several strong leads may arise from your conversations with attendees. After any services are provided for these clients, you can contact other audience members. Inquire about their current business operations; determine if they might eventually use your services. If not, you may still have created a valuable reference, provided they enjoyed and learned from the seminar. They might recommend your consulting firm to friends or others in the same business.

Summary

Seminars can provide you with a valuable means of building your client base. In addition, a substantial portion of your consulting revenue can be generated from these seminars. Once you have defined your target market, you can proceed alone or join efforts with local computer businesses or other establishments. The advertising media, location, time, day, and price must be chosen with your target market in mind. You should be adequately prepared for the seminar through rehearsal and by verifying all arrangements (see Figure 7-1). The seminar session itself should use demonstrations and visual aids as appropriate to increase your audience's understanding of the presented topics.

End Notes

1. "Training: A Built-In Market Worth Billions," *Business Week,* November 1, 1982, p. 84.

CHAPTER 8

Developing a Client's Computer System

When a client or prospective client expresses an interest in having a computer system designed, how should you proceed? There are several steps in the process known as the *computer systems life cycle*, the procedure that takes you from the preliminary analysis of a customer's business to the implementation and fine-tuning of a computer-based information system. A thorough understanding of the life cycle is essential to your performance in designing a useful and cost-effective computer system, which in turn will serve to perpetuate your business through a growing base of satisfied clients.

The steps of the systems life cycle are: (1) analyze the business of your customer and determine the problem areas and possible computerized solutions, (2) create a preliminary design for a computer system, (3) conduct a preliminary cost-benefit analysis of the proposed system to determine the feasibility of continuing, (4) investigate software availability, (5) determine hardware requirements to meet selected software, (6) implement the complete computer system and test for meeting the specified requirements, (7) train the system's users, and (8) maintain the computer system.[1] This chapter will discuss these life cycle steps, as well as writing proposals, maintaining existing systems, and other systems analysis methodologies.

Proposals

Back in Chapter 5, we discussed face-to-face selling techniques. Later in this chapter, we'll discuss some of the topics of concern when you first meet a client. This verbal communication, however, is usually accompanied by written communication in the form of a *proposal*. Together, interviews and proposals help win a client's business.

You are likely to write a proposal for one of two reasons. First, you are competing with other consulting firms or a client's internal staff to acquire a project. Alternatively, you may be the only outside consultant involved but the client company's policy requires a written proposal for reference or main-office approval.

A completed proposal should demonstrate that you understand the client's problem or opportunity and are competent to successfully complete the project. Additionally, you should state what actions you intend to accomplish, as well as any benefits to the client.[2]

There is always the possibility that even though you submit a proposal the contract may already be locked up by someone else with a built-in competitive advantage (maybe the prospect's sister-in-law's consulting firm). Why then would proposals even be requested? It may be a company requirement or a legislated one in the case of governmental agencies. Therefore, you should try to assess any potential competition. If you feel another party has an insurmountable advantage, you should either not submit a proposal or, if you wish, submit one but don't devote too much time to its preparation. It should still be a quality proposal, however; never submit shoddy work as it may find its way into circulation among other prospective customers.

Several formats exist for your written proposals; the submitting party may specify a required format in order to facilitate its competitive analysis. Generally, a proposal should include some or all of the following segments:[3]

1. Table of contents
2. Introduction
3. Purpose of proposed engagement
4. Estimate of benefits
5. Your approach to the problem
6. Project schedule and management plan
7. Nature of final output
8. Progress reports during the project
9. Pricing summary
10. Your qualifications
11. Use of outside support
12. Role of your client
13. Expected client support
14. Functions of client steering committee (if any)
15. Disclaimers
16. Appropriate references
17. Summary and closing

Your proposal should include charts, graphics, and flowcharts whenever possible. This enhances both the attractiveness of your submission and your perceived professionalism.

Sometimes you will be responding to a formal request for proposals (RFP); other times, your planned action will be based on personal interviews. Whatever your proposal states that you will accomplish, *never* commit yourself to actions based on ambiguous or incomplete requirements.

Assume an RFP states the need for a "custom accounting system," without further details. Does this include a general ledger system? Payroll? Accounts receivable and payable? How about inventory? All of the above? Two of the above? Answers B, C, and D above? Well, you get the idea.

The point is not to commit yourself to, for example, 40 hours of work thinking you will just be implementing a payroll system, when the client really wants an integrated five-application accounting package. Similarly, a 250-hour bid for an entire system when a simple payroll system is desired is just as bad.

You should attempt to obtain clarification of major points whenever possible. If this can't be accomplished, your proposal in this instance could state alternative time schedules and estimates based on one or more subset combinations; be sure to allow time for integration of common menu drivers and data environments.

In summary, then, the proposal should be used as a marketing tool to convince its reader that you are the one to implement the project and to formalize a course of action you plan to undertake. Assuming your proposal is accepted, the next step is a formal contract between you and your client, which is discussed in Chapter 13.

Business and Requirements Analysis

The starting point in developing any computer system is *knowing your client's business*. Many clients we have worked with have related stories of retail computer salespeople or computer vendors' sales representatives recommending specific computer hardware or software without attempting to determine the customer's needs and problems. In order to establish your reputation as a knowledgeable and competent consultant you must serve the needs of your client base, and recommending ill-fitting computer systems is the same as a custom tailor designing a business suit that is three sizes too large.

There are several reasons why understanding a client's business is essential. Most important is that no one understands a business and its problems like its owner or manager. You are not being hired as a management consultant to analyze the operations of the business with an eye for change. Rather, you should make recommendations where necessary as a service to the customer, but the primary emphasis should be on understanding current operations and problems to match the best possible computer system to the business.

Additionally, involving the client as much as possible provides a measure of protection for you, the consultant. As your client checks off requirements that you agree upon together, you are less likely to have an irate customer insisting that the completed system doesn't meet his or her needs.

The first step in the business analysis phase is the *interview*. A 2- to 3-hour interview should be scheduled with the client. The site of the interview is unimportant; it may be the customer's office, your office, a restaurant, or any other place conducive to exchanging ideas and information. Both you and the client should prepare for the interview prior to the actual meeting. The client should bring copies of important reports, invoices, often-repeated form letters, and other documents to the meeting. For each document, the client should note (1) time involved in preparation of the form, (2) how frequently the document is generated, (3) amount of retyping or re-creation required, and (4) how many employees currently work with the document type. The client should additionally consider why he or she is contemplating a computer system. Is it because of an increasingly backlogged work load, which results in overtime by present employees or the hiring of temporary help to keep up with the work load? Or is it to allow for planned future growth of the business? Your client should also attempt to analyze backlogs in current operations in addition to paperwork problems.

The consultant also needs to prepare for the first meeting. You should familiarize yourself with the client's type of business through reading, talking with friends and other customers in the same business, and any other sources available. Even though you want the client to describe his or her business situation, the interview will be of greater value if you are prepared than if you depend on your client to supply you with all background information. Less time will be spent attempting to understand details of the business operations that you would be able to investigate on your own. This serves a dual purpose. You and your client can start discussing problems and situations without regressing through as much background discussion as you would if you weren't prepared, and it serves to increase your esteem in the eyes of the client; you consider his or her business important enough to perform background investigation. You should also conduct a preliminary analysis of software and computer systems that have been implemented for the application being investigated, including systems you have designed for other customers in the same or similar businesses. This will acquaint you with the area under study so you will have a general idea of current efforts. Keep in mind that you are not limited to current software or hardware configurations, but you should be aware of what has been done in the area, along with any successes and failures.

These topics should be addressed in the preliminary interview:

1. Why is the client investigating a computer system?
2. What are current problems as the user sees them?
3. What is the volume of transactions performed in daily operations and periodic and special reports that must be produced?
4. What amount of information is currently stored in file cabinets or other media form, and what is the projected growth of transaction and storage volume? How many people perform similar tasks and how much time is spent working on the various functions?
5. What current communication of information takes place among various business sites (warehouses, branch offices, suppliers and customers, etc.)?

A sample evaluation form that I utilize during client interviews is illustrated in Figure 8-1. This form provides a convenient checklist to ensure that relevant topics are covered.

You should let the customer lead the discussion, but keep in mind the topics to be discussed and ask questions or inquire further at appropriate times. Having a written checklist as well as a mental one aids you in keeping the discussion on track. Don't be afraid to let the conversation drift to related topics, but make sure the main points discussed here are covered.

Back in Chapter 5, we discussed positive and negative motivators that lead toward computerization. The answer to question 3 in Figure 8-1 will provide you with the reason your client wants a computer. Depending on whether it is to exploit opportunities or solve problems you have a clue to how to proceed with the negotiations and subsequent development.

For example, Ms. Johnson of LTA (Looking To Automate) Building Supply Company, a Tucson, Arizona, building materials warehouse, asks you to design a computer system for her business. Using the above interview guidelines, you determine the following information:

1. Ms. Johnson is interested in a computer system because she expects her business volume to double in the next 12 to 18 months. Invoice preparation for builders is taking much longer than before due to

COMPUTER EDUCATION AND CONSULTING
P.O. Box 127
Colorado Springs, CO 80901

1. Name _____

   Address _____

   _____

   Phone _____

2. Application(s) _____

   _____

   _____

   _____

3. Reason for computerization: _____

   _____

   _____

4. Client's computer background (include current systems): _____

   _____

   _____

5. Existing hardware, if any (include internal and external memory sizes): _____

   _____

   _____

6. Number of system users: _____

7. Multiuser/network requirements (include number of simultaneous users; type and location of other nodes) _____

   _____

   _____

   _____

   _____

8. Installation time frame: _____ Desired   _____ Mandatory
   (if mandatory, state why)

   _____

   _____

   _____

   _____

Figure 8-1 Requirements analysis form.

9. Desired/budgeted system price range: _____

   _____

   Is amount a fixed budget requirement?   _____ Yes   _____ No

   Is hardware included in above price?   _____ Yes   _____ No

10. Desired user interface: _____ Menu _____ Command/query _____ No
                                                                      preference

11. Custom programming desired: _____ Yes   _____ No

    If yes, state why: _____

    _____

    _____

12. Software already reviewed (include comments and reactions): _____

    _____

    _____

13. Is there a projected need for subsequent add-on applications?

                          _____ Yes   _____ No

    If yes, what interaction with existing or proposed applications is desired?

    _____ None _____ Data sharing _____ Windowing/applications switching

    _____ Other (state) _____

14. What degree of postinstallation training and support is desired?

    _____ None   _____ Operational instruction   _____ On-call support

    _____ Other (state) _____

15. Projected data storage volume: _____

    _____

    _____

    _____

16. Special requirements that *must* be met (not already mentioned):

    _____

    _____

    _____

    _____

Figure 8-1 Requirements analysis form (*continued*).

increasing transaction volume, and three employees must now spend their entire work shift preparing invoices.

2. LTA currently processes 75 to 100 invoices per day, and each one takes approximately 10 minutes to prepare. When a builder calls LTA requesting building supplies, the employee must search the file cabinet for the appropriate inventory sheets. Each sheet contains product information (part number, size, estimated quantity in stock, price, and reorder point), manufacturer information (which vendors can supply the product, addresses, and wholesale prices), and which of LTA's customers use the material in their building.

It takes about 2 minutes to find each inventory sheet, and each invoice is normally for three different products. Once the file forms are pulled, the in-stock count is decremented by the number of parts ordered and the invoice is prepared with appropriate information (part numbers, quantity ordered of each part, price per unit, and total sales price for the invoice). A desk calculator is used by the invoice preparer to total dollar amounts.

3. LTA divides its product line into three main categories: windows, doors, and fixtures (kitchen and bathroom cabinets, countertops, etc.). There are approximately 2000 different windows in stock, 800 different doors, and 1500 fixtures. Though the quantity of invoices is expected to double, the number of different products will remain fairly constant in the foreseeable future.

4. If a clerk tries to fill an order and insufficient stock exists in the warehouse, he or she must call the main warehouse in Phoenix to check if they can loan the Tucson division stock to fill the requested amount. If so, the Phoenix office enters the amount requested on their local computer and a special interdivision transfer form is produced for next-day shipping of goods. If the Phoenix office needs to inquire about Tucson's availability of a product, an employee will call Tucson and a manual search will be performed on the inventory supply sheets.

5. When employees update the inventory sheet, they are supposed to check if reordering is necessary. Because of the growing backlog, however, LTA's clerks often forget to perform the check and on-hand inventory is usually below the safety-stock level. This has caused more frequent shipments from Phoenix than are necessary (along with increased transportation costs) as well as missed sales when builders purchase the supplies from a competitor rather than wait for LTA to restock.

6. When there is breakage of windows and other spoilage of goods the respective inventory files must be updated. Ms. Johnson has noticed that breakage reports often pile up for several days before the actual updates are performed, and often the reconciliation takes place after normal working hours, forcing overtime pay for the union employees.

After the interview, you compile facts from your notes and come to the following conclusions about LTA's business situation:

1. LTA is losing business because of untimely filling of orders. This situation will probably deteriorate as invoice volume increases.

2. Despite the projected increase in invoice volume, data storage requirements (either manual or automated) will remain relatively constant because of the stability of LTA's product line.

3. Having a quicker method of filling invoices will allow LTA's business volume to increase without a corresponding doubling in employees to process orders. This will provide greater operating leverage; that is, the same amount of fixed costs (salaries and equipment that do not change with increasing units sold) can produce a greater amount of revenue, thus increasing the net income of the business.

4. A means to automatically search Phoenix's inventory (and allow Phoenix to search local inventory) would be desirable.

Once you have conducted the preliminary interview, a short report containing original notes and the above conclusions should be presented to Ms. Johnson for her feedback and approval. Again, this is important because when the client is involved in the project from the beginning there is less risk of having a dissatisfied customer when the final system is delivered. Assuming that no major corrections are necessary or omissions are discovered, you are ready to proceed to the next step.

Preliminary System Design

The computer systems life cycle concept distinguishes between *logical system design* and *physical system design*. Logical system design means that a computer system is developed without regard to the specific hardware, software, and communications interfaces used. The analyst concentrates on the logical relationship among proposed system components. Physical system design superimposes actual hardware and software on the logical configuration to meet the specified system requirements. It is extremely important for you to concentrate on logical design prior to working at the physical-design stage. If you begin the design process with preconceived ideas of the specific hardware and software necessary to meet the requirements you often lock yourself into a specific configuration that may not be the best available (or may wind up not working at all). At the preliminary design stage you should analyze your interview notes and facts and concentrate on *general* solutions to problems.

For example, Ms. Johnson expressed a desire to automatically search Phoenix inventory when Tucson stock was insufficient to fill an order. Rather than specify a requirement for a "1200-baud modem, synchronous communications protocol software, and automatic remote database searching capabilities (transparent to user)," you should merely specify "communications interface between Phoenix and Tucson." Note that no specific hardware or software is mentioned; this allows a full range of options to be explored.

It is also important not to become too immersed in details because the preliminary design should be performed as quickly as possible; there is no guarantee that your client will hire you to design and implement the computer system, because your client *may not even need a computer system.* If Ms. Johnson had expected only moderate invoice growth over the next 5 years and little or no backlog in updating inventory sheets existed, the manual system at LTA would probably be sufficient for the near future to handle business requirements. As a consultant, you have an obligation to your clients to serve their best interests. If a computer system would not, in your opinion, improve current or expected business operations, your report to your customer should reflect that (see the Ethics section in Chapter 13).

What should you look for when conducting your preliminary analysis? One approach is to begin by identifying four key factors: (1) all relevant personnel involved in the current system, (2) the functions performed by these personnel, (3) the current information systems being used (manual,

Organizational Entities	Business Functions
Internal: Local manager (Ms. Johnson) Invoice clerks (3) Inventory pullers (5) Truck drivers (2) Phoenix warehouse External: Suppliers	Invoice preparation Inventory sheet updates Reordering inventory Packing inventory Delivering inventory Accounts receivable Accounts payable Customers
Information Systems	**Data**
Invoice filling (manual) Inventory updating (manual) Remote invoice filling (manual) Accounts receivable (automated) Accounts payable (automated)	Inventory sheets Remote inventory (Phoenix) Invoice copies Customer list Supplier list

Figure 8-2 Analysis factors for LTA Company.

semiautomated, or fully automated), and (4) the data considered important to operations.[4] Figure 8-2 illustrates the factors for LTA.

Once these factors have been identified, the next step is to determine the relationship among them. Who performs which functions? Who works with the important data? Which information systems operate upon which data categories? Figure 8-3 illustrates two of the relationships for LTA. You would draw similar charts cross-referencing information systems with system data, organizational entities with information systems, etc.

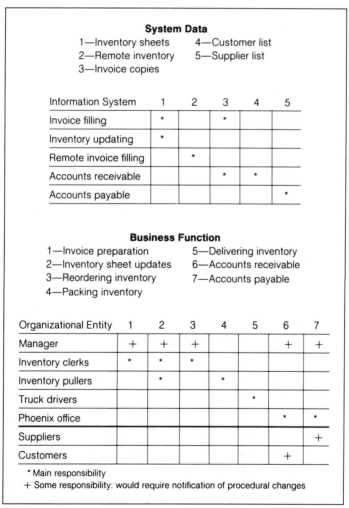

System Data

1—Inventory sheets	4—Customer list
2—Remote inventory	5—Supplier list
3—Invoice copies	

Information System	1	2	3	4	5
Invoice filling	*		*		
Inventory updating	*				
Remote invoice filling		*			
Accounts receivable			*	*	
Accounts payable					*

Business Function

1—Invoice preparation	5—Delivering inventory
2—Inventory sheet updates	6—Accounts receivable
3—Reordering inventory	7—Accounts payable
4—Packing inventory	

Organizational Entity	1	2	3	4	5	6	7
Manager	+	+	+			+	+
Inventory clerks	*	*	*				
Inventory pullers		*		*			
Truck drivers					*		
Phoenix office						*	*
Suppliers							+
Customers						+	

* Main responsibility
+ Some responsibility: would require notification of procedural changes

Figure 8-3 Relationship of analysis factors for LTA Company.

It should be noted that identifying and relating system factors is an iterative process. That is, continual refinement (with the assistance of your client) is necessary to make the logical design reflect the current environment as accurately as possible.

Now that a picture of the organization has been obtained, computer-based equipment can be superimposed on the critical areas. For LTA, the first step is a computer system at the Tucson warehouse. Note again that no specification as to brand of hardware or software is made; the computer system may consist of one or several microcomputers, a minicomputer tied to several micros, or one of many other architectures. This will be determined at a later stage. Since communication is desired between the Tucson and Phoenix warehouses, you can specify communications hardware at both ends of the network (it would be useless for LTA to install a modem in Tucson without a corresponding modem in Phoenix). Figure 8-4 reflects the preliminary system configuration.

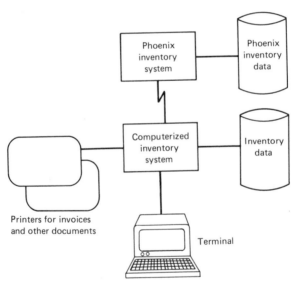

Figure 8-4   Preliminary system configuration.

An important step in refining your preliminary design is *capacity analysis*. Simply stated, capacity analysis is the process of determining storage and processing requirements for system components. Ms. Johnson has provided the following information regarding LTA's data. For each part in the inventory (2000 windows, 800 doors, and 1500 fixtures), there is a five-digit part code (one alphabetic character and four numbers), a quantity in stock that is never more than 500 for any one unit, a part name that is 10 characters or less, a price between $10 and $500, and a reorder point (somewhere between 50 and 150). Similar information produces the manufacturer and customer data used in the calculations.[5]

By simple mathematical calculations, we can roughly determine computer storage requirements. For simplicity, assume that we are dealing with 8-bit ASCII characters: 1 byte equals one 8-bit character.

Part data
Part number	5 bytes
Quantity	1 byte (integer number)
Price	4 bytes (room to store 1 floating point number)
Reorder point	1 byte
Part name	10 bytes
Total	21 bytes

21 bytes per record $\times$ 4300 records = 90,300 bytes

Manufacturer data:
Name	15 bytes
Address	45 bytes (including city, state, zip code, and phone number)
Cost	4 bytes
Minimum order	1 byte
Total	65 bytes

65 bytes per record $\times$ 100 suppliers = 6500 bytes

Customer data
Name	15 bytes
Address	45 bytes
Rating	1 byte
Total	61 bytes

61 bytes per record $\times$ 200 customers = 12,200 bytes

Total bytes of permanent storage: 109,000 bytes

We have already seen that the number of different parts is not expected to increase substantially. Assuming a 50 percent growth rate in new customers over the next 18 months, 6100 bytes can be added to the total, giving 115,100 bytes.

An important decision must now be made: What other storage requirements exist? For example, if LTA must keep the past 18 months' invoices online (immediately accessible), it is easy to see how storage requirements will increase drastically. However, Ms. Johnson decides that since past invoices are referred to infrequently, they may be stored in file cabinets. She can make this determination because all accounts receivable are controlled from the Phoenix office. They currently reconcile all payments against outstanding invoices on their own computer system and wish to continue this practice. If it were determined that Tucson's LTA warehouse would handle their own accounting functions (payroll, accounts receivable and payable, etc.) additional storage would be needed to allow for the extended online data. Note that we are not dealing with a question of technology here. It is certainly technically feasible for Ms. Johnson's new computer system to handle these accounting functions, but the *political* decision has been made to keep these functions in Phoenix. Again, you need to design a system to meet the requirements of your clients, not your own ideas of how their business should be operated. You should make your clients aware that certain capabilities exist that they are not utilizing, but the final decision is up to them.

You can now make a preliminary decision on what class of hardware is needed. Owing to the data storage requirements calculated, a microcomputer would probably be sufficient for LTA. If storage of 5 million bytes had been calculated a microcomputer could still be installed, but you now know that a hard disk (or some other storage medium capable of handling large amounts of data) is required. However, if 80 million bytes of data were to be put online, you should start considering a machine in the minicomputer class.

Similar logical design criteria can be superimposed over LTA's communication requirement. Ms. Johnson has two major options in connecting the proposed computer system with the Phoenix office's hardware. If a search for a part determines that insufficient stock exists locally to fill the order, an *automatic* search (no human intervention) of the remote data can be performed. This requires natural or imposed compatability between the two computer systems. If both systems run the same inventory software, automatic searches can be performed chiefly through the communications software. If, however, different software is used in Tucson than that which is currently used in Phoenix, some type of front-end program is required to translate data interrogations from one software form to another. We have now entered the realm of distributed databases, a complicated and expensive system design criterion.

Ms. Johnson's other option is for the local software to notify the operator of the insufficient stock condition. The operator must then access the remote computer (through dial-up lines, for example) and, using the remote software, access the inventory system.

Several complications arise because of this decision. If Ms. Johnson prefers option number 1 (automatic search), LTA must either use the same software (and possibly hardware) in both cities or provide for an expensive front-end program to handle the dissimilar accesses. Phoenix's existing software will probably need to be modified (or totally replaced) because of the system changes.

After studying these findings, Ms. Johnson determines that owing to the improved reordering system resulting from the new system, LTA will not be out of stock as frequently as now, causing less inquiries of Phoenix's system (Phoenix calls Tucson only five to ten times per day despite handling three times as many transactions as Tucson). For such infrequent remote access, you should recommend option number 2, manual intervention to access the remote computer system, which may be more cost-effective despite the slower access. Now a modem and simple communications software can allow access to the other system.

Another advantage of this decision is that LTA is not limited to certain hardware or software systems. During the physical-design stage you are free to explore the full range of hardware and software available.

Together with Ms. Johnson you decide that two employees would be able to handle all current and projected invoice processing and other inventory preparation. Ms. Johnson would also like one terminal to be free for correspondence, memos, and other word processing functions. A simple diagram of the proposed system is shown is Figure 8-5. Notice the lack of detail because we are at the early stage of design.

One word of caution: If you determine that storage, communications, political, and other requirements that surface during the interview and preliminary design stages are far beyond your capabilities, you should

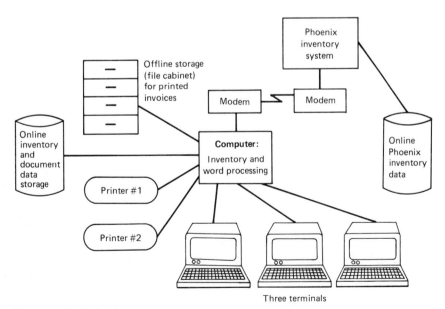

Figure 8-5 Refined system configuration.

seriously consider referring your client to another consultant specializing in that class of systems. For example, a nationwide distributed database covering 50 nodes over a packet-switched value-added network may be a bit too much for a consultant experienced in installing simple microcomputer-based information systems. No doctor, lawyer, or accountant is an expert in *all* areas of his or her profession, and computer professionals are no different. Rather than damage your business reputation (and your image) by undertaking a task that you are not experienced enough to complete successfully you should direct the customer to the appropriate specialist. You may be able to work with the other professional in an apprenticelike relationship on the consulting contract and increase your knowledge of that area; after all, you sent business to him or her. The other consultant may also direct clients looking for services in your area of specialty to you. This way, good professional relationships are created and nurtured.

Preliminary Cost-Benefit Analysis

This is often the hardest step in the systems life cycle process. How can all the benefits and costs be quantified as accurately as possible? Because of the problems associated with this process it is recommended that a preliminary estimated analysis be performed. If the incremental cost and benefit figures are close to one another you can proceed to the next stages of design.

In LTA's sample situation you tentatively decided upon the following configuration (based on Figure 8-5):

Hardware	*Software*
One microcomputer	Multiuser operating system
Three terminals	Inventory system
Two modems (one for Phoenix)	Communications software
Two floppy disk drives*	Word processing package
Two printers	

*Disk drives may be built into the microcomputer.

Since you have deliberately not chosen any hardware or software prior to this stage in the design process, how do you estimate costs of the configuration? The best method is to estimate prices based on average current market prices. By researching vendor price lists, current periodical hardware-software summaries, and similar publications, you can determine the average market price for various system components. Naturally, there is wide range in prices of both hardware and software. A microcomputer may range from $50 to $12,000, while inventory software may be as inexpensive as $50 or as costly as $10,000. Fortunately, you already have a general idea of what narrow band of price categories to consider. For example, the microcomputer must support a multiuser operating system and at least six peripheral devices (the printers, terminals, and modems). Your basic $150 home computer will not be able to support this configuration, so you can assume that your eventual purchase will be in the $4000 to $8000 price range. Similar assumptions can be made of all system components.

Based on your research, you formulate the following cost estimates:

Microcomputer and disk drives	$ 5,000
Terminals	2,000
Modems	500
Printers	1,500
Operating system	1,000
Inventory software	1,500
Communications software	300
Word processing software	300
TOTAL	$12,100

We can assume that since LTA's business volume is expected to double, the current staff of three invoice preparers would probably double also. Each employee's annual salary is $15,000. Since you have already determined that the current staff could process the increased transaction volume with computer assistance, it is easy to see that first-year savings alone will be approximately $32,000 ($45,000 in salary savings less the $12,000 equipment expenditure). The after-tax savings would actually be more since we have not allowed for investment tax credits on equipment (see Chapter 13).

Not all preliminary cost-benefit examinations will give you such a clear-cut answer to the question of whether to computerize, of course. For those with murkier distinctions, the intangible factors (mentioned next) will play an important role in determining the go-ahead decision.

As was just mentioned, the intangible costs and benefits must be considered. How do you attach a dollar figure to the benefit of the owner not having to work on weekends? Can you quantify such benefits as worrying less about business problems? The best approach to intangibles is to produce a list of all intangible costs and benefits that you and your client can think of, attaching weights of importance to each entry. If Ms. Johnson can now avoid working on Sundays to catch up on backlogged business (and avoid paying overtime) she may consider the improved work situation as a very important benefit and weight it heavily on the list. After all intangibles have been examined a clearer picture of the overall costs and benefits can be obtained.

With all the imprecision we have seen (estimates only of costs, intangible benefits and costs), how could this preliminary cost-benefit analysis be of any use to you? You should view this preliminary stage as simply a screening procedure to determine if your customer should continue the computerization process further. One of the first consulting services I performed was for a retail phonograph record store in Arizona. The owner was interested in installing a small business computer to assist with record keeping and general functions. A preliminary analysis of daily operations showed that bookkeeping functions took one employee approximately 30 minutes per day, including reconciling the cash register balance with the cash count. The only other tedious task was physical examination of records and tapes for weekly reordering. This task was usually performed during morning hours when business activity was light and was often performed by the owner, who was paid a fixed salary. At the time of the study (1979) a microcomputer would not have been cost-effective since little, if any, salary, time, and other savings would have been realized from computerization of bookkeeping or other functions. By 1983 the advent of the under-$100 microcomputer might have led to a different decision. Given the general hardware and software costs of the late 1970s, however, cost-effectiveness would not have been realized.

Note again in the previous example that no specific hardware or software had been investigated yet, and intangible factors were examined. By now, you should realize that the main result of the cost-benefit analysis is to conduct a preliminary screening to determine if you should continue to the next stage in the computer systems life cycle process.

Software Analysis

Nearly every computer book, magazine article, or report you read will tell you to choose your software first; then pick your hardware. There are very good reasons for this. Many commercial software packages will run on a wide variety of machines, depending on such factors as operating system and microprocessor. If you lock yourself into a certain hardware configuration, however, you may find that the software will not run on your client's machine. Since the software will determine the eventual usefulness of the computer system to its users (after all, a computer without good software is as useful as a radio tuned in to static) choosing good software is a key part of developing a computer system.

What makes a good software package? Evaluating software is not as easy as it may appear. Just as a 10-minute test drive of a new car may not reveal all the idiosyncrasies of the vehicle (such as continual stalling on a cold morning), spending 10 to 15 minutes with a software package will not provide you a comprehensive evaluation of it. Of course, 10 minutes may be enough for you to eliminate a program from further consideration. Prior to any online evaluation, though, you should conduct preliminary analysis of software in the target application. By studying specification sheets, vendor brochures, and reviews you can narrow your search range before you ever sit in front of a keyboard. Of course, you risk eliminating potentially useful software from consideration, but if you are careful and don't let one bad review turn you away from further investigation you can spend less time reviewing software that obviously will not serve your client's needs.

By now you are aware of the requirements of your software. For LTA's inventory system, the software must be able to perform economic order quantity (EOQ) modeling, breakage updates, and invoice generation. Any software that does not perform at least these minimum functions can be eliminated from further consideration.

After you study written material about the applications packages you are ready to begin hands-on evaluation. You may find that software vendors or computer store salespeople may insist on demonstrating the software for you. While there is nothing wrong with a demonstration, you should not base your purchase decision solely on any demonstrations. Software can have partially hidden bugs that someone could demonstrate their way around. These problems would not surface until the sale is made and the system is installed, causing headaches for both you and your client. Since your client (and his or her working staff) are the eventual users, you should test the software with their goals in mind.

Every program you test should be evaluated on the following factors:

1. *Meeting requirements:* The first test any software must pass is being able to complete the desired tasks. As stated previously, a computer program must be able to meet the minimum requirements of the user to be considered further.

2. *Ease of use:* Much discussion in computer literature has been devoted to the topic of user friendliness, with friendly software featuring online help, menu-driven interfaces, and understandable error messages. These features of user-friendly software are not an absolute standard, however. An experienced computer user may consider a menu-driven system both too slow and too restrictive. Users of a menu are limited to a set of predefined choices and usually do not have a what-if capability that a command-query system like that of most query-oriented database management systems have. Experienced users often feel frustrated by menu-driven software because they feel that the program is controlling them instead of serving their needs. "User-friendly" is a relative term; what one user considers friendly may be threatening or overly simplistic to another. By this stage of the design process you know how experienced your client is in using computers. When evaluating software keep this in mind. Figure 8-6 illustrates sample menu and command systems.

3. *Error recovery facilities:*   *All* software should allow users to recover from errors in a smooth manner. Computer users make mistakes like anyone else. When a person types in a 9 in response for a number between 1 and 8, he or she should be informed that the response was invalid and be given a chance to correct the entry. At no point should boundary errors, such as accessing illegal memory addresses at the machine language level, cause the program to spontaneously abort into the operating environment (operating system, BASIC language system, or other underlying system). Error messages should be understandable and preferably offer a solution or refer the user to the documentation for further help.

4. *Online help:*   It is inconvenient for the program user to refer to the documentation for every question that occurs. A good program should provide help at *any* level of operation by answering H or HELP to a menu question, typing in HELP in a command system, pressing the question mark key, or a similar mechanism. Help messages should be informative enough to add to the user-friendly concept of software; they should increase the usefulness of the software to the user.

5. *Speed:*   If a user must wait several minutes for a response to a menu choice or query, the software may not operate quickly enough to be useful. *Real-time operation* means that the time from query to response is within an accepted time interval that the user defines as allowing him or her to make a useful decision or perform a task. Like user-friendly, "real-time" is a relative concept. Several minutes' response time may be sufficient for certain applications requiring extensive reports, while a computer system in an aircraft may require a response time of less than 1 second.

6. *Easy exiting:*   Nothing is more frustrating than entering the wrong choice from a menu and having to answer an endless series of questions before you are asked if you would like to exit to the previous menu level. Any level in a menu-driven system should allow at least two exit

```
                    Menu-Driven Software System


                           Main Menu Level

        Choose one of the following:     I

        I - Insert new part data into the
            inventory
        D - Delete a part from the inventory
        C - Change part data
        H - HELP!
        X - Exit program

        _____


                      Data Insertion Menu Level

        Enter new part number: 12345
        or:   Choose one of the following:

        H - HELP!     X - Exit program

        R - Return to previous menu level



                    Command-Query Software System


            Welcome to ABC inventory system
            Enter date: ⟩⟩7/28/84
            Enter command:⟩⟩ Insert

            New part number:⟩⟩ 12345

            New part name: ⟩⟩ Computer

            Quantity on hand:⟩⟩ 34

            Correct? ⟩⟩ Y

            New part inserted into database:
            Press ⟨CR⟩ to proceed:
```

Figure 8-6   Menu-driven versus command/query software.

levels: one to the previous menu level and one to the operating environment (exiting the program).

7. *Documentation:* Many well-designed programs come packaged with extremely poor documentation. Long the scourge of the computer industry, poor documentation may reduce a valuable program to a useless scrap of bits. Unless the eventual users of software have thorough, conveniently organized, and descriptive documentation, users (especially inexperienced ones) will quickly become frustrated and the computer system will never provide its full potential benefits to the customers. An online interactive tutorial is an excellent way to learn a new software package, but it is usually included only in command-driven software rather than a menu-driven system, since the menu driver acts as a pseudo tutorial.

8. *Capacity:* Software capacity refers to the maximum number of computer records, number of user-defined fields, or other system-dependent criteria that may limit the application of the software to the user's environment. Although not as critical as hardware capacity, you should review the specifications sheet and documentation to determine what (if any) capacity constraints exist.

9. *Company:* How long has the publishing company been in business? What other successful software products have they marketed? What is the financial situation of the firm? Are periodic "bug fixes" or other software updates offered?

10. *Local support:* If you purchase this software from a local computer store, is any local support (answering questions, investigating problems) available? If not, is a hotline phone number available to the publisher or technical support staff?

11. *Current users:* You should attempt to contact current users of the software packages being investigated. How has the software been working? If any problems have occurred, how quickly were they resolved? How has using this software improved business operations? These questions should be asked. Request that the computer store or software vendor provide you with references of current users and try, if possible, to investigate on your own any other users.

After you eliminate the candidates that do not meet the various evaluation criteria you should let your client try the remaining packages to obtain feedback. After reducing the list further, you should strike any packages that are far outside any budget constraints your client faces. An inventory package that costs $25,000 not only may be too expensive but may include many features that are not needed in the current system. A realistic appraisal of all software within a specified budgetary range will usually yield several finalists.

How do you make the final choice? If all of the finalists contain the same features and meet all requirements, price may be the final deciding factor. Once you choose the best software for all applications (in LTA's case, we are looking for an operating system, inventory package, communications front-end, and word processing) you may find yourself facing a problem. Nonstandardization has been a plague in the computer industry to both hardware and software. Assume that you determine that inventory package ABC and word processing software DEF are your top choices. ABC runs under operating systems X, Y, or Z, but DEF only runs under operating system W. In our case the driving factor behind computerization is automation of inventory, so ABC should remain as the inventory choice and an alternative word processing program that operates on operating system W should be selected. The same criteria exist for the next step, evaluating hardware. If your software selections run on the different versions of the same operating system that require different hardware a similar ranking must be determined.

Occasionally you may find a situation where no commercially available software fits the determined needs. In these instances custom software may be required for part or all of the software needed. Chapter 10 discusses writing custom software for your client's computer system.

Hardware Selection

Selecting a computer for your client is now a matter of finding hardware that will support software. Your list of choices may be a long one if your software runs under a widely implemented operating system such as CP/M or MS-DOS, or if you select programs that are limited to a proprietary operating system implemented on a narrow range of hardware. In either case your hardware should be evaluated on various criteria.

1. *Capacity:* Internal memory must support your applications software and operating system. External storage (floppy disks, hard-disk system, or another technology) must be sufficient for current and projected data storage, including all programs.

2. *Expandability:* Can additional central processing (CPU) power be added or upgraded? Can further external storage be interfaced if needed?

3. *Peripheral support:* Existing ports should support all terminals, printers, modems, and other peripheral devices. If not, expansion capability must be able to raise the support level to connect the required devices.

4. *Good documentation:* As with software, clear and understandable documentation is critical for the user. All commands should be illustrated with examples. System initialization procedures should be clearly defined, as should error messages and recovery methods.

5. *Company support:* A hotline number should exist for users with questions that aren't resolved by the documentation. The company should also be financially sound (if that can be determined) to ensure continued postsale support.

6. *Local support:* If the hardware is purchased from a computer store the retail outlet should assist with installation. They should also be willing to answer any questions that may develop to prevent contacting the manufacturer for every problem.

7. *User references:* Current users should be contacted to obtain their opinions of the computer's performance. If none can be located, think very strongly about considering another computer; limited use may reflect certain inadequacies in the system.

8. *Features:* You should look at screen clarity, keyboard configuration, special function keys, and similar features to determine ease of use.

9. *Price:* Many computer stores offer packages consisting of a computer, printer, other peripherals (modem, extra disk drive, etc.), and sometimes software. These prices should be compared against the cost of configuring the desired system piece by piece. You should know by your defined requirements what general price range you are looking at (under $1000; $1000 to $5000; $5000 to $10,000; more than $10,000), so that you can compare prices of total systems within your target price category.

Implementation

A critical part of implementing a computer system in a business is making the transition from current methods of operation to new ones using the new system. Problems need to be resolved in many areas, including validating new system results, overcoming any employee resentment, and possibly redesigning report and paperwork formats. You should run the new system side by side with old operations for a trial period to ensure correct results. While this may entail additional costs in labor and equipment during the trial period it is usually cost-effective over the long term if problems are detected that otherwise would have remained hidden.

Training

During the trial period and prior to complete integration of the new computer system all eventual users must be trained in new operating procedures. This may be a simple task if only one menu-driven applications package will be on the system, or it will be considerably more complex if several programs requiring user queries will be used. All training should, of course, be hands-on, with sufficient supervision to ensure correct use of the system. The supervision can decrease as the users become more proficient.

Maintenance

When a computer system is designed by an in-house programming-analysis staff it is usually assumed that they, with assistance from the vendors and possibly third-party contractors, will maintain the system, including program modifications and implementing additional applications. As a consultant, your obligation normally ends when you have successfully installed the system and trained the users. This should be specified in the contract between you and your client.

Some clients, however, may desire continual modifications of their system, especially if the software was custom written. In these cases you should negotiate some type of retainer fee or additional hourly rate for continued postinstallation support.

Maintenance of Existing Systems

In addition to those clients' systems you build yourself from the analysis stage, you may also be called in to enhance or fix existing computer systems. Having spent much of my own computer programming career in maintenance environments, I can personally tell you that maintenance is an important yet difficult function.

Computer systems tend to evolve over time due to changing needs and requirements of their users. Even though recent design methodologies such as structured programming have emphasized modularity for ease of maintenance as well as the initial design effort, it still is a relatively difficult task to take someone else's programming effort and make changes. Computer programming is both an art and a science, and many different programming styles exist; mind reading should be a required skill for anyone involved in system maintenance. Few tasks are as frustrating as trying to understand the coding actions of a talented but mischievous programmer who didn't want anyone else to decipher his or her work.

To further complicate matters, the phenomenal growth of commercial software has made software modification even more difficult. Consider the following situation: A client requests that you make some changes to their integrated accounting system. Payroll deduction rates will be changed, new reports are desired, and bookkeeping procedures will be modified to accommodate new accounting principles. Unfortunately, the client's commercially purchased program does not include the means to make these changes.

Normally, an in-depth analysis of the program's source code could help an experienced programmer understand how the program works and where changes must be made. But wait! How many commercially available programs include source code listings on the disk? Not too many! So what's a consultant to do?

You may be able to persuade the program's developer to provide you with the source code, but don't count on it. If a programmer is willing to allow modifications to his or her work, normally he or she will insist on performing that modification. There is also no guarantee, given the volatility of companies in the computer industry, that the developing firm is still in business.

You may be forced to recommend new software, either commercial or custom-built, owing to the inability to modify the currently used program. Now you have the problem of switching existing systems data to the new software's format. This may be a relatively simple task of reformatting standard ASCII data files, or it may require a complicated database revision.

Some programmers may be able to "reverse engineer" a program by using a debugging tool to examine the object code's use of memory locations and registers. Though this method is infinitely more difficult than examining poorly documented source code, some programmers can still patch a program to make the desired changes.

Whatever options you choose, the same rule of initial systems development is applicable; be sure of your ability to accomplish the task. My firm was recently involved in a situation where a local beer distributor's accountant requested consulting assistance with his client's accounting software. The software, which ran on an IBM minicomputer, was so full of bugs that the firm's accounting data was extremely unreliable. Balance sheets didn't balance, outstanding accounts data was not current, etc. In addition to the individual software problems, the program had been integrated with a delivery routing system through a custom-written interface that was causing extremely slow response throughout the entire computer system.

The programs were written in RPG II, which none of the partners in my firm were familiar with. The task at hand was difficult enough without the added complications of an unfamiliar programming language and foreign hardware. Our recommendation was to find someone qualified in the hardware and the language who could conduct an in-depth analysis as to whether any software changes could help the situation.

Finally, your client should also be aware of the difficulties of system maintenance. Your client contract should state exactly what you are to do: produce new reports, change processing actions, or fix system bugs. As with all other client-consultant relationships, a clear understanding by both parties of exactly what is to be accomplished will hopefully prevent subsequent headaches.

Other Analysis and Design Methodologies

The process presented in this chapter to conduct logical systems analysis and design is one of many that can be utilized. It seems that every systems analysis–oriented university computer department has developed one or more alternative methodologies, accompanied by those used in industry. It can't be determined which process is best; as with most things in business and life in general, a methodology may be appropriate for some situations but ill-fitted to others. One of the drawbacks of the BSP/BASE system is a lack of data flow representation; that is, we can view the matrices and see who interacts with what data, but we can't see any logical flow among system entities.

The data flow diagram (DFD) methodology of Gane and Sarson[6] overcomes this shortcoming by charting the flow of data into the system from the outside environment, following the data through the internal system and subsystems, and showing any places they exit the system and are no longer under process control.

The DFD shows data at a logical level without regard to physical devices. That is, a customer order entering the system is shown without regard to the physical medium by which it appears (mailed-in punched card, manually transcribed telephone order, videotext, autoanswer modem, or another means).

Additionally, the DFD may be shown at various levels of abstraction. That is, an overall system can be diagrammed, yet individual sections can be enlarged into detailed, lower-level DFDs. For large design projects involving several analysts, this provides a means to modularize a project by specifying input, processing, and output of a given subsection and allowing a designer to create the data flow within his or her assigned section.

Gane and Sarson go on to discuss how to further define system processes and use data dictionaries, structured English, and other tools to implement the logical design. For further information, consult their book *Structured Systems Analysis: Tools and Techniques.*

Another widely used design system is the Michael Jackson design methodology (no, not the singer!). In his book *Principles of Program Design,*[7] Jackson proposes a data structure–based system to (1) build hierarchical trees of input and output data; (2) create a logical programming process to convert the input to the desired output, including any necessary intermediate data forms; (3) compose the logical program instructions; and (4) translate the logical program structure into an optimized physical structure.

Notice that like BSP/BASE and data flow diagrams, the Jackson method places a weighty emphasis on the data in the system as well as the procedures involved; the analysis takes place without regard to physical medium, physical data structures (linked lists, relational databases, flat files, etc.) or any other constraining factor. The key to successful design of any computer system is conversion of raw data into useful information. By logically mapping the entire system, from data gathering to transformation to output, any discrepancies (such as insufficient data collection) can be spotted, hopefully avoiding costly revision of a program that is almost complete.

Many other methodologies exist, each with an appropriate place in the system development life cycle. You should have an understanding of several analysis and design methodologies, their respective tools, and their appropriateness to different situations. By using a system (or systems) that you understand, you will facilitate your system-building process into a productive machine.

Prototyping

Prototyping can be considered a subset of almost any methodology. Once the specifications and logical design phases have begun, a series of screen mock-ups (50 to 100, for example) can be generated to provide the user with a view of the proposed system.

By placing these mock-ups on a computer and paging through them with dummy data, the user can obtain an idea of the system's features and friendliness. Feedback provided by the client can help you adjust the system to meet their unaddressed needs and tastes.

Algorithms that convert proposed input data to output information can then be added, to replace the dummy data. This process provides a feasibility analysis of the system, proving that the data necessary to produce the desired results has indeed been collected.

Finally, this prototype can be used as an on-site (Beta) test release to collect further user feedback and final adjustments can then be made.

Although prototyping's primary use is for program development, it is still applicable if commercial software will be used. Mock-ups of proposed screens for several commercial programs, as well as prototyped data sharing (if required), can be developed. This way, the client can get an idea of what the combined system's user interface will be like before it is implemented.

Alternative Consultant-Client Relationships

There are no set rules stating that every contract you accept must call for the development of an entire computer system. Some very large projects may not be suitable to an accurate estimation without much more detailed research than that allowed by a cursory problem analysis. Your first phase might be to conduct a feasibility analysis, with system development covered under a separate future contract for which you may competitively bid against other firms.

Additionally, many owners of small businesses are not accustomed to dealing with consultants or contractors and may be hesitant about committing a critical project to a nonemployee (despite the fact that a well-structured consulting contract could protect a client more than an employer-employee situation if performance criteria and milestone payments clauses are included).

An alternative approach for you and a prospective client is a contract for development of a small portion of a complete computer system. This may include complete development of one of several desired applications; complete logical design, but not implementation, of the system; or another combination of functions.

These approaches allow you to become familiar with a particular customer's working relationships and payment patterns, while the client can evaluate your work: whether you can complete a project within time and budget constraints, the quality of your work, and your professionalism.

Through this working relationship, you may become involved with a small aspect of a large project you otherwise wouldn't be able to accept. Your sole responsibility for a client's $3 million development contract may be development of specifications for the system's accounting portions, for example. Even if you are not involved with the rest of the system development process your expertise in this one small area allows you to partake of the consulting dollars pot.

Summary

Many of the contracted tasks that you will undertake as a consultant will be for installation of computer systems of varying size and complexity. The design methodology presented in this chapter is applicable to any analysis and design project.

Once user needs and requirements are investigated and specified you can proceed to the logical system design phase, being careful not to prematurely decide on specific hardware and software. Software can then be chosen, followed by hardware and peripheral devices. Finally, the system is installed and users are trained in the new operations.

Of course, no single chapter can cover all aspects of computer systems analysis, design, and implementation in detail. Further information about these areas can be found in the references listed in Chapter 14.

End Notes

1. Several variations of the systems life cycle have been proposed by systems analysts, and they differ in the categorization and grouping of the life cycle steps. Most analysts are in agreement on the major order of the life cycle processes: preliminary business analysis, logical systems design, physical systems design, implementation, training, and maintenance.

2. Robert E. Kelley, *Consulting: The Complete Guide to a Profitable Career,* Scribner's, New York, 1981, p. 144.

3. Ibid., pp. 145–149.

4. This systems analysis approach is an outgrowth of research conducted by the author while a graduate student at the University of Arizona in Tucson, Arizona. The methodology is based on IBM's Business Systems Planning (BSP) and Honeywell Information Systems' business analysis for system effectiveness (BASE).

5. The data format that is presented is a result of normalization of the filed data. That is, data redundancy has been reduced by formatting the data to facilitate cross-referencing rather than repeating common material. The data normalization process is discussed in many database management books.

6. Chris Gane and Trish Sarson, *Structured Systems Analysis: Tools and Techniques,* Prentice-Hall, Englewood Cliffs, N.J., 1979.

7. M. A. Jackson, *Principles of Program Design,* Academic Press, London, 1975.

CHAPTER 9

The Hardware World

Let's digress for a bit from the products and services of your consulting practice to take a look at the different classes of hardware available. As was mentioned earlier, you should choose one or two classes of machines and specialize in them—know as much as you can and become an expert.

The primary reason is that when you are investigating a computer system for a client or installing that system, you can't afford to learn the basics from scratch. Making the transition across some machines is relatively easy; if you are familiar with CP/M-based 8-bit machines, using MS-DOS or its derivatives (PC-DOS, ZDOS) should be easy. Learning an IBM System 38 minicomputer "on the fly" without any prior multiuser experience would probably be somewhat more difficult.

In this chapter, we'll look briefly at the various categories of hardware currently available. Some brands and models will be listed, but the emphasis will be on the relative features and complexities of the categories rather than each machine. Owing to the rapidity with which new computers are introduced, any comprehensive list I could develop at this moment would be incomplete and partially out of date by the time you read this book.

Basic Microcomputers

The area offering the most opportunity for computer consultants today is probably that of single-tasking machines: basic microcomputers. Less technical knowledge is required for these systems, in terms of multitasking, communications, job control language interface, etc., than larger, more complex machines.

One of the largest categories of basic microcomputers is that of the IBM PC and its lookalikes and workalikes. Much of the microcomputer software is being written for the MS-DOS operating system (and its different versions) because of the large installed base of these computers. Figures vary, but the IBM PC is estimated to possess around 25 percent of the microcomputer market by itself, with additional shares going to its clones. Therefore, a computer consultant specializing in these systems has a potentially large client base.

IBM's latest entry into the microcomputer arena is the PC-AT (Advanced Technology), introduced in August 1984. Currently available in two major configurations (based on the amount of disk storage desired), the PC-AT features an Intel 80286 microprocessor that runs considerably faster than the 8088 used by the rest of the IBM family. The higher-priced configuration features a 20-Mbyte internal hard disk, as well as the same 1.2-Mbyte high-density floppy drive and 360-kbyte standard drive as the lower-priced model. Main memory (RAM) is expandable from the 256K baseline to 3 Mbytes. Additionally, a slot for the Intel 80287 math coprocessor is built into the system. The PC-AT will also be able to be used as a multiuser system as soon as a multiuser operating system is available.

Beginning in late 1983 and early 1984, Digital Research's Concurrent CP/M gave the IBM family multitasking capability, and similar operating systems were scheduled to be released by other vendors. IBM announced its PC-Net network to accompany already existing networks. Therefore, the computer consultant specializing in these machines has the capability to develop more complex systems than were possible before.

Another large base of basic microcomputers is the Apple II world (Apple II, II+, IIe, IIc, and Franklin machines). Much software has been developed for these machines and, like IBM, they have a large installed base. Just as with the IBMs, the Apple can be part of a larger network so that sophisticated work is possible.

Before the advent of the IBM PC generation, the main competitor to the Apple machines was the vast array of 8-bit CP/M computers. These machines were based on either Zilog Z80 or Intel 8080 (and later Zilog Z80A and Intel 8085) chips and much of the microcomputer software was written for these systems. Even though the more powerful 16-bit machines have stripped market share from the 8-bit CP/M computers, many customers still have existing Kaypros, Osbornes, NorthStars, and others.

Another early competitor was the Tandy TRS computer series: models I, III, etc. Using their own proprietary operating systems they ran software similar to that of the Apple and CP/M machines. Tandy's newest computers have joined the 16-bit world, however, and possess some degree of compatibility with IBM machines.

The basic microcomputer usually has a simple, easy-to-use operating system. Without enhancements such as connection to a network or multitasking features, the machine can perform one task at a time: run a program, perform an operating system command, or print a file. When connected to a printer buffer or spooler, simultaneous program execution and long file printing is possible.

One or more floppy or hard disks are connected to the machine. Newer innovations such as RAM disks are also used for storage. In the "old days" cassettes were commonly used for program and sequential data file storage.

Again, communications capabilities and other advanced features increase the technical knowledge required of a consultant to design, install, and program these systems.

Special Machines

Once upon a time, a clear distinction could be made between microcomputers and minicomputers: microcomputers were single-user and single-tasking, while minis were multiuser and multitasking. Then along came Altos, Compupro, and Televideo hardware, accompanied by MP/M and UNIX operating systems. Suddenly the lines between the two system classes blurred. Minicomputers were still more powerful and could support more users, of course, but what was the actual differentiation between a mini and a micro?

Many people have proposed their own definitions. Suffice it to say, however, that as 32-bit microcomputers with Z80 cluster controllers became realistic (featuring over 1 Mbyte of main memory) the distinctions blurred further.

Regardless of actual definitions, however, any consultant who specializes in these systems needs to understand concurrent applications processing, shared databases, and similar advanced topics. When choosing or designing software to be shared among users, you need to be certain that access to common data areas doesn't destroy data validity or cause database deadlocks, just as if you were working mainframe or minicomputer software.

Some of the multiuser operating systems, such as UNIX, are far more complex to use than CP/M or MS-DOS. Even MP/M, the multiuser version of CP/M, has operating system commands equivalent to those of larger minicomputers.

In addition to multiuser and multitasking systems, other microcomputers exist that can't be truly classified as a basic personal computer. An example is the Apple Macintosh and its cousins in the Apple Lisa family. Use of the mouse as a user interface accompanied by icons (pictures on the screen replacing menus) provide a radically different user approach from traditional systems.

Another type of special computer is the portable Workslate, which has been described as a spreadsheet computer. It has a built-in modem and plug-in modules for various spreadsheet applications.

Two other special machines are IBM's 370/XT and 3270-PC. The 370/XT can run both PC-DOS microcomputer software and VM mainframe software; the 3270-PC can emulate the IBM 3270 terminal. These computers are leading the way toward integration of mainframe and personal computer functions.

Home Computers

There is a somewhat blurry distinction between a home computer and a small business computer. Some home computers, such as the Commodore 64, feature 64K of internal storage, a powerful 8-bit processor, and optional disk drives that allow powerful applications to be run. Generally, though, a home computer is a relatively inexpensive machine categorized by an 8-bit processor and application software emphasizing personal finance, games, and simple business applications. Hardware such as the Atari 1200XL, Coleco Adam, and Commodore's C64 and VIC-20 belong in this category.

Any consultant emphasizing home computers should concentrate on commercial software development or education (such as children's computing classes) rather than traditional consulting; it's difficult for someone to spend $199 for a computer and then spend $35 per hour for advice in selecting $25 software!

The Other Machines: Minicomputers and Mainframes

Ten years ago, if anyone had predicted that a computer book would one day categorize minicomputers and mainframes as "other machines," the straightjackets would have been quickly ordered. However, the emphasis of this book is on microcomputer hardware and software. In the interest of completeness, though, let's spend a bit of time discussing the other machines, including IBM's other systems, Sperry, Honeywell, Burroughs, DEC, Prime, and Data General.

As was mentioned in Chapter 2, most businesses with these large machines have at least one on-site programmer or analyst. Therefore, you aren't likely to be dealing with the same level of expertise as you would with a grocery store owner who purchased an Apple IIe for business accounting. You need to specialize in database management, communications, operating systems, or another extremely technical and narrow specialty. Alternatively, you could develop sophisticated custom or commercial software directly for end users or licensed through hardware vendors. You could specialize in systems analysis or designing and building computer systems.

There is a wide range of activities you could perform as a large system specialist. The important point to remember is that if you eventually choose this route, your activities and clients will be different from those of a microcomputer specialist.

Choosing Machines

Alright, you decide to emphasize basic microcomputers in your practice. Does it really make a difference whether you choose a widely used system such as the IBM PC or Apple IIe to emphasize in your activities, as opposed to a less popular machine? After all, many other consultants probably specialize in the popular machines, and software developers concentrate on the same hardware.

Consider this: Suppose you were a mainframe commercial software developer 25 years ago and decided to specialize in Philco hardware. What's a Philco computer, you ask? It was one of the mainframe competitors to IBM, Sperry, and Burroughs. Then there was General Electric's venture into computers. If you had invested scarce resources in developing software for hardware that wasn't widely accepted, you probably would have had little chance for success.

One might argue that without third-party software vendor and consultant support, a machine may have little chance of marketplace survival. I firmly believe that a consultant should not select name hardware or software solely on the basis of popular acceptance. I've seen commercially successful software that was poorly written and occasionally aborted into the operating system; upon inquiry, local retailers say, "Well, it sells great!"

Chapter 8 discussed selection criteria for hardware and software. You should choose computer hardware that meets your selected software; if the software runs on a less popular but less expensive computer of sufficient quality and vendor support, by all means consider that hardware for your client.

Summary

This chapter has attempted to outline the different classes of hardware you might deal with as a computer consultant. We've also looked briefly at the different skill levels you should possess for each category, as well as define your probable client bases and product-service mix. The key points are: (1) hardware technology is rapidly advancing, resulting in a blurring of the distinctions among classes; (2) different categories require different levels of expertise on your part, meaning you should choose your specialties with care; and (3) you should select your specialties with an eye toward the marketplace and probable demand.

CHAPTER 10

Writing Contract Software

Given the amount of commercial software currently available, along with the explosive growth in the number of software packages coming to market, why would a client contract to have custom software developed? Isn't it faster, simpler, and less expensive to purchase an existing program to meet the user's needs?

In this chapter, we will discuss why a client may consider purchasing a customer-written software package rather than pick one off the local retailer's shelves. We will discuss the mechanics of developing a contract package, including analyzing requirements and developing system specifications, choosing your developmental software, and determining an implementation time frame. We will also review managerial considerations such as obtaining client feedback and support, determining your software's price, postinstallation support, and hiring assistance.

Reasons for Contract Software

We already asked why a client would desire contract software rather than a commercial package. The three most common reasons are:

1. The customer has a specialized application or variation of a standard application for which little or no software can be purchased. An example would be a restaurant that requires a specialized inventory system, differentiating food and nonfood processing, with online menu (the restaurant menu, not a computer menu) updating, and a specially interfaced accounting system. The driving force behind a custom system would be the special industry-specific nature of "standard" inventory and accounting applications, as well as the integration of several applications.

Even if a "restaurant system" was available that performed most or all of the desired functions, there may be special problems such as inflexibility of the stored data (i.e., the manager wishes to add certain fields to the inventory record but the software package won't permit this) or intercomputer access to other systems from the software. In short, if no commercial software is available to meet all of the client's critical problems, the client may wish to have a customized package written rather than settle for insufficient software support.

2. The client already has a computer system but can't obtain applicable software for that computer. This is common among computers using a proprietary operating system rather than a multiple-hardware one like CP/M, MS-DOS, or UNIX. Many software houses and independent programmers prefer to develop software for the more common operating systems with a larger hardware and user base.

3. Occasionally a computer owner prefers the support of knowing who developed the software (and who can fix it if problems result) as well as wishing to provide for easy integration of additional applications at a later date.

Developing Software Specifications

Every computer program must be developed according to a set of specifications to ensure compliance with the eventual user's needs and desires. To develop a useful software system, you must determine the following:

1. *Data:* What information will the user need to store? Will it be retrieved by querying individual records, producing reports of all data items, or a combination of both methods? How much data is projected to be stored? How volatile will the types of data stored be (will frequent changes in data field types occur)?

2. *Reports:* What formats will reports take, on both paper and the computer's screen? An advantage that custom-built software has over many off-the-shelf packages is that reports can be designed to utilize existing preprinted forms or meet organizational format requirements with greater ease than with commercial systems.

3. *Algorithms:* What functions must the software perform and through what means? What formula must be used to compute interest payments, inventory values, or other quantitative amounts?

4. *Integration:* Will the program be integrated with either existing or future software? If so, the degree of integration must be determined, such as simultaneous operations, data sharing, or common user interface.

5. *User interface:* When an interactive computer program is being developed from ground-up specifications the users can specify *exactly* how they would like to "talk" to the program. It was mentioned in Chapter 8 that software interfaces could be of the query-command variety or operate through a series of menus, and people with different levels of computer experience may prefer different systems. The user could also specify exactly what commands are desirable (do we use DELETE or ERASE? CHANGE or MODIFY?) or whether letters or numbers are preferable for menu selections.

While this may seem trivial, the purpose of developing a computer system with either commercial or custom software is to produce a useful and "friendly" tool for the user. The more input the users have the less reluctant they will be accepting the computer system. Remember, the person who approaches you with a request for systems development may not be the only user of the system; there may be, for example, order entry clerks who view the computer as a threat to their jobs. Much has been written about user resistance to computers; it is theorized that the more input the eventual users of the system have regarding design considerations the less resistance there will be.

6. *Backup and recovery requirements:* The critical nature of the data will determine the backup and recovery procedures. You must determine the frequency of backup copies and how long they will be retained, along with recovery procedures in case of a catastrophic error.

7. *Special requirements:* You must also determine needs for remote access to other computers, simultaneous multiuser requirements, and multitasking needs, such as print spooling. The need to implement special requirements would affect both the system's software and hardware. A system that should allow two users to simultaneously access the same data record must maintain data integrity while preventing deadlock situations (these topics are discussed in most database management texts).

Once these requirements are fully specified, you have the blueprints from which a well-designed and functional software system can be developed. It can't be stressed enough that the most successful custom software is like a custom-tailored suit; it fits the customer's needs while allowing for future modifications.

Now it's time to create a software development plan. You need to determine what will be done, how it will be done, and over what time frame. It is *extremely* difficult to accurately determine how much time it takes to write a complex computer program. Many complexities may arise such as interface problems among software modules and any existing software, including the operating system, windowing system, or database manager. If you have developed a complete set of specifications that have been reviewed for software engineering soundness, implementation is much easier than if you begin by writing a program. The computer systems life cycle reviewed in Chapter 8 still applies if contract software is being substituted for commercial software; the software selection phase is replaced by a program development stage, consisting of software design, coding, testing, and refinement.

The time alloted for project completion should take into consideration:

1. *Frequency:* The frequency with which you will be working on the software (number of hours per day, number of days per week).

2. *Expertise:* Your expertise in the system being developed—how much research must be done on the target hardware, developmental software, and the application itself?

3. *Accessibility to the computer:* Sometimes the client will only allow you access to the hardware after normal business hours owing to operational requirements. Developing the system in your spare time may also limit access to the machine unless you have your own software-compatible machine for developmental purposes.

4. *Deadline:* If the software *must* be online as soon as possible, customizing the user interface or implementing extensive HELP screens become subordinate to the critical mass of code that will perform the basic input, processing, and output. This development method is known as prototyping; your goal is to implement a useful system as soon as possible.

The rules presented in Chapter 8 regarding your competence in completing the contracted tasks also apply here. You assume a large risk to your personal and professional reputation (not to mention potential legal liability) if you accept a task and fail. You should possess whatever basic tools and skills are necessary for the contract, including some familiarity with the hardware and application. Additional research can further clarify how well you may perform this job. If you don't feel you have the expertise to complete the assignment, subcontract the job or refer your client to another consultant or software developer.

Choosing Developmental Software

The choice of a computer language for your program is critical. As most programmers are aware, computer language have different strengths and weaknesses. Assuming that you are not confined to a particular language by the client's contracting policy (or system limitations), you should choose a computer language that will facilitate your program development.

This decision can be expanded into the choice of an entire software development system that includes database managers and front-end user interfaces. Let's examine the features and relative advantages and disadvantages of different classes of developmental software.

Assembly Languages

Once upon a time the majority of "serious" software projects were written in the machines' respective assembly languages because of a combination of factors (such as limited internal memory, lack of sufficient high-level languages, and interfacing with the operating system). These programs ran faster than those written in interpreted BASIC, the other primary language available.

With the proliferation of machines with larger memory capacities, much development (even for systems programs like compilers, operating systems, and database managers) has been done in high-level languages.

Why would you want to develop software in assembly language? Some applications require a close interface with the host operating system that isn't available with some high-level languages. Additionally, a client who already has a computer but has limited internal memory may need to have every byte of storage managed as efficiently as possible and can't afford to have a complex application developed in a memory-hogging compiler language. You can control segmentation and overlays as well as squeeze instructions together in as efficient a manner as possible.

What are the disadvantages of using an assembly language? The primary one is the additional development time required, which is due to the nature of assembly languages. The number of statements in an assembler program is several times greater than that of a similarly functioning

BASIC or PASCAL program. The software development process is likely to last much longer in an assembler environment than in a high-level one. Even if you are charging by the hour, your customers are likely to balk at 90 hours versus 30 hours of development time just because you choose to use assembly language.

Second, the assembly program's complexity is far greater than a corresponding BASIC or COBOL one because of the cryptic nature of the assembly statements and the heavy use of the machine's registers. The probability of program errors increases, as does the difficulty of locating the error. Therefore, the debugging phase of development is likely to be more tedious and difficult.

Third, assembly languages are different among all types of microprocessors. A program you develop for an IBM PC running under an 8088 processor must be extensively translated prior to implementation on an Apple IIe with a 6502 chip.

Since most microcomputers have extensive memory capacity (whether utilized or not) and a vast array of high-level languages exists, assembly language program development should be avoided in a contract environment.

Owing to the added time it usually takes to develop and debug a program in assembler rather than a high-level language, each project will require more of your time, resulting in fewer contracts you can complete and less revenue. Many newer high-level languages provide access to the bit level in computer words as well as operating system interfaces. Those that don't can often be combined with assembly language subroutines to provide these features, as we shall soon see.

High-Level Languages

A high-level language is any computer language that provides either English-like or mathematical statements to take the place of several assembler loads, stores, and jumps. Rather than loading a register with the contents of memory location A, adding the contents of a second memory area B, multiplying the result by a third value C, and storing the result back in the first memory location, you can write

$$A = (A + B) \times C$$

rather than code four or more cryptic assembler statements.

There are many high-level languages available for program development. Some of the more common ones are BASIC, COBOL, FORTRAN, PASCAL, and C. Most programmers are aware of the advantages and disadvantages of the languages relative to one another (COBOL was developed for business applications while FORTRAN is used for scientific projects). For further comparisons, you may wish to consult various computer periodicals' special reports on computer languages, such as the one featured in the September 1983 issue of *Popular Computing.*

What are the advantages of using a high-level language? You can choose a particular language that is tailored to your application. A business program might use COBOL while a statistically laden program may be written in FORTRAN.

The portability of the resulting software is another benefit. Unlike assembly languages, high-level languages are mostly alike among different computers. BASIC on one computer may be slightly different on another in terms of input-output and system-dependent procedures, but the bulk of the language is the same among different versions. This provides benefits to both you and your clients. Parts of your software can be reused in different projects to decrease your development time, even if a different computer system is being used. Your clients benefit by being able to upgrade to new hardware without requiring massive rewrites of their custom software because only those system-specific parts must be rewritten.

The primary disadvantage of using a high-level language is the decreased hardware and operating system control as opposed to the control you get with assembly languages. Newer versions of compilers (as well as new languages) are providing mechanisms for these operations, but the programmer may still run into problems with memory capacity; the compiler needs to fit into the memory as well as the program during compilation (or at least *parts* of the compiler and the program need to fit if the compiler contains overlays or the program is being written in small segments or subroutines). The compiler may also provide some memory-intensive system subroutines for input, output, and screen management that crowd the available space. In short, the programmer has less control over what will be in the resulting executable program than if he or she develops the program in assembler.

Another disadvantage is that the data access methods provided by the language may not be sufficient to allow for complex data manipulation; the software developer must then either write his or her own routines or utilize an outside database manager.

Finally, it is rare to find compilers (other than an occasional BASIC one) included in the computer system purchase price. Most computers have a BASIC interpreter, which may not be appropriate for development because of execution speed limitations. Therefore, a compiler may need to be purchased by your client for that particular computer and language, thus adding to development costs. Of course, if you are writing a program in IBM FORTRAN and you already have an IBM FORTRAN compiler on your own machine, you can develop the software there and transport the resultant object code to your client's machine.

Database Management Systems (DBMS)

Many of the DBMSs available today for microcomputers contain a built-in programming language to simulate the functions and features of high-level languages such as BASIC or PASCAL. Some are more sophisticated than others, containing structured programming constructs such as IF-THEN-ELSE, DO WHILE, and CASE statements. Others merely provide a simple user interface (responding to prompts, for example) and the ability to selectively do other groups of command statements without having to repeatedly type in every command.

The primary advantage to using a programming DBMS (as we shall refer to these systems) is that applications with complex data handling requirements can usually be implemented much faster than if the programmer must manage trees, linked lists, indices, and other data structures. Rather than having a BASIC loop, for example, to locate the first freshman in a student data file and follow pointers to every other freshman, you may be able to substitute a statement like FIND ALL CLASS = FRESHMAN in your program. The maintenance of these data structures upon additions, updates, and deletions is also automatically performed by the DBMS, allowing for even more time savings during development (and far fewer headaches!).

A second feature that many developers find useful is a report generator, which is contained in many DBMSs. By "drawing" your desired output formats on the terminal screen or by answering system prompts regarding what fields you would like totaled and subtotaled (and by what criteria), the programming process is further simplified. Modification can usually be made by respecifying or modifying your displayed formats rather than going into your source code and changing display rows and columns, data items, and calculation specifications.

Still another useful feature of a development DBMS is the ability to quickly and easily modify the types or characteristics of the data being maintained. By modifying the structure, or schema, of a database, fields can be expanded or shortened in length, new ones added, and data typing (numeric, alphanumeric, date, etc.) can be changed without rewriting major sections of your programs and creating reload programs to convert your old database to its new format.

Various DBMSs allow you to specify data editing features (for example, only allow numeric digits for a zip code) that permit you to "idiot-proof" your software without the usual tedium involved in such a task.

With such wonderful features, why would anyone develop software in anything other than a programming DBMS? There are some disadvantages associated with the development method. As mentioned earlier, some of the languages aren't really languages: they're a means for repeatedly performing a similar set of queries. Unless the selected DBMS has a good complement of programming building blocks, the resultant software systems may not be as flexible as if they were constructed using a traditional programming language (high-level or assembler).

Another disadvantage is the execution speed of the developed program. Most DBMS command files are treated by the operating system in a manner similar to interpreted BASIC; that is, each statement must be reread repeatedly and *then* translated into a series of machine instructions to perform the desired operations. Some DBMSs, however, such as dBASE II and Knowledge Manager, have released "run-time" versions of their systems that, acting like a compiler and linker, take your command files and perform a one-time translation into machine code. The resulting product is the same as any other executable file on your computer system.

When would you want to use a programming DBMS for your software development? In most instances when your client needs very complex data manipulation these systems are likely to be time savers for you and cost savers for your client. Be cautioned, though: In most cases, unless the publisher has a special run-time cost arrangement, your client is paying for both your development work *and* the underlying DBMS, which may be expensive and contain many features he or she is not using. Therefore, these development systems may not be applicable for small, relatively inexpensive computer systems unless the client has already purchased the DBMS software for another use.

Applications Generators

While the days of true automatic program generation have not yet arrived, program generators such as The Last One and Quickcode (which generates dBASE II code) can be of assistance in generating standard applications or reducing the tedium of software development.

The software designer or user typically answers questions regarding important data, processing requirements, and output formats and a skeleton application is produced by the generator. While we are still a long way from parameterized generation of complex applications, these tools can be useful in producing a program base from which the programmer can enhance the application. It is strongly recommended that you sample the production code from an application generator prior to purchase or use, as the products may vary in sophistication, efficiency, and other factors.

Combinations

An alternative you have as a program developer is to use a combination of two or more development systems we've discussed. You may develop the bulk of your code in a high-level language while interfacing assembly language subroutines to do screen input and output or operating system interfaces. Or you could combine a BASIC program with a DBMS that acts as a data management subroutine for host language programs.

The key is to treat your program development process in the manner that computer science and information systems students are taught in college-level programming classes: figure out what you need to do and *then* pick a development system or combination of systems to best meet that task within your time, ability, and user-defined constraints.

Naturally you must deal with these real-world constraints as best you can. If you are developing a package for a client's computer with a proprietary operating system you may not have access to certain languages, DBMSs, or applications generators. Though this would be the most efficient development manner on paper, in this case you are limited to what is available for the given hardware.

Costing and Timecharting

How long will it take you to design, code, test, and implement your client's contract software? Many methodologies have been proposed to determine software engineering and development factors.

A simple method is to analyze your application in terms of (1) your experience, (2) the experience of anyone else working on the project, (3) the complexity of the application, and (4) the sophistication of your development tools. If you have substantial experience in both the application being generated and your developmental software (the language, DBMS, etc.), your total development time will be less than if you have only a cursory knowledge of both the application and the software. This is also true of anyone else working on the project, whether a partner, subcontractor, or employee.

The complexity of the application will also affect the development time. A program with complex graphics, sorting, file searching, and calculations will take longer to complete than one with simple calculations and file work but no graphics or sorting. The time will also vary according to the experience level of programmers (you and others) performing these complex tasks. Few programmers are experts in all aspects of programming: database manipulation, graphics, algorithm generation, and others. You may be very experienced in complex data management schemes and can develop programs in this area very quickly, but a graphics development program may be much more tedious and time-consuming.

Your development tools play a role in reducing your programming complexity. A good graphics generator or DBMS will significantly reduce turnaround time as opposed to performing these tasks in BASIC, assembler, or another language. Therefore, after you have an idea of what needs to be done in terms of data storage and access, user interface, calculations, report formats, and special requirements, you should make a close examination of the application, the development software, and the relative complexity of both, as well as your own level of expertise (or that of the programmer, if someone other than you) with these factors. Try to calculate how many hours the associated research, development, and testing will take based on these factors but leave room for unexpected problems and complexities.

User Feedback

Throughout the programming process you should attempt to work as closely as possible with your client. To ensure understanding of your client's needs and problems periodic reviews should be scheduled to obtain feedback of the development done to date. Sample menu screens should be demonstrated periodically to ensure that your client is comfortable with the user interface. Sample reports should be examined for data validity, ease of understanding, and conformity with standards.

As with choosing commercial software, the system being designed and built is for your client and the end product must be as useful to him or her as possible.

Contracts

Except for rare occasions, any software developed for a client should be *licensed* to the client, with ownership (and copyright) retained by you. This ensures that your customer doesn't turn around and resell your program to several other users, recovering his or her costs and profiting from your efforts. License agreements are covered in detail in Chapter 11 but briefly, your client should sign a nondisclosure agreement to prevent leakage of your source code (if you choose to provide it) and your contract should clearly state the terms of license (exclusive, nonexclusive, etc.).

An exception to the licensing and nondisclosure agreements may occur when your client and you agree to develop a software package for the client's use but also to jointly market the program to other potential users. In this case, your client may recover his or her costs by making an investment in the software development and sharing the proceeds of resale to others.

If this situation occurs, the resulting software may be marketed on a limited basis to the client's business associates and contacts or developed as a commercial package to be self-published or licensed through a software publisher. If the former is the case, be sure to examine *Commercial Versus Custom Software* in Chapter 11 to make the transition from a single- or limited-use program to one used by many buyers.

Your contract should state that the only applications and features to be included in the completed software are the ones previously and mutually agreed to by your client and you. This will prevent confusion and disagreement at a subsequent time if your client were to say, "Oh, by the way, I'd like this feature added also."

Pricing Your Software

A task almost as difficult as determining total implementation time is setting a price for your contract software. Should you charge a flat fee? How about charging on a per-hour basis? Should you place a ceiling on the number of hours?

While many consultants may use different methods, an approach I favor is to take your estimate of development hours (with a buffer to handle unexpected difficulties), attach an hourly rate, *and* place a ceiling in the contract on the number of hours (as described in Chapter 4). I favor this approach because you are guaranteed a fair wage based on the number of hours estimated for the project. Since you have a reasonable estimate (hopefully) of the development time with built-in protection for overruns, the total development process is handled in much the same manner as a normal consulting contract: your compensation is based on the time and effort you devote to the project.

Your client also benefits in two important ways. First, the possibility exists that the project may be completed in less time than projected, resulting in some (or substantial) savings. Second, he or she is protected, in case you have made miscalculations of the time involved, by the ceiling of hours. There is no reason the client should pay substantially more because your estimate, based on mutually agreeable specifications, was inaccurate.

How do you benefit from this type of arrangement? Remember our marketing lesson: A satisfied client usually leads to many more satisfied clients. If a project is brought in under budget or a client realizes that he or she is protected by your "outstanding" sense of fairness in the form of a price ceiling, your reputation as a fair businessperson (as important as your reputation as a knowledgeable professional) will spread among prospective customers.

If, however, you find unsuspecting (or gullible) clients, contract on a straight hourly basis, and consistently complete the project at double or triple the orginal cost estimate, it won't be long before your reputation also spreads, and I don't mean as a fair businessperson. Even though you can legally collect these exorbitant fees (if your contracts are structured so), in the long run you will end up as the loser.

What hourly rate should you use? Since the computer program development process almost always involves some trial and error in the form of testing and debugging, I favor a slightly lower hourly rate than your normal consulting fee. If you normally charge $35 per hour for consulting services, you may quote $25 or $30 for each hour of contract programming.

This is dependent on the market and demand for your services, however. If you have a reputation as an outstanding consultant and designer, you may be able to charge your regular hourly fee for programming. If, however, you charge upwards of $75 per hour, the resulting price for any software project may be too high to compete with alternative bids. The key is to know your market and the demand for your programming services.

Subcontracting

There are several reasons you might wish to subcontract part or all of a contract software project. First, you may be involved in several other ongoing projects and don't have the time to devote to this particular project. Rather than turn down a contract, you can hire a programmer to accomplish the required programming.

Second, a particular software project might be so complex that one person would have a difficult time completing it by the required deadline. By adding one or two other programmers to the project the development time can be decreased, even though the accumulated programmer hours will be roughly the same. Be aware, though, that adding too many programmers to a particular task can be counterproductive because of the increased interpersonal communication necessary.

Finally, you may not possess the programming expertise required for this (or all) complex software assignments. Again, rather than bypass the project, you may find that subcontracting provides the answer.

How much should you pay your subcontractor? This should be a function of the programmer's experience and (again) the market supply and demand. An experienced software developer should receive a larger proportion of the consulting dollars than a student programmer, for example. If you are receiving $30 for each hour of program development and, out of 75 total hours, 45 hours will be devoted to coding, the programmer should receive a percentage of the *actual programming hours,* not your own design and implementation efforts.

The percentage is determined by the old economic laws of supply and demand. It would be difficult to find an experienced programmer willing to work for $5 per hour, of course, so don't expect to keep $25 out of each $30 hourly charge to your client. On the other hand, it is possible that the programmer (depending again on supply and demand of contract software services) wouldn't have the task to perform without your willingness to subcontract the work. Divisions of 50–50 and 40–60 are fairly common.

Occasionally my firm has received software development contracts from customers of local retail computer stores. In these cases, we act as a programming subcontractor for the store's system implementation and receive, for example, 90 percent of the total custom software dollars. We specify our estimate of hours and from our normal hourly fee pay 10 percent to the retailer as primary contractor. You may think, "Why give up 10 percent of your earned dollars to someone else?" but without the store we likely would have no contract and no dollars to pay anything from. Also, there is considerably less unpaid overhead than there is with our own contracts: initial meetings, phone calls, the prorating of advertising expenses (remember indirect costs?), and the general effort put into a project while unsure if it will become a reality. Knowing this will help you both understand your subcontractors' position better and prepare you for the times when you are the subcontractor. As a computer consultant you will likely find yourself wearing both hats.

Selecting Hardware

For those custom programming clients who don't already have computer hardware, your system development task may include selecting a computer. The rule to go by is to choose a system that supports your to-be-developed software in terms of internal and external storage, multitasking capabilities (if desired), adequate number of peripheral devices supported, etc.—the same way you would choose hardware to match selected commercial software.

If your client will probably have all subsequent programs developed under contract rather than commercially purchased, you don't have to worry much about finding a computer that runs one or more popular operating systems (CP/M, MS-DOS, etc.). Rather, you can purchase a computer with a proprietary operating system that may be less expensive than a more commercially successful one.

When choosing a system, the same evaluation criteria we discussed in Chapter 9 (vendor support, reliability, etc.) still apply. Of course, price is also very important.

Postinstallation Support

Is your job completed once you finish your software development and testing? Probably not. Most custom software purchasers want or need training in the operation of their programs.

When you are doing your time estimates near the beginning of the project these training hours should be included. You should be able to determine the amount of training needed by the project's complexity.

In addition to the designated training program, a good consultant should be available to answer user questions by phone or, if desired, in person. Depending on the structure of your contract you may provide a certain amount of additional support time at no cost to the user, followed by billable hours.

You will, however, be expected to investigate and correct any suspected system bugs the user reports (i.e., if your software performs incorrect calculations, aborts unexpectedly, or otherwise causes problems that weren't uncovered during your testing). To protect yourself from user complaints many months (or years) later, your contract should specify, for example, that any problems discovered during the first 30 days of normal operation will be corrected at no charge while the purchaser will be billed for any subsequent time spent.

What happens when your client decides during the first month of operation that this isn't really what he or she wanted or he or she would like a report added? This is where your contract and user-agreed specifications provide you with protection. As long as the client has agreed in writing to various specifications and lists of features throughout the development process, you should not be responsible for your client's indecision. Naturally, any program modifications can and should be made, *but under separate contractual arrangements*. Often, your client may later wish to have additions or modifications to the program. These should also be handled under a separate development contract.

Summary

This chapter covered the basics of software development for individual clients. Rather than purchase commercial programs, some people prefer or must have custom-developed software. This development replaces software selection in the computer systems life cycle (Chapter 8).

Many important decisions must be made about the development process, including developmental software, program features, and cost estimates. The more decisions you make in conjunction with your client the less likely you are to face later-stage or postdevelopment problems.

Well, Bernie Jordan has been resting for a couple of chapters, so it's time to check in on him. Bernie's first contract, as we saw previously, included development of an integrated legal office package. While meeting with his clients, Bernie was able to determine the desired features of the system as well as the relative complexity. After his initial design efforts he modified his configuration slightly with feedback results from his clients.

Since the hardware choice was his to make within client-specified budget constraints, Bernie chose a popular hardware brand that was compatible with his own system. Using his database manager with a programming language, Bernie was able to develop the database-dependent features quickly, providing time savings to him and cost savings to his clients.

Since Bernie plans to modify the software for resale, his clients have allowed him the freedom to implement commercial-like features such as idiot-proof menu drivers and a HELP facility. They will be sharing in the development and marketing of the final product and wish to have the program as well written as possible.

CHAPTER 11

Commercial Software

The author will receive a royalty; the rest of the retail price will be split among the publisher, the distributor, and the retailer.

Books? Phonograph records? No, we're discussing the software industry. The computer program marketplace is rapidly evolving into a multi-tiered structure similar to other publishing industries. The days when a programmer could write a simple software package accompanied by five pages of photocopied instructions, place a classified advertisement in a computer hobbyist magazine, and mail program copies when requested are rapidly disappearing.

Software entrepreneurs must understand proper advertising strategy of the software as well as find the most profitable distribution channels and set a competitive but profitable price—in other words, they must apply the marketing principles we looked at in Chapter 5. The documentation must be of the highest quality.

Additionally, there are many different routes programmers can pursue in bringing their program to market: should the program be marketed through an independent software publisher, bundled with hardware and sold as a package, or self-published?

Needless to say, the legal considerations involved are extremely complex; entire books have been written discussing the legal issues of software marketing and protecting both your rights and your investment.

In addition to these many topics, this chapter will also discuss the features commercial software should have, how to price your program, the postsale support you should provide, and the pros and cons of using outside help.

The Commercial Software Market

One of the first questions you may be asking yourself is, Is there still a market for software? There are thousands of commercial sources of microcomputer software; isn't the market saturated already? How many word processing programs and spreadsheets are really needed?

There *is* still an outstanding market for independent computer programs for several reasons:

1. Every time new machines and operating systems are introduced software must be made available. Often, existing programs that run on popular machines are converted (as was the case when the IBM PC came to market; most of the popular microcomputer software was adapted for the PC). When the new computer runs an existing operating system on a standard CPU chip with few or no modifications (MS-DOS, CP/M, etc.) the applications software modifications tend to be relatively minor. However, when a new operating system or computer chip is introduced that is incompatible with existing applications, major rewriting is often needed for existing software.

This brings us to the first reason the commercial software market is still lucrative: when new computer systems are introduced, the opportunity exists for new software to be marketed that runs on those machines.

2. New applications are introduced. The industry buzzword of 1983, for example, was "integrated applications." This meant software that combined the previous stand-alone functions of word processing, database management, spreadsheet analysis, graphics generators, and communications capabilities into one program (but not all integrated software contained all functions). A repackaging of existing applications, made possible in part by increased microcomputer memory size (a technological advance), allowed many new and existing companies to battle for new customers. Even though there were many existing programs available for the individual applications, the combining of these functions into a new applications package allowed companies such as Lotus, Context, and VisiCorp (among others) to battle for the many dollars being spent on this type of software.

Though it may appear at times that new applications would be difficult or impossible to come up with ("OK, we integrated word processing,

database management, etc., into one system, so what else is left to do?"),
you never know what ingenious new software idea someone may bring to
the market. How many people in 1970 could have envisioned a system like
VisiCalc? Who in 1980 could have foreseen Lotus 1-2-3?

The advent of a true artificially intelligent system (if and when it happens) could provide the impetus for a whole new class of smart, "thinking"
software, for example.

3. As computers became more powerful in terms of CPU speed,
internal memory, external storage capacity, etc., applications that previously were only able to run on larger systems can be downloaded to
smaller computers. Our example of integrated software package would
have been extremely difficult in a 64K, 8-bit environment (though one
recently introduced system from Arktronics, Jane, reportedly performs
these functions on 8-bit systems).

With a large internal memory capacity, for example, word processing
programs can keep more of the current document and the program itself
"in core," requiring fewer disk accesses for program functions or other
parts of the file; spreadsheets can be larger; and more levels of applications menus can be accessed without going to disk. Larger external storage
allows for a large database, which, when coupled with a fast CPU chip,
provides quicker file searches than were previously available. Larger computer words (16- or 32-bit machines, for example) provide for greater
memory access ranges than were available with 8-bit machines.

The point is that as the hardware technology advances, existing applications can be improved to take advantage of those technological
advances. Coupled with the fact that most new hardware requires new
software, this provides excellent opportunities for talented programmers
to exploit the new hardware technology and provide software that is big-
ger, faster, and easier to use than that currently available.

More and more microcomputers are featuring multiuser and multitasking functions. Along with the systems software that is being developed
primarily by existing companies (multiuser or multitasking operating systems are coming out of Digital Research and Microsoft), a whole new
range of applications software must be developed. What happens when
two users of an inventory management system attempt to simultaneously
update the same inventory item record? While mainframe and minicomputer software has dealt with this situation for years and provided file-
locking capabilities, password protectors, etc., the microcomputer programmers have been dealing with single-user systems until recently: why
provide file-locking capabilities when the computer itself can only have
one user at a time?

These problems must be resolved prior to full acceptance of multiuser microcomputer systems by end users. Again, technological advances provide an opportunity for new computer software to enter the market.

As long as technological breakthroughs continue to occur in the computer industry new software will always be needed (in fact, necessary) to make the machines as useful as possible to their users. An apparently saturated software market could suddenly have gaping holes begging to be filled by insightful and talented programmers.

Commercial Software Areas

Off-the-shelf software can be divided into several main categories. The price, user interface, and the features of the software package often depend on which areas the system can be grouped into.

One of the primary applications for microcomputers has been "personal productivity" tools such as spreadsheet analysis, database management, time and schedule management, and word processing. While these applications have definite uses in most business enviroments, the primary use has been to improve the productivity of individual managers and employees, mostly through stand-alone, single-user machines.

A second category is traditional business applications, such as accounting, inventory management, and real estate property management. Small businesses that find a mainframe or minicomputer impractical and don't wish to subscribe to a time-sharing service have been greatly aided by the implementation of these applications programs on small business computers in the $1500 to $6000 class.

Educational software has received much attention lately as the United States attempts to revive a stagnating educational system. LOGO, a language devoted to educational applications, has been implemented on a wide range of machines. Many software firms are attempting to develop computer-based "courseware" for a wide range of educational topics, from first-grade-level mathematics to college accounting.

Games have been a strong software area on home computers, with many of the popular video arcade games existing for Atari, Apple, Commodore, and other machines. In addition to video games, other entertainment software such as adventure games and trivia quizzes have come on the market.

The above four major categories can rightly be considered applications software; that is, the computer user will use the programs for business, educational, or entertainment purposes. Two other classes of software can be grouped as systems software; that is, they assist the computer system in performing its functions so as to provide a useful product for the user but aren't the primary reason why the user purchases a computer.

Systems software such as the operating system, language compilers, communication programs, and operating environments provide useful and necessary tools for applications programs to function.

Let's consider an investment analysis program, written in PASCAL, that downloads data from an outline information retrieval database and allows the user to search for stocks that meet specified criteria. Without a compiler, the PASCAL source program could not have been translated into the machine's native assembler language. Without an operating system, the program's object code would have to do *everything,* including disk access and terminal screen management, rather than use preprogrammed operating system functions. A communications program is necessary to access the remote database and perform important error checking and other data communications functions.

As you can see, most applications would be extremely ineffective without underlying systems software to support both the development and execution of applications programs.

Finally, programmer's tools, such as screen generators, host language–imbedded database management tools, graphics programs, and applications generators, assist computer programmers in developing software by alleviating many of the tedious and repetitive functions. Thus, programmers can concentrate on the function of the program without getting tied up in as many details as if, for example, they had to generate every interactive terminal screen by appropriate operating system calls.

One final note: Software often overlaps two or more of the broad categories we've reviewed. Games are often educational, database managers are often used for business applications as well as personal productivity, and compilers can also be considered programmer's tools. The purpose here is not to take every piece of commercial software and force it into a set category; rather, it is to make some observations about the distinctions among the various classes of applications and system software. As we shall see, your intended software category will affect your package's price, software development system, and user interface type, among other features.

Does Your Program Have a Market?

We saw that despite the huge amount of software currently available, new and unique programs should always have the potential to capture a significant portion of certain market niches. The key word here is niche: the ghost of Chapter 5 is still with us because selecting a market niche is the same as defining your target market. Just as your consulting services need to be developed around a projected marketing strategy that includes defining a target for your services and meeting that market's needs, commercial software development demands the same concentrated effort.

Let's say you develop a word processing package for the IBM PC. Regardless of the technical aspects of your program (execution speed, user interface, etc.), you need to consider the following:

1. How many word processing programs are currently available for the PC? What are their prices? Which are the most popular and why?

2. Will the hardware itself become obsolete soon? If so, can its software be upgraded to a follow-on machine? What, if any, modifications must be made to the program to enable it to run on a new machine?

3. How is your program different from existing packages? Why would someone want to buy your software rather than a currently available system?

Ideally, these questions should be explored *before* embarking on a lengthy, time-consuming program development process. If you estimate your program will take 9 months from the design phase to completion, try to project the market 9 months ahead. This is where trade publications become very useful; they often have industry projections based on both public and "leaked" knowledge. Information about future plans of your target hardware's manufacturer regarding system upgrades and new operating systems can drastically affect the success of your program.

Digressing for a minute, a strong argument can be made here for a high-level language as your development system. If, for example, your hardware manufacturer upgrades to a new microprocessor chip, massive translation of an assembly language program would be necessary to utilize the new instruction set. A source program in COBOL, for example, would likely require only minor modifications to the code and then could be run through a new compiler to produce new object code.

An interesting problem could occur here, though, since you may find yourself waiting a long time until a new compiler is developed by the hardware manufacturer or a third-party source. Whereas you could have begun translating an assembly language program immediately upon publication of the new processor's instruction set, now you are dependent upon someone else's software development to enable you to pursue your project.

Features of Commercial Software

Ideally, commercial software should be the perfect system for every user, from computer novices to experienced persons. In practice, however, that is rarely the case.

We saw in Chapter 8 that a menu-driven program with all user choices derived from a multitiered menu system may be far too tedious for an experienced user, who may prefer a command-driven program. Remember your target market, however. For whom are you writing the program? What is their projected level of computer experience?

Ideally, a program could have both menu and command interface that the user can switch between, but it is often too time-consuming and impractical to include both systems. A strategy you may employ is to offer the system with a menu interface, which allows the user to purchase an inexpensive command interface as a later add-on option.

In addition to an appropriate user interface, commercial software should feature:

1. *Online help:* In the course of running a program, the user shouldn't have to refer to the reference manual every time a question or problem arises. Through a standardized (more about that in a bit) process, such as pressing a question mark or the escape key, help should be available to explain what the possible situation and actions are at this point.

2. *Standardized commands:* In a letter-driven menu, the user gets a choice of a one-letter code for each possible action. Therefore you don't want to use C for "create" and A for "alter" in one menu, while showing C for "change" and A for "add" in another. As people become more familiar with various processes, they won't always read each menu screen completely prior to making their choice. Without standardization among the various levels of the program for the same functions (ADD versus CREATE versus NEW; DELETE versus ERASE versus PURGE; MODIFY versus CHANGE versus EDIT versus ALTER) frustration and confusion can set in for the novice user, anger for the more experienced one. The same is true if commands themselves are entered rather than menu choices; be consistent!

3. *Easy escape and error recovery:* What happens if a person accidentally winds up in the middle of a menu or data addition screen? Should the user have to press 35 carriage returns in response to questions or data requests just to arrive at a means of escaping from the mistake? Of course not. Software should contain a way (standardized at all levels, of course) for the person to tell the program, "Sorry, I didn't mean to do this"—by pressing the escape key, for example.

Similarly, errors should be easy to recover from. Suppose, while using an inventory program, John Clumsy orders 40,000 jackhammers instead of 40. This mistake should be easy to correct, either by voiding a whole order (if other mistakes are present) or selectively changing that one item's quantity.

Other error recovery techniques should include notifying the user that an invalid command or menu selection has been chosen, an alphabetic zip code has been entered, or negative hours worked has been typed. Most beginning programming classes deal with error recovery and data validation.

4. *"Uh-oh" processing:* Related to error recovery, software should have a means to undo a previous transaction. If you erase 50 records from your database via a qualified deletion, such as all those with a zip code in the 40000 to 49999 range, then discover you meant a different set, such as 50000 to 59999, you don't want to either retype all 50 records or reload your backup database (many legitimate transactions performed since the last backup would have to be redone). A simple way to say, "OK, I messed up; please retrieve this data I so carelessly tossed out" is helpful. This process usually requires maintenance of some type of translation log file.

Note that in addition to trying to maintain data validity, you are also attempting to influence and win over a variety of users, many of whom are beginning computer users. If they find a software package that is "unfriendly" they are likely to stop using it if they are in control of which software will and won't be used. Additionally, this dissatisfaction will spread to other potential purchasers of your program, thus crippling your target market.

However, extremely satisfied users are likely to tell others about your remarkable program (remember what we said about word-of-mouth marketing?) and also provide an audience for your follow-on software ("I had great performance from my Ford, so I'll get another one when trade-in time comes").

5. *Interactive tutorial:* Even easy-to-use, menu-driven software requires that the user know what can and can't be done, and at what stages. Rather than being subjected to a 75-page description of the program's execution, the user can get a feel for the program through an online instructive tutorial that integrates various steps of the program with constructive feedback and mistake correction. Tutorials should use dummy data and instructions, and ideally they should be broken down into various parts, with the user choosing which ones to work on and when.

6. *Software-driven data backup and recovery:* While it may be tempting to say "Let the users back up their own files through operating-system commands and programs," the software itself should perform file maintenance and archiving. A pharmacy that needs to transfer all people who haven't ordered a prescription in 1 year from the active to the inactive file should be able to perform that through the program itself, as well as make duplicate end-of-day or end-of-week file copies. Similarly, recovery of archived or backup material in the event of a system crash or hardware failure should also be accomplished through the applications software.

7. *Mirror the activity:*   The purpose of a computer is to function as a tool to assist the person using it in performing some type of action, whether it is calculating personal finance assets, managing an accounts payable system, or even writing programs. The "electronic desktops" of window-managed software are meant to mimic peoples' actions closely, not force them to switch program and data disks each time a new task is to be performed. A manager without a computer may be interrupted while analyzing a financial statement by a phone call that requires him to access both personnel and vendor files. In a computerized environment, the manager shouldn't have to save financial data, exit that program, insert a file manager disk and personnel disk booting the database program, find personnel information, replace the personnel disk with the vendor file, and so on and so on. Before long, the "productivity tool" has become a hindrance rather than a help.

Whatever program you are developing, spend some time talking to and observing the projected users of that program. Understand their business activities, both in terms of *what* is to be done and *how* these functions are performed. Your software should mirror the activities of these users as much as possible.

Commercial Versus Custom Software

Software meant for commercial sale has a different development procedure from that developed under a single-site contract. While none of the differences are major, the commercial software developer needs to be aware of these topics.

The most important thing to remember is that you don't know your expected software users personally. While a contract program can truly be customized to your client's tastes and needs (as we saw in the last chapter), it is unlikely that many purchasers of commercial software will have the same data and report requirements, let alone use interface preferences.

Therefore, you need to anticipate as much as possible what your users need and like (remember target market analysis?). If your program is likely to be used primarily by computer novices a menu-driven interface will probably be a good interface choice, while a system for more experienced users might be command driven. Similarly, report formats can't be coded according to customers' unique preprinted forms, though a flexible program may allow for report forms generation.

A custom program can easily be modified if your user decides new or different features are necessary. Once several hundred or thousand copies of your commercial program are distributed, however, this personal customization becomes impossible.

The same is true for software bugs: while *all* software should be bug-free when installed, contract software can at least be modified if errors slip through the testing phase. A flaw in a program that resides in the hands of 5000 users isn't fixed as easily.

An application program must be an optimum mix of the most desirable features for that process. An inventory management program should handle order processing, spoilage, receivable and payable generation, back ordering, and EOQ modeling, as well as many other features that the typical user might need. An incomplete program is less likely to sell than one deemed to have too many features.

There are exceptions to this rule, though. A real estate investment analysis program can contain many different modules for lease-back analysis, raw land management, and other features that many users wouldn't need. They may prefer to purchase a less expensive program with standard income-expense analysis, cash flow management, etc.

"Personal productivity" programs, however, can and do feature subsets of functions. Someone who needs only an index card-type file manager may prefer to purchase a simple data management program at a cheaper price than a full-feature relational database management system.

One way to market any applications programs you develop is to provide several modules that are available separately. Accounting software is usually offered this way, with separate programs for accounts receivable, accounts payable, payroll, and general ledger (among others) that integrate into one large program.

A plus for the developer of a successful off-the-shelf program over someone who deals solely in custom software is the dollar return per resources invested. A property management system sold to one user may bring $1500 in revenue, while the same system sold commercially may bring in thousands of times more. True, more effort must be put into documentation, research, testing, and other developmental functions, and possibly a greater financial investment on your part as well, but the reward for effort ratio increases dramatically.

Speaking of documentation, commercial software *must* contain tutorial and reference material for a far greater quality than that of custom software. Custom software, of course, must contain complete instructions and references, but its sale is usually accompanied by personalized instruction (as well as phone calls if problems occur). Since you can't personally instruct every user of your commercial programs, a complete written tutorial (preferably accompanied by an online one) is necessary.

Finally, commercial software may be run on a variety of machines or interface with many types of peripheral devices. Software written for the IBM PC, for example, is run on a wide range of compatible machines with varying degrees of code modification required for each machine. Off-the-shelf software s usually accompanied by some sort of installation program to control terminal and printer configuration, standard forms modification, etc.

Documentation

The most imaginative, helpful, and complete online tutorial and help facilities are no substitute for comprehensive documentation. Increased emphasis is being put on documentation as part of a complete software package. The reference material should be well-written and consist of the following sections:

1. *Introduction:* Explain the major features of the package, how its use will benefit the user, and what hardware and operating systems this version runs on. Potential customers often review the documentation before testing or purchasing a package, so this section can serve as publicity for your software.

2. *Configuration:* Any special configuration programs that enable the software to run on a variety of computers or terminal types should be mentioned. Examples should be included of special configuration runs. Any special design of input and output forms (if applicable) should be used.

3. *Tutorial:* Step-by-step instructions, progressing from starting the system to ending a session, should be clearly explained and shown. Major subsections include how to start the program; how to enter, update, and delete information; how to print reports, use archival and backup features; and how to access any advanced features. Sample screens should be included as the user steps through the system. Sample reports should be shown.

A word of caution: If subsequent versions of the software change menu choices or the order in which screens appear, be sure to change this part of the documentation to reflect that; otherwise, new users may become extremely confused and frustrated.

4. *Reference section:* In addition to the tutorial material, a comprehensive reference section should be included. If your system is command-driven, an alphabetic list of commands should be included with usages demonstrated.

The major difference between the reference and tutorial sections is that while the tutorial is directed toward the first-time user of this package, the reference section provides quick but detailed information without the instructional emphasis.

5. *Examples and run sessions:*   Though the tutorial should feature many examples, a series of sample runs combining the software's many features should be included, possibly in an appendix. Typical applications should be used; include entering and modifying data, printing reports, and any other situation the user is likely to encounter.

6. *Comprehensive index:*   All documentation should have an index for easy reference to various topics. This is especially important as the software becomes more complex.

7. *Error messages:*   Any error messages you have built into the software should be listed, alphabetically or numerically, along with possible recovery actions. Additionally, any operating-system error messages the user may find while installing or using the software (for example, a DISK FULL message while copying data files) should also be listed.

8. *Problem feedback:*   Though your software will go through many phases, it's possible that some bugs may go undetected and uncorrected. A problem report for the consumer will provide you with feedback to test and validate reported problems.

9. *Reference card:*   An especially useful feature for a command system is a reference card with an abbreviated summary of the systems commands. This may preclude having to refer to the manual for syntax checks or other simple matters.

While some software documentation is still printed on a dot matrix printer and photocopied, higher-quality software usually contains professionally typeset documentation. Colors are helpful. A looseleaf binder should accompany the documentation so users can insert their own additional information (technical notes, helpful hints, and sample programs published either by you or in periodicals). Also, program documentation should be well-written and grammatically correct, like any other written material; no spelling errors or sentence fragments should be present.

Remember again that software users are not concerned with what programming language you used to write your software nor the marvelous algorithms you've implemented. Their only concern is that the software assists their business or personal tasks and is easy to use. Comprehensive documentation is a critical element of this ease of use.

The Marketing of Commercial Software

This chapter's introduction mentioned the complexities involved in producing and marketing commercial software. As a programmer with a software package you would like to bring to market, you are faced with many options for your production and marketing strategy. You could attempt to publish the software yourself, assuming responsibility for placing advertisements, collecting revenue, and distributing the product. Alternatively, you could contract with a software publishing firm for them to market and distribute the program, paying you a percentage of receipts under a royalty (license) agreement. What are the trade-offs of this decision? Let's look at some of the choices you face and analyze the factors involved in making your decision.

Should You Publish Your Program Yourself?

What is involved in bringing a self-published program to the market? The first task that must be completed is development and completion of the program itself. (The development stage should include necessary research to support the market for the software, of course.)

Following completion of the program, advertisements must be placed in the appropriate media (business and computer magazines, for example). Sample copies should be sent to major computer periodicals for evaluation. A good review of your software, which, hopefully, you should receive if your program has been carefully developed, is bug-free, contains clear documentation, etc., is excellent publicity for your software.

As orders begin to trickle or pour in, you must make copies of the program and mail the diskettes, documentation, and other material to the purchaser. Meanwhile, you may find yourself dealing with postsale functions such as tracking down previously unknown bugs or manning a software hotline for users' questions.

The self-publishing approach has two main drawbacks: it takes both time and money. If this program is the first one you've brought to market you may not have much capital for the necessary advertisements, which in turn generate interest in and orders for your program. (Sounds almost like when you begin your consulting practice with minimal capital, doesn't it?)

Conceivably you could borrow money or dip into your personal or business savings to finance advertisements. If your software could potentially generate a large user base, you could also seek venture capital to finance the marketing and postsale functions necessary for self-publication.

Of the above financing alternatives the most desirable one, in my opinion, is seeking venture captial (unless you have *extremely* large capital reserves as a result of successful consulting operations, previous software sales, or personal inheritance). Sometimes, though, venture capital or other financing from outside investors may not be easily found.

Even if sufficient capital is available the time involved in self-publication may be substantial, if done alone. You may want to proceed to another software project or expand consulting operations after completing your program. The time involved to successfully complete your software marketing may preclude these activities.

If it seems like I'm discouraging self-publication of your software, I'm not. Rather, I'm pointing out the major pitfalls you may face. Additionally, you may be so burned out after completing a commercial computer program that you may not be able to give the marketing your best effort; this in turn, could hurt the program's sales.

It may be, however, that you feel you can fulfill the necessary tasks involved in self-publication and would rather invest time and money than share the proceeds with other parties in the product-to-consumer chain. If that is the case, then you should strongly consider publishing the software by yourself.

Your other main alternative is to contract with a publishing firm. Again, this procedure is very similar to writing and publishing a book. Book authors can publish their work themselves, but most use the traditional method (as I did) of contracting with a book publisher.

Let's look at books for a minute. A publishing firm has considerably more bargaining leverage with individual and chain bookstores regarding any negotiable agreements than most individual author-publishers have. Most bookstores carry a limited number of books (in relation to the total number of books in print), and will carry those that are projected to sell the best. Most authors don't have the necessary experience or time to handle printing, binding, and distribution arrangements.

The same factors are true for the software industry. Retail computer stores (both full-service and software-only outlets) have very limited shelf space in relation to the amount of software currently available. They will, therefore, carry the programs that they hope will sell the best and have reputable distribution channels. Remember that computer programmers are sometimes viewed as "flakes" with little business savvy. If a retailer is unsure of the availability of a product, why keep a demonstration copy and take up shelf space?

Major software publishers with a number of bestsellers under their belts are usually viewed favorably by the retail market. Presumably a program marketed by a reputable publisher has been thoroughly tested, contains quality documentation, and is generally a useful package (and potentially successful seller). This is one of the strongest arguments that can be made in favor of utilizing a publisher's service.

Another is that a publication firm with expertise in the marketing of software can perform all of the functions we've seen, while you can go on to another project in your own area of expertise (or take a much-needed vacation).

What are the disadvantages of contracting with a publisher? The first is that you may not receive as much of the total revenues as you would with self-publication. Remember, though, that by using a publisher less of your own time is put into the postdevelopment functions, so a per-hour calculation would likely yield somewhat similar figures (depending on contract terms, of course). And, as was just mentioned, your subsequent projects can begin and be completed earlier than if you self-publish.

Other disadvantages are that you may find yourself locked into unfavorable contract terms and the publisher may not market the software in a manner with which you feel comfortable. Both of these can be somewhat alleviated by your own diligent research while selecting a publisher.

Summarizing, the choice between self-publication and using a publishing house is one you will have to make based on your own expertise, financial strength, and available time.

How Do You Find a Publisher?

Various software publishers advertise in computer trade magazines and solicit material from programmers for publication consideration. As a rule, though, these have been a small subset of the available publishers, whose ranks are constantly increasing. For years *Writer's Digest* has published various books listing book, magazine, and music publishers. Recently they published *The 1984 Programmer's Market,* which contains a comprehensive list of software publishers, noting addresses, preferred hardware, typical fee structure, current needs, recent publications, and currently available contract work. (Note: Many publishers have contract work available, including program conversion and new program development, that an independent consultant could investigate as an important revenue source.) By matching your program's specifications (machine type, applications category, and other factors) with the listed publishers (several indices provide useful cross-reference information) you can narrow your search to several publishers who are strong candidates for marketing your program.

Your next step is to submit a query letter to each candidate firm. The letter should state your program's application area, the target hardware, special features, and intended users, as well as a bit about yourself (and any other programmers involved, if they have impressive credentials).

There are two main categories of software publishers: independent firms and hardware vendors. Traditionally, the hardware vendors have favored software developed in-house for publication, though this is changing rapidly as more and more talented independent programmers appear.

One of the primary advantages to contracting with a hardware manufacturer is that the program has a high probability of making it to the dealers' shelves because of the manufacturer's endorsement. However, the programmer often winds up with less favorable contract terms than an independent firm offers. Most hardware vendors also look for nearly complete programs with complete documentation.

Independent publishers, on the other hand, sometimes assist an author with program and documentation development, making suggestions to improve the software's usability. Contract terms also tend to be more favorable to the programmer than a hardware vendor's.

The ideal situation for an experienced author is to utilize an independent publisher's services *as well as* contract with hardware vendors for specific machine versions through nonexclusive licenses (see the upcoming section on legal topics). These terms may not always be available for an unproven programmer, but they do bear consideration.

Assuming that several publishers express interest in marketing your program and, following testing and evaluation, offer you contracts, upon what criteria should you base your decision? The contract terms are important, of course; you should attempt to negotiate as favorable a contract as possible.

Other considerations include the firm's distribution channels, author and customer support, and marketing capabilities.[1] You don't want to enter into an exclusive licensing agreement with a firm that will half-heartedly market your program or, worse yet, put it on a shelf somewhere and forget about it.

Another criterion that is sometimes important is the publisher's computer language preference. For a publisher to provide useful support for you in the program development and refinement stage, its staff should be intimately familiar with both the target hardware and how the programming language interfaces with that hardware's operating system. This match between your software and the publisher's preferences will help facilitate the program's market debut.

When submitting a program to a publisher for evaluation, a nondisclosure agreement should be signed by both you and the publishing firm and separate nondisclosure agreements should be signed by anyone who has access to the software. The purpose of these agreements is to protect both you and the publisher. You want to ensure that your program doesn't leak to a potential competitor and be able to recover damages if it does. The publisher wants to make sure that your program has been kept secret during development, thus protecting its own investment. Different types of nondisclosure agreements will be reviewed later in this chapter.

The question also arises as to whether you should submit a commercial software candidate exclusively to one publisher or simultaneously submit the product to several firms. While you may gain more bargaining leverage if more than one publisher is interested in the software, some firms may not consider programs that they know someone else is evaluating (remember, testing and evaluation cost them time and money).

Whether you submit your software to more than one firm is up to you; however, you should notify each publisher that this is not an exclusive submission to avoid the nasty situation where one firm offers you a contract but you notify them you have signed with someone else they weren't even aware was evaluating the software.

Remember that these guidelines are primarily for the software newcomer; your first priority should be to get published. If you become a "software superstar" with a number of bestsellers, you can then hire an agent and negotiate among the various publishers for the best contract terms, including advance payments against royalties.

Speaking of agents and advances, these are two features of other publishing industries that are gradually entering the software publishing business. Most programmers do not have agents, though representatives are available; those seeking outside help usually use their attorneys to review and negotiate contracts. Some publishing firms are now offering advances against royalty payments to programmers who appear to have extremely promising programs.

What Contract Terms Should You Negotiate?

The primary contract feature that most programmers are concerned with is the method of payment. The two main payments are *outright sale* and *royalties*. Of the two, outright sale is not recommended except in extraordinary circumstances. Witness Paul Lutus, author of the word processing package Apple Writer. He sold the program outright to Apple Computer, Inc. for $7500, whereas a royalty agreement would have paid him 10 to 20 times more money.[2] (Not to worry, though: Apple Writer II and Apple Writer III were negotiated as royalty agreements, probably leading to six-figure receipts.)

Royalty agreements (formally known as license agreements) pay to the author either a certain percentage of the publisher's net sales price or a fixed amount per program sold. The primary difference between the two agreements is how much control the programmer wants over the program's retail price; a fixed dollar amount per sale forces the publisher to set a high enough price to cover these front-end expenses. A percentage agreement, however, leaves the author little negotiating room in setting the software's price. If the publisher should choose to use this software package as part of a promotional giveaway the author may realize little revenue from the product's marketing.

In his book *Legal Care for Your Software,* attorney Daniel Remer suggests a combined agreement specifying a minimum fixed payment per unit plus a percentage clause; in other words, you set a floor beneath which your receipts per program cannot fall.[3]

In addition to the programmer's compensation, Remer devotes an entire chapter to license agreements. I will summarize the major contract terms you should be concerned with, but for detailed information please consult Remer's book or an authoritative legal source.

1. *Introduction:*   This section should denote all parties involved in the agreement, what type of agreement it is, and what programs are involved.

2. *Definitions:*   Clarify any ambiguous terms.

3. *Items provided by software developer:*   This will state if the publisher receives a copy of the source code, source documentation, user manual, and other material. It also states what the publisher is not entitled to.

4. *Delivery schedule:*   This will state when the publisher receives the items from the above section.

5. *Program maintenance, modification, and training:* This section states what responsibilities you (the program developer) will have once the publisher takes over, who pays for fixing bugs and recalling programs (hopefully this won't ever happen), and terms for any program updates.

6. *License:*   This part describes the subject of the license (usually the material described in section 3), the duration of the license, and any limitations of the license. These limitations include geography (is a United States or worldwide license being granted?), hardware, and whether an exclusive or nonexclusive license is being granted (can you sign an agreement with another publisher for different versions of the program or a different market?).

7. *Acceptance:*   This will note the terms for accepting or refusing the final program, including procedures for requesting modifications.

8. *Royalties:*   In addition to how royalties will be calculated, other topics include timing of royalty payments, a contingency section (for example, what happens if a minimum number of copies is not sold, or royalty payments are late), any advances against your royalty account (including whether the advance is refundable or not), and royalty treatment of dealer demonstration copies.

9. *Accounting:*   You should reserve the right to inspect the publisher's records regarding your particular program to verify accurate royalty payments.

10. *Warranties:*   You guarantee the publisher that you have the legal right to grant this license, no pending lawsuits exist concerning any aspect of the program, and that the program is fully functional.

11. *Indemnification:* You usually agree to pay the publisher's legal fees if the publisher is sued regarding the program, but the publisher will defend the developer (you) against any claims regarding the program's quality.

12. *Copyrights:* This will state who owns the copyright (you or the publisher). The copyright should be in your name, and we will discuss shortly how to copyright your software.

13. *Termination:* Under what conditions shall the contract be terminated, and when shall termination take effect?

14. *Arbitration:* This states how any contract disputes are managed.

15. *Source-code escrow:* This is an optional section that states how the source code will be stored for the publisher if it isn't initially provided to the publishing firm. An alternative is to keep the updated source code in a safe-deposit box to which the publisher has a key but have the publisher promise in writing not to use the code unless certain circumstances occur.

16. *General:* Anything that hasn't been mentioned so far in the contract is discussed in this section.

When negotiating a contract with a software publisher, you may be presented with a standard contract form and told that all of the publisher's contracts are based on this form. The key word is "based"; don't be bashful about asking for changes in any of the presented terms if they are unsatisfactory to you.

Because many contracts are written in a hybrid of English and hieroglyphics, you should have your attorney review the contract. Hire an experienced contracts lawyer who is familiar with the computer industry. You may even wish to have your attorney conduct contract negotiations in your place, since he or she is more experienced in these matters. At the very least, have the contract reviewed by a lawyer prior to signing it.

How Should Your Program Be Tested?

Needless to say, extremely comprehensive testing of your program should take place prior to submitting it to a publisher. You should be on the lookout for any type of bugs, programming inconsistencies (for example, using CHANGE in one section and MODIFY in another), and any functions that you now find confusing or time-consuming.

If your program was developed with the assistance of an expert in the applications area, such as a real estate developer or accountant, have them try the program to see how useful and easy they find it; unbiased eyes can often spot things that you may not see.

Once in-house testing is complete, field testing (called beta testing) can commence. Often the publisher does the field testing, but you may find it worthwhile to conduct some beta testing yourself for additional feedback prior to submission. Of course, if you've decided to take the self-publication route, you will be responsible for this task.

Beta test sites are often found by taking potential program users and asking them to try the software and provide feedback regarding both good and bad features. Some form of compensation is often included, such as a free copy of the finalized software package. (Remember our marketing lesson of how people tend to value the opinions of others in their fields; a satisfied field tester may be a walking advertisement, sparking interest once the program is marketed.)

Everyone who has access to the program prior to publication should sign a nondisclosure agreement, or a clause should be included in the field-test agreement notifying the tester that confidential information is not to be released.

It's clear from this section of the book that bringing a computer program to market is not just a matter of being a clever, resourceful programmer. A thorough understanding of the commercial software marketplace as it currently exists (and being able to recognize industry trends) and publisher-developer relations are essential to the successful marketing of your software.

Setting Your Software's Price

If you decide to license your program to a software publisher, the publishing firm will likely determine the programming price. This decision will be based on factors such as desired profit margins, prices of similar software, and hardware-software price relations.

If you choose to distribute the program yourself, you will need to set the price. The aforementioned items need to be considered. A spreadsheet program for a $150 home computer, for example, probably wouldn't sell many copies at $350 each. If the target machine is priced at $7500, however, software costing $350 would not be considered outrageously expensive by the hardware owners. Therefore, the software should be priced such that it will be within the projected budget of an owner of the matching hardware.

Prices of similar programs play a factor in your program's costs. If you write a word processing package for the IBM PC, it is unlikely that you could charge $1000 or more when most comparable programs are priced in the $250 to $500 range.

Your program's features are another price factor. If you have developed an easy-to-use file manager that accepts simple queries from the user and manipulates single-file records, your price should be less than that of a full database management system. However, a system that contains features "never before seen in the civilized world" may command a premium price, provided market research has supported the intended price.

Naturally, you need to make a significant profit to justify the software development effort. Chapter 4 discussed different types of costs: direct and indirect, variable and fixed. The projected income based on expected unit sales must cover fixed direct costs (that is, those expenses directly attributable to creating the program and unavoidable once the project has started). You need to analyze possible revenue flows based on a number of different scenarios, adjusting units sold, variable costs, amount of overhead, etc.

The last thing to be aware of is that your software's price may need to be adjusted because of changing market conditions such as competitors' products or your own follow-on programs. You should keep abreast of falling unit sales or other factors that might require software price reappraisal.

Legal Considerations

It is not possible to fully cover all of the pertinent legal topics in this book. Rather, I will summarize the main points you should be aware of. Most of the material is adapted from Daniel Remer's *Legal Care for Your Software*, an excellent reference source for most of your legal questions.

Trade Secrets

A trade secret can be defined as a "secret used in your business that gives you an edge over the competition."[4] Keeping your software classified as a trade secret could be summarized as "don't show anybody anything anytime, but if you must, make them sign." This basically means that your program's source code should be stored in a secure container such as a safe or locking file cabinet.

Listings should be stamped confidential, as should the program disks and their storage sleeves. A warning notice stating that the program is a trade secret should be included at the front, back, and in several locations within the code. The notice should warn against disclosure of the contents.

Sometimes, however, having people review your source' programs is unavoidable. Your employees may be assigned to work on program projects or a software publisher may wish to review your source code to make suggestions. In these cases, a nondisclosure agreement (discussed in the subsequent Contracts section) should be signed, and periodic written reminders of the trade-secret status sent to them.

Other measures include keeping a written record of all accesses to your trade secret programs and keeping a generally secure atmosphere. Copies of the source code shouldn't be left lying around or casually discarded in everyday trash.

Remer's book illustrates various types of nondisclosure agreements: general, specific, outsider, and end user. If you use the book's models, be sure to select an appropriate skeleton agreement.

Remer also states that trade-secret protection can apply to object code as well as source code, coexisting along with copyright protection (though some attorneys disagree). These cases would arise specifically when a program is meant for very few users rather than the commercial market.

Software publishers should only be sent a copy of your program's object code for evaluation. Sometimes they may have a staff member review a program's source code to make programming suggestions (on a program consulting basis) or to make sure algorithms and formulas are correct. In these cases, nondisclosure agreements should be signed.

Copyrights

Possibly the number 1 controversy in the legal computing arena today is copyright protection, both of source code and object code. The battle between Apple Computer, Inc. and Franklin Computers has resulted in decisions being made and then overturned. At this writing, Franklin Computers had agreed to abide by an appeals court decision that object code can be copyrighted and pay Apple Computer several million dollars, in addition to refraining from using the copyrighted code further.

Copyrights are usually used to protect your programs' object codes rather than the source codes (though just as the trade secret doctrine can do double duty, so can copyrights). You automatically gain copyright protection for your programs the moment they make the transition from idea to paper or machine-readable storage media (disk or tape). To enforce your copyright, however, you need to perform many tasks, such as placing a correct copyright notice in several places and filing with the United States Copyright Office. Let's first review what you can copyright.

According to Remer, copyright law "protects the expression of ideas" rather than the ideas themselves.[5] That is, the ideas must be in a published form such as handwriting or machine-readable form. The work must be of original authorship (i.e., not copied from another source) and not in the public domain. To forfeit copyright protection by placing software in the public domain, you must either state this fact or omit a copyright notice and not correct the error.

The first step you should take to create a copyright is to place the copyright notices in certain places (similar to the trade secret notices we just saw). A copyright notice contains (1) the copyright symbol ©, (2) the effective date, (3) the owner's name, and (4) an "all rights reserved" notice. The effective date should be the year the program will be published (available for sale), even if the program was written in an earlier year. The owner's name will be the program's author, unless a work-for-hire situation (to be discussed later) exists. In that case the copyright owner is the company.

If you wish to publish your programs through your own corporation, *don't* copyright the software in the corporation's name; if you sell all or part of your business, you sell all or part of your copyright ownership. Copyright the work in your own name and license it to the corporation.

A copyright notice, therefore, should be attached to all disks and their jackets. It would look like this:

```
© Copyright 1984 Alan R. Simon
All Rights Reserved
```

A similar notice should appear on the computer's video display unit when the program begins running. A (C) can be substituted for the © in this case.

Remer gives many examples of how to correct deficient and missing copyright notices; please refer to these examples for any problems you might encounter. The simplest way to correct errors, however, is not to make them in the first place. Don't (1) forget the date, (2) predate or postdate the copyright notice, or (3) omit or misspell your name, etc. Reasonable caution should prevent these problems.

You have up to 5 years after publication to correct any mistakes or publish a copyright notice, but these actions should be taken within several months after publication.

Your next step is to fill out Copyright Office Form TX, available from:

```
U.S. Copyright Office
Library of Congress
Washington, DC 20559
```

This form contains information regarding the program, authors, dates of completion and publications, copyright claimants, and registration history. Basically, the same information as appears in the copyright notice is included on Form TX, but in more detail.

Send in a registration fee of $10 with Form TX, as well as a listing of your object code in hexidecimal or binary. If your source code is not being treated as a trade secret, it too should be included (first and last 25 pages only for very long programs).

Copyrights can be purchased from others. If you are considering buying someone else's copyright, check with the copyright office to ensure that you are the only purchaser.

Copyrights are in effect for either a single author's life plus 50 years or, for joint works or work-for-hire situations, the shorter of 75 years from publication or 100 years from creation. In the case of computer software, this period of time is almost sure to far exceed the commercial life of the software.

Documentation should be copyrighted also, especially in cases where its author is not the same as the accompanying software's author. Even if you choose not to file Form TX, you can still place the copyright notice on the documentation. The same is true for the software itself, but problems arise if Form TX is not filed within 3 months of publication. Statutory damages and recovery of attorney's fees can be lost by procrastination.

We now come to another controversial area: copyrighting source code. If you choose to take this action, secret algorithms and formulas should not be included in the mandatory first and last 25 submitted pages if possible. Internal documentation (i.e., comments) should be removed, and possibly replaced with false ones. Deliberate misspellings, nonfunctioning code, and other tactics can also be employed.

Just as noncommercial software intended for a few users can employ trade secrets to protect the object code as well as source code, that same software should probably rely on trade secrets solely for source code protection rather than copyrighting that source program. In these cases, your trade secret notices can be modified to include a warning of copyright, even though you do not register the program itself. That is, you would warn that the program is an unpublished work that is both protected by U.S. copyright law and considered a trade secret.

Remer discusses several legal gray areas that can affect you. Can unpublished source code be copyrighted, and can trade secret protection coexist with copyright protection? Please refer to his book or your own attorney for a discussion of these issues.

Finally, the Computer Software Copyright Act of 1980 allows program users to make archival and backup copies and covers many topics of concern to copyrights and software.

Patents

Usually patents are not applicable to software. The few patented cases tend to be operating systems and languages that are closely related to hardware. The U.S. Patent Office specifies that in order for software to be patented, conditions of subject matter, novelty, and "lack of obviousness" must be met. Software usually fails one or more of these tests. Therefore, trade secrets and copyrights provide the usual protective measures for your software.

Trademarks

The purpose of a trademark is to distinguish your product from other similar products. Two registration systems exist: the Principal and Supplemental Registers. Though the Principal Register is more desirable to be listed with, those ineligible for it can register with the Supplemental Register.

Whether or not trademark registration is desirable is a matter of how important it will be to sales. Remer suggests that often software that does not possess a registered trademark sells as well as those programs that do. If, however, you choose to trademark your program, use a lawyer who specializes in trademarks.

You (or your attorney) must conduct a trademark search to ensure nonduplication. You must then sell your software in the course of interstate commerce prior to registering your trademark. Once these tasks have been accomplished you can register your software. You will, however, wait for a long time for trademark publication owing to the Patent and Trademark Office's massive work backlog. Depending on whether your program winds up on the Principal or Supplemental Register, certain benefits accrue. If no one challenges your right to a trademark following publication in the *Official Gazette,* it is entered into the Principal Register. In other cases, the Supplemental Register will still provide some protection.

If your mark is listed in either register, you use an R symbol. Otherwise, you would use the TM symbol and note the state in which it may be registered (as opposed to federal registration).

When you use someone else's trademark, the common practice is to acknowledge the trademark and its owner in order to avoid potential problems.

You may notice that our legal topics, beginning with licenses in the last section and continuing with trade secrets, copyrights, patents and trademarks, appear to be getting more complicated and murkier. We'll now take a turn back toward some more substantial areas of law.

Contracts

We've already discussed several types of contracts the software developer needs to be concerned with, including license agreements, nondisclosure agreements, and software testing agreements.

I previously promised to discuss nondisclosure agreements in more detail. A *nondisclosure agreement* ensures that those who have access to your program for development, testing, or evaluation purposes do not disclose trade secrets that belong to you or prematurely disclose your operating plans. To be able to recover damages in court you must be able to prove that the person who leaked your secret information was aware of its secret status, and the best way is by written contract.

Noncompetition contracts ensure that your employees don't work for you, siphon your technical expertise and client list, and then go into business for themselves at your expense. You need to be reasonable in these contracts because you can't really inhibit someone's desire to earn a living. However, you can try to ensure that your former employees don't use your firm as a training ground and then cripple your business. Consult your attorney for reasonableness of noncompetition agreements in your particular situation.

Work-for-hire contracts specify the employer-employee relationship, including who owns software developed for the company, trade secret protection by employees, payment methods, and other topics. Variations of the contract will be in force for independent programmers or consultants, staff workers, and other independent help.

You may find yourself dealing with other types of contracts in the course of your business, such as client agreements (discussed in Chapter 13). To avoid subsequent problems you must be sure that all terms are clearly understood by all parties involved.

Limiting Liability

One of the most important legal considerations is how to protect yourself from dissatisfied customers. Remer states that most software publishers will replace the medium of a defective program (i.e., the disk itself) but not assume the cost of damages arising from the program.

In the commercial software business, you will find yourself faced with different types of *warranties:* express and implied. Express warranties are those that you explicitly state or advertise; for example, "This program will sort 10,000 records in under 5 minutes," or "Up to 10,000 property records can be stored and recalled by the software." Often retailers create express warranties through their demonstrations and statements. If these are extracted from your own publicity brochures and technical publications, you may also be creating this express warranty.

An implied warranty doesn't have to be stated or demonstrated; you are implicitly guaranteeing certain facts unless you disclaim them. These include merchantability, a vague term meaning the program should perform as well as other programs of the same type, and fitness, which is when a specific program is recommended for a specific situation.

The best way to limit your liability is to ensure that the program is both well-tested and reliable. Any advertising claims should be true and not deceptive. Serious problems that were undetected during testing may trigger a program recall or a "patch" fix sent to program users.

Additionally, a *disclaimer of warranty* should be attached to the software indicating that the software is sold without warranties as to performance or merchantability and any statements made by salespeople do not constitute a warranty. No express or implied warranties are included with the program, especially since users may attempt to adapt the software for use on hardware not supported by the publisher (which, of course, could lead to problems with different screen managers, operating systems, or other systems software).

The disclaimer must be placed where it can be read *without* opening the program's package and should also be included with the documentation. Remer points out that many warranties are legally invalid owing to location, readability, or other factors.

Occasionally, you may wish to include a limited warranty, usually for the transportable media rather than the results of the software. Be very careful in these cases.

Finally, Remer suggests that errors-and-omissions insurance be purchased to ensure that any problems that do occur do not cause financial ruin to your company or yourself (remember that unless incorporated, your business liabilities ripple through to your personal obligations). Additionally, as we've seen earlier in the book, your customers should probably consider insurance to cover their own business losses in case of catastrophic situations.

As you can see, the legal considerations of commercial software play as important a role in the marketing of your program as the marketing choices and the program itself. Even if you decide not to self-publish your software, you will still be responsible for knowing about license agreements, copyrights, trade secrets, nondisclosure agreements, work-for-hire contracts, and just about everything else we've seen; even if you are not a party to certain contracts, you should be certain your publisher conducts business properly and in your interests.

I've hinted several times during this chapter that consulting a lawyer may be appropriate. Chapter 13 discusses the pros and cons of using an attorney (along with accountants and other outside help); however, I can say that unless you are an attorney yourself or have a *very* strong legal and contract background, the price you pay for professional expertise is well worth the benefits you receive.

Again, as I've stated before, Daniel Remer's *Legal Care for Your Software* has been a valuable resource both in preparation of this book and in my own consulting practice. Rather than consult with your attorney on every matter that arises, you can use the book as a helpful reference source for most situations with which you would be concerned. A quick reading of the "Trade Secrets" and "Copyrights" chapters prior to embarking on a software development effort will probably prevent you from making serious errors that could hinder both your software's potential success and your ability to recover damages if you are wronged.

Hiring Outside Help

Expanding business operations, including adding personnel, is discussed in Chapter 15. I will briefly review here those topics applicable to commercial software development.

Though you may begin writing programs alone, you may find that as the programs become commercially successful, much of your time is occupied by tasks such as software maintenance, telephone and mail program support, and public relations efforts. As was mentioned earlier in this chapter, self-publication introduces many more time-consuming tasks.

Additionally, as your programming efforts become more ambitious and the projects more complex, one person, no matter how talented, may be insufficient for software development efforts.

When you find yourself overwhelmed by the amount of work to be done in all aspects of commercial software, from market research to system design to selling the program to a publisher, it is time to consider hiring others to assist you. There are many ways of expanding your firm's human resources, as we will see in Chapter 15: subcontracting, part-time employment, forming a partnership, or simply hiring programmers or administrative staff. The deciding factor should be that the dollars paid for assistance will provide benefits to your firm, both tangible and intangible, in excess of the amount paid.

Make sure that all help, whether employees or independent workers, understand and sign a work-for-hire agreement.

Postsale Support

Does your obligation and effort end the moment a customer purchases your program or you sell software rights to a publishing firm? Hardly. Commercial software postsale support may be different from that of contract programs because you do not know and train all of your customers personally, but the quality of that support should nonetheless be impeccable.

Depending on the contract with your publisher, you may or may not be responsible for fixing uncovered program bugs. If you are, your customers deserve to receive fixes to their software when issued. They did, afterall, have faith enough in your promises of excellent program operation to purchase your software.

Answering users' questions when questions and problems arise is also important. A customer support hotline is helpful in answering questions and determining if software problems exist. The user may be experiencing a problem unrelated to the program code—for example, a bad disk copy of the program.

If your software becomes obsolete—as would an income tax preparation program that is only accurate for one tax year—you may offer updates to current users at a below-retail price. In these cases, a constant software maintenance effort is necessary to ensure that changes in financial information, laws, and other factors are reflected in the most recent software version.

Additional postsale support may include training seminars for program purchasers, a user newsletter for your firm's software customers, and program modification to run on upgraded hardware or operating systems.

Therefore, your efforts (your own and your company's) do not cease when contracts are signed and money changes hands. A true professional, as you are, backs his or her products with support, add-on products, and a generally helpful atmosphere. Remember, every satisfied customer is walking advertising for you, but every dissatisfied one can cause severe damage to your operations.

Summary

Well, this certainly was a long chapter, but it contained a lot of information. Commercial software development can be the key to turning your small, one-person consulting firm into a major force in the computer industry. With more sophisticated hardware and operating systems, as well as more qualified programmers, than were around several years ago, the competition for users' computer software dollars is becoming very great.

However, a talented programmer, gifted with exceptional insight into the mechanics of software development (from market analysis through program creation through successful marketing effort through legal protection), is a step ahead of the competition that lacks the understanding of the critical success factors of the commercial software market.

One of the main advantages commercial software development provides the consultant is a means to balance your revenues with steady earning from program royalties. This can provide very important capital for your business, allowing for expansion. If you are consulting part-time, the successful sale of one or more programs can lead to a full-time consulting and software development career.

In the last chapter, we saw Bernie Jordan working on his contract legal system, with an eye toward marketing the program commercially. Working with his clients, he made modifications to the software to enhance its features. Additional error checking was added, as well as help menus and screens.

Several attorneys were then selected as beta test sites. After signing nondisclosure agreements, the lawyers were asked to use the software for several months, commenting on favorable and unfavorable features.

After further modifications were made, incorporating beta test site comments, Bernie was ready to market his software. He chose a well-known software publisher who was interested in vertical market (industry-specific) applications. One of Bernie's attorney partners conducted contract negotiations, arranging for beneficial terms.

Bernie has decided to handle postsale support by himself for now; if the program should become a great commercial success, he will then hire a technical support employee to aid customers and several programmers to develop further software. Hoping for success in the market, he proceeds with his plans.

End Notes

1. Steve Ditlea, "Marketing Your Software," *Popular Computing,* May 1983, p. 101.

2. Ibid., p. 100.

3. Daniel Remer, *Legal Care for Your Software,* NOLO Press, Berkeley, Calif., p. 99.

4. Ibid., p. 11.

5. Ibid., p. 25.

CHAPTER 12

Writing Books and Magazine Articles

As your consulting practice expands, one of the profit centers you may wish to add to your repertoire is writing both books and magazine articles. When discussing seminars in Chapter 7, we saw that conducting seminars provides you with several benefits; in addition to the revenue earned, the publicity and visibility for your consulting business is invaluable in making contacts and building your client base. The same is true of writing; you will be generating revenues and simultaneously building your (and your firm's) reputation.

There is an outstanding market for books and periodicals in the computer field; the next time you walk into a well-stocked bookstore, gaze upon the vast number of computer books and publications. We will see in this chapter how the mechanisms of being published work; we will discuss how to choose a market to write about, write a query letter, and review book contracts and periodical agreements.

Choosing a Market

Picking an area of computing to write about is similar to choosing what applications your business will concentrate on. Most likely, you will write about topics that you are familiar with. If, for example, you specialize in CAD/CAM (computer-aided design/computer-aided manufacturing) applications, it would be natural to write about subjects within this area. You are (or should be) an expert in this field; while you may not know everything there is to know about the topic, you are generally more knowledgeable about CAD/CAM than most generalists.

Other markets you can target aside from your applications area include:

1. *Home computing:* Emphasize the low end of the computer market, including games, home environment control, "checkbook-class" applications (that is, simple software used for financial and other home applications), and, of course, the machines themselves.

2. *Small business computing:* This is probably where your own applications specialties would fit. Other areas include personal productivity products (spreadsheets and database programs, for example), hardware and peripherals, mainframe interfaces, and topics of concern to users like insurance and catastrophe prevention.

3. *Industry analysis:* These articles and books would chart the courses that technology and the companies are taking, the goal being to keep readers informed about the constantly changing computer business.

4. *Computer professionals:* These subjects would be of interest to those who actually design, build, and maintain working computer systems and would be more technical than those directed toward the end users.

5. *Hobbyists:* The mainstay in the early days of personal computing, these subjects would include interfacing various peripheral devices to your computer and building computers from scratch. You can always tell a hobbyist-oriented article or book by the schematic diagrams included that most of us can't understand.

Naturally, you could probably think of other general areas under which your writing could fall. The point is that you should try to find a market, whether it be end users, programmers, or hobbyists, and become established as a respected author in that field. Notice how the same marketing lessons keep surfacing in the chapters dealing with the various products and services of a computer professional? The lessons of Chapter 5 are alive and well.

Finding a Publication Medium

Once you have a general idea of what you want to write about, you should now think about where you will see your efforts in print. The first decision is whether to make your first effort a magazine article or a book. To be very honest, it is extremely difficult to get a publisher to contract for a book if you don't have a track record of prior publications. There are, however, many computer magazines with a vast need for outside contributors.

In reality, though, the publication medium should be determined more by your subject matter than by how many times you've been published. Remember, you are an entrepreneur, a risk taker, and will make the extra effort to sell a good idea. The subject matter of this book, for example, would have to have been dramatically reduced to fit into a magazine article. Since the goal was to provide a comprehensive reference for computer consultants, a book seemed to be a more appropriate form for the subject matter.

One thing to keep in mind is that writing a book is a *very* time-consuming task. The end result of a finished product is very rewarding (or at least I hope it is; while I'm writing these words, I still have six chapters to write and a mass of editing to accomplish). However, let's look at a situation where you've begun consulting within the past year or two and are still operating your practice on a part-time basis and working at your full-time job. In addition to working with your clients, you are spending a lot of time doing preliminary market research and financial analysis as well as learning the ropes of the business. The time involved in writing a book at this stage of your career may be overwhelming with everything else you must do. This, again, is from experience; all I can say is thank heavens for partners!

An occasional magazine article, though, takes far less time and provides a nice source of revenue to fill in the gaps between consulting jobs. Remember revenue patterns? If you can become a regular contributor to one or more periodicals these additional spurts of revenue can become regular streams.

Over a long consulting career you should attempt to publish as many articles as possible. Remember that every article means additional earnings. Once you feel comfortable enough with article writing, it's probably time to expand into the world of books. By the very nature of the consulting profession, a successful consultant can usually be a successful author. That is, consultants must be able to write well, recognize and exploit opportunities (or create the opportunities in the first place), sell their ideas to others, be knowledgeable, and persevere through long projects. Think about how several books and widely used commercial software systems will provide you and your firm with significant earnings! For the times during your career that you may wish to take a break from the continual soliciting of new business and the effort you must put into business operations, the royalty checks will contribute greatly toward making up for otherwise lost revenue.

Query Letters

After you have decided what you want to write about and in what form, your next step is to convince a book or magazine publisher that your text will be welcome in their publication or catalog. You *don't* want to sit down one day, begin working on a book, finish it 8 months later, and then see if anyone would like to publish it. The accepted process in the publishing industry is to submit a *query letter,* stating your proposed subject matter and how it will aid the publisher as well as the author.

A query letter should also state a bit about your background and publishing history. Even in the case of magazine articles, most editors don't want to be surrounded by manuscripts from prospective authors; they would rather review a query letter to see if the proposed article would fit in the magazine's format before evaluating the written material. The letter submitted for this book is shown in Figure 12-1.

Alan R. Simon
8225 Cutter Terrace
Colorado Springs, CO 80918
(303) 594-9535
September 3, 1983

McGraw-Hill Book Company
Attn: Mr. Tyler G. Hicks
Editor in Chief
Computing and Software
1221 Avenue of the Americas
New York, NY 10020

Dear Mr. Hicks:

Attached is an outline for a proposed book titled How to Be a Successful Computer Consultant. I am sending you this outline for publication consideration by McGraw-Hill Book Company.

I am founding partner of Computer Education and Consulting, a Colorado Springs, Colorado, computer consulting firm. Our firm is involved in a variety of activities, including seminar training for both beginning and advanced users, custom software development, and general consulting services. I formed this organization as a sole proprietorship and recently added three partners to the firm. While organizing Computer Education and Consulting, I spent many months researching small business management, tax considerations, marketing strategies and seminar techniques. Because there was no one book

---

Figure 12-1 Sample query letter.

dealing specifically with computer-related consulting, I relied on general consulting material and small business management references, coupled with my experience in the computer field.

The explosive growth of computer use in businesses and homes is well documented. The advent of the "personal computer age" has, in addition to providing computer owners with powerful tools to manage their information and environments, afforded an outstanding opportunity to provide computer-related services to others. "Computer literacy" has become a common industry buzzword. Many personal computer owners have a unique chance to find a niche in this growing field developing custom programs, conducting educational services, and writing articles for the many computer magazines being published. How to Be a Successful Computer Consultant conveys pertinent and timely information in several areas: starting and organizing a consulting operation, managing a growing firm, and an in-depth look at computer services.

Because most personal computer owners already have full-time jobs that may not even be related to the computer field, a theme I intend to emphasize throughout the book is the part-time operation of a consulting firm. Computer Education and Consulting was started while I was a full-time U.S. Air Force officer and all four partners are still USAF computer officers. I am, therefore, extremely familiar with the problems, such as conflict-of-interest situations, that may surface when organizing a business while still employed by another company. However, the advantage of having job security while embarking on a new venture often outweighs these problems.

In addition to my experience in the consulting field and as an Air Force computer officer, I have been employed as a computer programmer, systems analyst, and consultant by the Arizona attorney general's office and the University of Arizona. I taught computer classes at the University of Arizona during graduate school and currently teach computer classes for the Chapman College (California) residence education center in Colorado Springs. I have both bachelor's and master's degrees in College of Business computer programs from Arizona State University and the University of Arizona.

I hope I have conveyed the importance of a book such as How to Be a Successful Computer Consultant to both the potential readers and McGraw-Hill Book Company. I feel that a large, untapped market exists for this book and that many people would be able to benefit from this information being provided in one concise location. A sample chapter is available upon request. Thank you for your consideration of my submission, and I look forward to hearing from you.

Sincerely,

Alan R. Simon

You'll notice that the query letter shown is addressed to a particular editor rather than a generic "Dear Editor." Where do you obtain the appropriate editor's name? Where do you find the publisher's address? The answers lie in the annual *Writer's Market,* published by Writer's Digest Books. Remember the *Programmer's Market* publication I mentioned in the last chapter? *Writer's Market* is the equivalent source for the book and magazine market.

In addition to the address and appropriate contact points for each publisher, each listing contains information about what types of submissions the firm is looking for, their query letter policies, the number of books or articles annually sought, desired manuscript lengths, and publication terms. You can also learn how long you can expect to wait for a response to a query letter or manuscript submission. Other publisher policies such as whether or not they will accept photocopied or simultaneous submissions are sometimes stated.

Magazine entries are classified by subject. The areas you are most likely to be interested in are home computing, data processing, and possibly business management (want to write about consulting or how to manage a small business?). Book publishers are listed alphabetically. Browsing in your local bookstore can give you an idea of what publishing firms are likely to be interested in computer-related books. *Writer's Market* also includes many helpful articles and sections discussing contracts, writing tips, agents, and many other topics. A new edition is published each year.

Magazines

What types of articles should you consider writing for computer industry publications? We saw earlier the general markets you can aim toward; the following topics can fit into one or more market groups. For example, software reviews can be of home computer applications or software development tools for programmers.

1. *Reviews:* Many computer magazines solicit reviews of both hardware and software products to supplement those of their staff. Review articles should be objective, so point out both good and bad features. You should discuss all of the evaluative features of hardware and software products we looked at in Chapter 8. Take a look at reviews in the magazine you are interested in.

2. *Tutorials:* In addition to reviews, instructive articles on how to use computer products are helpful to readers. The tutorials can be about specific products or about technology in general. For example, you may write an article explaining various types of external storage systems or communications technology.

3. *Sample programs:* Many publications carry articles about various computer applications and include program listings. *Programmer's Market* lists magazines that accept program submissions.

4. *Advanced topics for commercial software:* You may, for example, write an article explaining advanced features of software products. Tips on how to write advanced dBASE II programs or program function keys for WordStar are useful for owners of those software packages.

5. *Advanced topics for programmers:* Interfacing with operating-system features, utilizing math and I/O coprocessors, and combining assembler subroutines with your BASIC programs are among the many topics in which computer professionals are interested. Remember that as quickly as computer technology changes, those in the field need sources of information about the latest technological advances, programming theory, and products.

6. *Editorials:* Some magazines print editorials submitted by respected authorities in the computer industry. Once you have achieved this status, these submissions can serve as a forum for your opinions about various subjects.

Check both *Writer's Market* and stated policies sometimes included in the magazines themselves for other ideas. You can get extra mileage from your writing efforts if your articles are published in periodicals that buy *first rights* rather than *all rights*. That is, a magazine that buys first rights will publish the submitted articles for the first time, after which the author controls all other publication rights. Therefore, you can resubmit the same article to other publications.

"All rights" means that once you sell your article the publisher owns the article's rights of publication. You cannot use the material elsewhere. Other types of publication rights are included in *Writer's Market* and should be consulted.

Books

We now come to the big one—the sign that you have indeed made it in your field of expertise. From experience, I can tell you that there are few greater feelings than having a major publishing firm inform you that they would like to publish your book. A tremendous effort must be put into producing a quality book. As I stated before, the perseverance and background that a successful computer consultant must possess are the same traits that make a successful author.

One look at the shelves of your local bookstore might make you wonder how publishers could possibly consider producing any more computer books. There are almost as many books as software packages. The reasons for a growing market are basically the same that a market for new software exists; the dynamic nature of the computer industry creates new opportunities.

If you've read the preface to this book, you'll recall that when I was forming my own consulting business, I was unable to find any books that dealt specifically with computer consulting. A search of the *Subject Guide to Books in Print* confirmed that, indeed, none existed at the time. Following basic marketing principles, I concluded that there was probably a market for a book of this nature. When Daniel Remer wrote *Legal Care for Your Software,* he probably performed the same type of analysis; many software entrepreneurs with little or no legal background could use a comprehensive source of legal considerations that specifically dealt with producing and marketing software.

In addition to new books that result from applying subjects specifically to the computer field, the rapidly changing technology in the industry leads to new books. When personal computers exploded onto the scene several years ago, many business executives were stymied as to choosing a computer. This confusion increased as the number of systems proliferated. A need for books discussing how to evaluate hardware and software was apparent.

As new machines reach the marketplace, a market is born for books that discuss the basic and advanced features of the machine. Remember that the quality of documentation is generally decried throughout the computer world. New users are often confused by the manuals, while experienced programmers often can't find instructions for performing advanced tasks.

The same is true of software; though manuals accompany the software, separate instruction books are a plentiful seller.

Just as you can write magazine articles about many subjects, the topics of computer books are just as varied. Among the major categories are:

1. *Textbooks and advanced topics:* Professionals in the field, often university professors, write books covering the latest advances in database technology or introductions to computing. These are often the hardest books to write, since you should be an experienced educator familiar with course curricula.

2. *General computer books:* These include the "how to pick a system" books as well as nontechnical explanations of computer topics. Caution: The market is rapidly becoming saturated in this area.

3. *Language tutorials and references:* I wouldn't recommend writing a book about how to program in BASIC; this market is as crowded as the above-mentioned one. An exception would be a book that covers BASIC as applied to a just-introduced computer system; since BASIC dialects sometimes differ among various hardware and operating systems, these books have potential to sell.

Books on new or emerging languages, such as C and FORTH, should experience an increase in sales as language use spreads. These books can sometimes double as textbooks. Remember your audience, though; don't write a book for a university computer science student in the same manner as one for a beginning home computer user.

4. *Hardware and software:* I already mentioned the market for supplementary reference material. The key here is to be *fast;* these books should be introduced as soon as possible following the introduction of a new computer, operating system, or applications package. This is especially true if the book is meant as a tutorial rather than advanced reference material.

5. *Specialized markets:* Examples include this book, material discussing legal topics, or the *Programmer's Market.* That is, even though all of the areas mentioned earlier would not be of interest to every computer book buyer, these books deal with more than just technology or new products. They are meant to appeal to people involved in certain areas of computing. Another topic would be computer crime and preventive techniques.

Take a look at both your bookstore and the *Subject Guide to Books in Print.* Even if the area you would like to write about appears crowded, don't be discouraged. If you feel you have a novel approach to a thoroughly covered topic, convince the publisher and editor through your query letter. A novel approach to a BASIC book is *Elementary Basic* by Henry Ledgard and Andrew Singer. The book follows the adventures of Sherlock Holmes as he tracks clues and utilizes BASIC programs; by the end of the book, the reader has been entertained and instructed in the BASIC language. Be creative in your efforts.

What if you develop a great idea for a book but you feel you don't have sufficient writing background to join the literary world or are too busy with other projects? Consider coauthoring a book, either with a professional writer or another computer professional. A coauthor may provide additional background for your subject as well as polish for the words. If you wish to have a professional author put your ideas into words, be sure to either choose someone with experience in the market you wish to exploit or preview a sample chapter or two to make sure that you like their writing style.

Contracts

Of course, this chapter wouldn't be complete without a brief discussion about book contracts. These are very similar to the license agreements I mentioned in Chapter 11 when discussing commercial software. That is, you almost always contract with your publisher on a royalty basis.

If a publisher is interested in publishing your book, you will probably be offered a standard publishing contract. How much negotiating room you have depends on your previous writing experience—how many of your books have been published—the novelty of and projected market for your material, and your own negotiating skills. At the very least, you should attempt to maintain the book's copyright in your own name, receive an appropriate advance against royalties ("appropriate" meaning whatever you can negotiate; remember, it will probably be a while between the contract date and the first royalty check), and favorable royalty terms. Both *Writer's Market* and *Law and the Writer,* also published by Writer's Digest Books, discuss contracts in detail.

Summary

Writing both books and magazine articles can be a rewarding experience, both financially and emotionally. Knowing that someone thinks enough of your writing skills and knowledge to put your words in print is quite an ego boost. Beware of the critics, though! Just try to write the best book or articles you can.

Again, owing to time and practical constraints, you may wish to work on magazine articles before embarking on a book effort. We looked at the major markets of both books and periodicals, as well as specific topic categories for each.

Having your work in print can be a substantial marketing tool for your consulting business. If a publisher is willing to print your efforts, you must know what you are talking about (or so the theory goes).

Bernie Jordan has decided to concentrate on magazine articles for the near term. With his extensive background in and research of the legal computer systems available, he queried several computer trade magazines and will be submitting articles to three of them. These articles deal primarily with legal applications, particularly productivity and office management systems. Once he has more experience with both writing and consulting, he may consider working on a book about legal computer systems or a similar topic.

PART 3

Continuing Concerns

CHAPTER 13

Managing Operations

During the early chapters of this book, we discussed many of the managerial and business topics that are important to you as the owner of a consulting firm. We dealt with these subjects from the viewpoint of beginning your practice: what decisions should be made to establish your company, build your client base, and define your product line.

We will now return to these topics, but address them as ongoing activities of an established firm. That is, once you have succeeded in building your practice from the ground up, how do you keep it growing?

We will discuss the importance of operational planning, accounting and tax-related activities, personnel management, insurance concerns, marketing, utilizing outside resources, and, if necessary, cutting back on unprofitable operations.

Operational Planning

During the early stages of your consulting activities, you developed a business plan that discussed plans for your services, marketing activities, financial needs, and other subjects. As time passes, your business plan needs reviewing to ensure that it reflects the state of your firm's operations. Additionally, an annual *operations plan,* based on your business plan, should be developed to identify special opportunities, problems, financial and personnel needs, and anything else of concern over the coming year.

For example, your business plan projected earnings and break-even points several years into the future from the time it was written. Are those estimates still accurate? Is more or less outside capital actually required than had been estimated?

Additionally, new markets and opportunities that were unforeseen several years earlier may have evolved; these should be included as an integral part of your operational plans.

Your operations plan for the coming year should include the following sections:

1. *Products and services:*   Will any new products or services be added to your repertoire this year? Will any be removed because of unprofitability, changing markets, or other reasons? Will new markets be exploited for existing products and services, such as expanding from medical and dental applications to legal ones?

2. *Marketing:*   What is your projected advertising budget, and through what media? What public relations methods will be employed?

3. *Financial:*   What are the upcoming year's anticipated revenues, expenses, and net earnings? Is any additional capital needed from operations? If so, from what sources? Will cash flow be sufficient to cover existing and projected expenses? Do you plan to invest your firm's assets in spin-off businesses or other investment opportunities?

4. *Personnel:*   Do you plan to hire any employees this year? If so, will they work full-time or part-time? Will they be operational (writing software, conducting seminars) or support (secretarial, administrative)? Do you project using any outside accountants or attorneys or subcontracting any work to others?

5. *Information:*   What new areas of both business and the computer industry do you feel a need to learn more about? For example, if you wish to seek venture financing 18 months from now, you probably need to learn more about venture capital firms, what industries they are currently investing in, and the mechanisms of selling public stock. Similarly, if you foresee a need to better understand new computer technology because you anticipate several major product releases, you might want to review the computer literature closely to learn about those new operating systems, hardware, or other products.

Your operations plan should serve as your short-term (1 year or less) guideline to ensure efficient management of your practice, just as your business plan should meet your long-range strategic planning requirements. By consciously forcing yourself to appraise all aspects of your company at least once a year, hopefully you will be able to plan for a continually growing firm that isn't surprised by foreseeable problems or missed opportunities.

Bookkeeping and Accounting

Not many topics strike as much fear in business people as bookkeeping and accounting. Words like "tedious," "difficult," "confusing," and similar adjectives tend to be in the forefront of thoughts.

Why, then, bother with maintaining a set of records? Of course, there's the obvious reason; you have a legal requirement to file tax returns, and the only way to obtain the necessary information is to keep accurate records of your income and expenditures. The more organized your records are the simpler it is for you or your accountant to complete your required federal and state tax forms.

There are two other very important reasons for maintaining accurate and informative records. First, prospective investors and lenders need to gauge the solvency of your business operations. An accurate accounting of your income and expenses, assets and liabilities, and cash flow provides an insightful picture of your financial situation. Well-organized accounting procedures also demonstrate your business prowess rather than portray you as a disorganized manager.

Additionally, your financial records help you effectively manage your operations by telling you if you have too much overhead cost, aren't earning enough from a particular service or product to make it worthwhile, or by identifying exceptional growth in another operations area. Pricing decisions can be based on recorded information. In short, it will be difficult to successfully run a business and almost impossible to make it grow without informative bookkeeping and accounting.

So, whether you view accounting as a necessary evil or as an invaluable management tool, we've established that it is required. In this section we'll look briefly at business bank accounts, discuss cash versus accrual accounting, and look at the difference between single- and double-entry financial ledgers. Then we'll look at how to automate your accounting as much as possible to alleviate some of the tedium and better organize your records.

Bank Accounts

Back in Chapter 3 we saw that among the tasks to do when forming a business was to open a business bank account. Again, this is important because you must establish your business as a financial entity separate from your personal finances, even though it may not be a different legal entity.

Accountant Bernard Kamoroff, in his book *Small-Time Operator,* lists several rules to follow regarding business bank accounts.[1]

1. *Keep your business finances separate from your personal ones:* Business expenses should be paid by check from your business account to provide accurate documentation. Inevitably, some minor expenses such as pens, file folders, or stationery may be paid by cash but they should be done so out of a petty cash fund.

I might add that you may wish to obtain a business charge card such as MasterCard, Visa, American Express. You may be in a bookstore, for example, and see a book entitled *How to Be a Successful Computer Consultant* and have an overwhelming urge to purchase it, but not have a business check with you (most business checkbooks are of the large three-ring notebook variety and are cumbersome to take everywhere). By charging your purchase to your business account directly, you have a record of expenditures as well as several weeks or more of "free" credit by paying for your purchase upon subsequent payment of your charge card bill.

2. *Deposit all income directly into your business account:* Most likely you won't be accepting charge cards for services rendered, since few consulting firms operate in that manner. Most payments will be by check, with a few by cash. Directly depositing the payments into your account provides an audit trail of all income.

3. *Any withdrawals from the business account should be in the form of cash transactions:* This means that you will either write a check payable to cash or yourself or directly transfer the funds into your personal account. If you write a check from your business account for a personal expenditure, the accuracy of your record keeping is complicated with possible confusion of whether any given payment was for business or personal use. Even if you note a payment was for personal use your end-of-month and end-of-year calculations are unnecessarily complicated by the distinctions you must make.

4. *Balance your bank account regularly, upon receipt of each statement:* This will help prevent bounced checks, endless hours of trying to figure where in the last 5 months a 17-cent error occurred, and is just generally good practice.

5. *Any expenses that are partly personal and personal business should be paid from your personal account:* Your business account can then reimburse you via cash transfer (and the appropriate notation) for the business portion of the expense. This is less complicated than reimbursing the business account for your portion and having to adjust the dollar amount appropriately.

Cash Accounting Versus Accrual Accounting

You are probably familiar with cash accounting (though maybe not the term) from your own personal tax returns. Simply stated, any income and expenses are recorded in the period received or paid, respectively. This means that if you perform a consulting service for someone on December 15, 1984, and collect payment on January 15, 1985, the income will be shown on your *1985* tax return. Similarly, if you purchase a book on December 20, 1984, and pay the bill on January 3, 1985, the expense will also be included with those for 1985.

Accrual accounting, however, states that revenue and expenses are recognized at the time they are earned or incurred, regardless of whether any funds change hands at that time. Our first income example would be reflected on the 1984 books, as would our book purchase.

Which method should you use for your business? Most consulting firms could use either method, but consult your accountant to determine any requirements you may have to use the accrual method. Those employing the cash method could time purchases and billings to some degree to provide a favorable tax picture depending on taxable-income patterns.

For example, if next year will likely provide less income than the current one, collections for services near the end of the year can be delayed until after the new year, shifting those earnings into a lower tax year. The opposite is also true: collections could be accelerated into the current year if next year's income will be substantially higher than this one's. Similar manipulations could be done with payment of business expenses.

Users of accrual accounting can perform similar financial magic by accelerating purchases or delaying billings, and they may have even more flexibility than cash accounting users.

Cash accounting provides a slightly less accurate picture of financial operations than accrual accounting. A given year's income or expenses may not be accurately reflected because of uncollected (but earned) revenue or unpaid (but incurred) expenses. It does, however, present a more accurate cash flow picture for a reporting period than accrual accounting.

Consider the situation where Bernie Jordan finishes a major contract on December 24, 1984 (just in time for Christmas Eve) that provides $5000 in revenue (payable January 2). Other revenue for the year was $3000, and all was collected. Total 1984 expenses were $4000, all paid.

Under an accrual basis, Bernie would show 1984 pretax earnings of $4000 ($8000 revenue less $4000 expenses). The cash basis, however, will produce a net loss of $1000 ($3000 collected revenue minus $4000 expenses). Which is correct? Bernie didn't really have a loss of $1000, but if he had to suddenly pay $2000 on December 30, 1984, he couldn't very well take the money from 1984 profit, since he hasn't collected all of his revenue yet.

There is no 100 percent correct answer, but it is recommended that you use accrual accounting because of the increased accuracy of effective earnings reporting and evaluation. In fact, for a firm with consistently increasing annual earnings the accrual basis offers a better means for accelerating revenue into the current, lower-earnings year: whether your client pays before or after January 1, by billing before the end of the year the revenue can be counted in the current year.

As should be obvious, the accrual accounting should be accompanied by accurate cash flow and working capital analysis. Potential investors (and you) aren't interested merely in reportable income; cash flow is important. As we will see shortly, the purchase of a $10,000 computer system will appear on current books not as a $10,000 expense but as a depreciation expense for a portion of the asset "used." To show the $10,000 cash outflow requires more than just an income statement and balance sheet.

Ledgers

In what form do you then record your cash or accrual accounting? You have two options here, also. You could use the standard accounting *double-entry* system or a simplified *single-entry* method.

Double-entry systems provide much greater accuracy of records than single-entry systems but are far more complex to learn and manage. We'll take a look at both systems shortly.

A single-entry system consists of a series of ledgers for income, credit, expenditures, and equipment.[2] A double-entry system typically has a continuous journal from which entries are "posted" to a general ledger. The double-entry system, as implied by the name, requires two entries for every transaction: a debit and a credit. These entries serve to offset each other so that when a *trial balance* is computed, the totals of debits and credits should be equal, providing a measurement of accuracy of transaction entry.

Confused already? Your best bet, then, is to organize your own books under the single-entry system presented next and, for now at least, skip over the double-entry section. Those of you who are at ease with accounting concepts should review the double-entry section, especially if your last exposure to journals and ledgers was in Accounting 101 during your freshman year of college.

Let's look at Bernie Jordan's transactions for the first month of 1985. Bernie completed three consulting contracts on the following dates:

January 10—Installation of legal system	$2000
January 25—Development of property management software	2500
January 28—Installation of real estate system	1500
Total	$6000

The first two payments have been collected, while the last hasn't been received yet.

During this month Bernie made the following purchases, all paid by cash or check:

January 3—Annual post office box rent	$ 25
January 10—Office supplies	15
January 15—Postage stamps	5
January 28—Box of 10 floppy disks	25
January 29—Computer printer	400
Total	$470

If Bernie were to calculate his business profit for January he would show $5530 ($6000 − $470), assuming he used the accrual accounting method. Right? Wrong. The computer printer purchase must be treated in a special manner since it is an acquisition of an asset rather than a periodic business expense. Let's look at the above transactions and how they are treated by a single-entry system.

The first ledger Bernie must maintain is the *income ledger,* a record of all business income. Since service industries are not normally subject to state and local sales tax on their revenue, no record of taxable sales and sales tax is necessary. Bernie's income ledger is shown in Figure 13-1.

Alternatively, a separate ledger could be maintained for credit sales but duplicate entry of each contract is required, once to the income ledger and once to the credit ledger. Since most of your payments will be received following an invoice billing to your client nearly every transaction will require two entries.

The preferred method is to combine these two ledgers as shown in Figure 13-1, filling in the date-paid column upon receipt of funds. A periodic search through the ledger will reflect those payments still due. This search process becomes even easier when you support your ledgers with a database management system or electronic spreadsheet, as we will see.

A similar ledger will be maintained for business expenditures. Figure 13-2 illustrates Bernie Jordan's expenditure ledger.

Income Ledger for January 1985

Contract date	Client	Date paid	Amount	Memo
1/10	Jones, Smith & Johnson	1/17	$2000.00	
1/15	ABCDEF Realty	1/26	2500.00	
1/28	GHIJKL Realty		1500.00	Billed 1/30
			$6000.00	

Figure 13-1   Income ledger.

Columns should be provided for all likely expenses of your business. If you don't have any employees, you don't need a payroll column, and if you work from your home an office-rent column is unnecessary. (Note: If you are taking a home office deduction on your tax return, a year-end reconciliation of home office expenses is necessary for your tax return.)

By providing a total column as well as individual ones a single payment can be recorded that contains purchases in more than one category.

The nondeductible column is for personal cash withdrawals, repayment of business loans (the interest payment is tax deductible), depreciable assets, accounts payable, and legal fines or penalties.

Wait a minute. Why is Bernie's printer purchase listed as a nondeductible expense? As we said, the purchase of an asset is not treated the same as a periodic business expense. *Depreciable assets* are considered to have a useful life longer than 1 year and must be used over an extended period of time. Depreciation will be discussed in the tax section of this chapter.

A lot of paperwork, right? Well, no one said running a business was easy!

At the end of each year (assuming your business operates on a calendar-year basis) you need to summarize your income and expenditures for your tax reporting and close the books on the year. By summing the columns on your expenditure ledger you arrive at summary amounts to be entered on your tax return in the appropriate places. The same is true for your income. Any expenses are supplemented by your calculations of depreciation, home office rent and utilities, and other adjusting entries we will discuss in the tax section. Any cash or check payments for last year's credit expenses (known as accounts payable) should not be included as a business expense for this year if you use accrual accounting, since those

Expenditure Ledger for 1985

Date	Method of payment	Payee	Office expenses and postage	Supplied	Advertising expense	Non-deductible	Total	Notes
1/3	Check 235	U.S. Post Office	$25.00				$ 25.00	Box rent
1/10	Check 236	Favored Office Supplies	25.00				15.00	Paper, folders
1/15	Cash	U.S. Post Office		5.00			5.00	Stamps
1/28	Check 237	By-Mail Computer Supplies		$25.00			25.00	10 disks
1/29	VISA	Downtown Computers				$400.00	400.00	Printer

Figure 13-2 Expenditure ledger.

expenses were included on last year's return; they would be entered in the nondeductible column.

Now, on to the torture. Bernie Jordan studied accounting in college (remember, he was a business school graduate) and decides to implement a double-entry system. Using the same transactions as before, his accounting journal is shown in Figure 13-3.

Wait a second! *This* is a more accurate system? It looks like the Tower of Babel compared with a single-entry system. Well, we're not finished yet. The journal is merely a transaction log from which entries are posted to the general ledger.

Each account has its own ledger entry, sometimes known as a "T-Account." All debits to an account are on the left side of the T, while all credits are on the right side. For example, assuming no beginning balance, the accounts receivable ledger account would look like this:

Accounts Receivable			
1/10	2000	2000	1/17
1/25	2500	2500	1/26
1/28	1500		
	6000	4500	
	1500		

The end of the month shows a $1500 debit balance, indicating that this amount is still owed to Bernie Jordan. Managing a complicated journal and ledger set is very tedious when done by hand, but much simpler when done with a computer *as long as you comprehend the underlying accounting principles.* Year-end processing is more complex than with a single-entry system because you must adjust some accounts and close others to prepare the books for next year.

If you are familiar enough with double-entry accounting (translation: you got an A or B in your college accounting class) you may find that, with computer assistance, you can obtain much more useful information than from a single-entry system. Consult one or more accounting books to refresh your memory. On the other hand, if you aren't familiar with accounting and this method is just too confusing, don't despair; use the single-entry method.

Automating Your Bookkeeping

There are ways of using your computer to assist you with bookkeeping and accounting without purchasing an accounting package. By using a

---

Accounting Journal, 1985

Date	Account	Debit	Credit
1/03/85	Office expenses and postage Cash (P.O. box rental)	$ 25.00	$ 25.00
1/10	Accounts receivable Revenue (Jones, Smith & Johnson)	2000.00	2000.00
1/10	Office expenses and postage Cash (Office supplies)	15.00	15.00
1/15	Office expenses and postage Cash (stamps)	5.00	5.00
1/17	Cash Accounts receivable (Payment from Jones, Smith & Johnson)	2000.00	2000.00
1/25	Accounts receivable Revenue (ABCDEF Realty)	2500.00	2500.00
1/26	Cash Accounts receivable (Payment from ABCDEF Realty)	2500.00	2500.00
1/28	Supplies Cash (Floppy disks)	25.00	25.00
1/28	Accounts receivable Revenue (GHIJKL Realty)	1500.00	1500.00
1/29	Equipment Accounts payable (Printer)	400.00	400.00

Figure 13-3   Accounting journal.

spreadsheet program, such as VisiCalc or SuperCalc, your single-entry system can be effectively managed. All of your ledgers can be put on a spreadsheet and entries can be easily made, automatically updating summary totals.

A database management system is helpful in managing a double-entry system. I use dBASE II to prompt for journal entries, check the equality of debit and credit amounts entered, and automatically post entries to the appropriate ledger account. Year-end summaries and adjustments are also easily done.

An integrated program such as Lotus 1-2-3 could combine the easy calculations of a spreadsheet program with the file storage of a database manager to provide you with a very useful home-grown system.

Taxes

So what happens after you manage your books and decide on an accounting method? You get to pay your taxes! If you're one of the many people who cringe when you fill out your 1040 and Schedule A, prepare for a shock: tax accounting for businesses, even small ones, is much more complicated than your personal income tax situation.

This section will present a brief overview of the major tax concerns for small businesses: what records you must keep, how to file your taxes, how to avoid having your business categorized as a hobby loss (resulting in tax-time disaster), major types of business deductions, self-employment taxes, retirement plans, and state taxes. As with many of our topics, the review presented can be supplemented with more detailed information from other sources, which are listed in the following paragraphs and in Chapter 14.

Record Keeping

Once your bookkeeping system has been established, you are well on your way to accurate and necessary record keeping. IRS Publication 552, *Record-Keeping Requirements and a List of Tax Publications,* provides the IRS guidelines for record keeping. Many accountants, however, feel the publication is not very useful because it is published by your number 1 adversary when it comes to tax regulations.

Your appointment calendar, listing your business meetings and trips, should be retained to support travel and other expenses. Business purchases should be supported by receipts *and* canceled checks (or credit card receipts). If you set up a room at home for business use, you should retain a photograph of the room supporting that business use. If you move and are audited 2 years later, how will you support your office claim?

Any business trips should be supported by hotel bills and plane ticket receipts (if applicable), as well as a record of activities during the trip. Any expenditures over $25, such as meals, must also be supported by receipts.

Records must be retained for 3 open tax years, along with tax returns for the same period. If you are suspected of falsifying your tax returns, they are open to inspection for 3 additional years (for a total of 6 years). Any continuing items, such as a 5-year depreciable computer, must be supported by records as long as the items are in use.

IRS Publication 583, *Record-Keeping for a Small Business* also provides information to supplement Publication 552.

Filing Requirements

For consultants operating as sole proprietors Form 1040 is supplemented by Schedule C, "Profit or (Loss) From Business or Profession," listing income and expenses of the business (see Figure 13-4). This form is filed at the same time you file the 1040 (long form)—by April 15 of the next calendar year.

Consulting partnerships are required to file Form 1065, "Partnership Information Return" as well as a Schedule K-1 for each partner (see Figure 13-5). Schedule K-1 shows each partner's proportional share of income and expenses and the net income or loss is "carried forward" to Form 1040, Schedule E, "Supplemental Income." Confused? Don't worry, there's more!

Since you are your own employer, you don't have a company to withhold social security (FICA) taxes. Therefore, you must file Form 1040, Schedule SE, "Computation of Social Security Self-Employment Tax," if you have $400 or more of self-employment net earnings.

Hobby Losses

One of your most important concerns is proving that you are actually operating a consulting business, rather than attempting to support tax deductions for a hobby. Fortunately, if you follow the guidelines presented in this book (business registration, letterhead and business cards, business checking account, etc.) and keep an accurate file of business correspondence and proposals, you should have little trouble proving your business intent.

The key is to establish a profit motive; you intend to make money rather than spend money on an enjoyable sideline. A full-time consultant is less likely to be susceptible to any problems in this area than someone consulting in his or her spare time.

If you show a net profit, you probably won't be faced with an angry auditor screaming "hobby loss." When you are losing money, though, the burden of proof is on you.

You may be presented with the "opportunity" to file Form 5213,

SCHEDULE C
(Form 1040)

Department of the Treasury
Internal Revenue Service (0)

Profit or (Loss) From Business or Profession
(Sole Proprietorship)
Partnerships, Joint Ventures, etc., Must File Form 1065.
▶ Attach to Form 1040 or Form 1041.　　▶ See Instructions for Schedule C (Form 1040).

OMB No 1545-0074

19
09

Name of proprietor ▶ Bernard Jordan

Social security number of proprietor　000 00 0000

A Main business activity (see Instructions) ▶ Computer Consulting Services ; product ▶ Services

B Business name and address ▶ Jordan Business Computer Systems
7300 NO. 27th Ave., Phoenix, Az. 85021

C Employer identification number

D Method(s) used to value closing inventory
(1) ☐ Cost　(2) ☐ Lower of cost or market　(3) ☒ Other (attach explanation) N/A

E Accounting method.　(1) ☐ Cash　(2) ☒ Accrual　(3) ☐ Other (specify) ▶

	Yes	No

F Was there any major change in determining quantities, costs, or valuations between opening and closing inventory? — — ☒ (No)
If "Yes," attach explanation

G Did you deduct expenses for an office in your home? — — ☒ (No)

PART I.—Income

1 a Gross receipts or sales	1a	6000	00
b Less: Returns and allowances	1b		—
c Subtract line 1b from line 1a and enter the balance here	1c	6000	00
2 Cost of goods sold and/or operations (Part III, line 8)	2		—
3 Subtract line 2 from line 1c and enter the **gross profit** here	3	6000	00
4 a Windfall Profit Tax Credit or Refund received in 1983 (see Instructions)	4a		
b Other income	4b		—
5 Add lines 3, 4a, and 4b. This is the **gross income** ▶	5	6000	00

PART II.—Deductions

6 Advertising	150	00	23 Repairs		50	00
7 Bad debts from sales or services (Cash method taxpayers, see Instructions)			24 Supplies (not included in Part III)		50	00
8 Bank service charges			25 Taxes (Do not include Windfall Profit Tax here. See line 29.)			
9 Car and truck expenses			26 Travel and entertainment			
10 Commissions			27 Utilities and telephone		100	00
11 Depletion			28 a Wages			
12 Depreciation and Section 179 deduction from Form 4562 (not included in Part III)	300	00	b Jobs credit			
			c Subtract line 28b from 28a			
			29 Windfall Profit Tax withheld in 1983			
13 Dues and publications			30 Other expenses (specify):			
14 Employee benefit programs			a			
15 Freight (not included in Part III)			b			
16 Insurance	150	00	c			
17 Interest on business indebtedness	100	00	d			
18 Laundry and cleaning			e			
19 Legal and professional services	200	00	f			
20 Office expense	100	00	g			
21 Pension and profit-sharing plans			h			
22 Rent on business property			i			

31 Add amounts in columns for lines 6 through 30. These are the **total deductions** ▶	31	1200	00

32 Net profit or (loss). Subtract line 31 from line 5 and enter the result. If a profit, enter on Form 1040, line 12, and on Schedule SE, Part I, line 2 (or Form 1041, line 6). If a loss, go on to line 33	32	4800	00

33 If you have a loss, you must answer this question. "Do you have amounts for which you are not at risk in this business (see Instructions)?" ☐ Yes ☐ No
If "Yes," you must attach Form 6198. If "No," enter the loss on Form 1040, line 12, and on Schedule SE, Part I, line 2 (or Form 1041, line 6)

PART III.—Cost of Goods Sold and/or Operations (See Schedule C Instructions for Part III)

1 Inventory at beginning of year (if different from last year's closing inventory, attach explanation)	1	
2 Purchases less cost of items withdrawn for personal use	2	
3 Cost of labor (do not include salary paid to yourself)	3	
4 Materials and supplies	4	
5 Other costs	5	
6 Add lines 1 through 5	6	
7 Less: Inventory at end of year	7	
8 Cost of goods sold and/or operations. Subtract line 7 from line 6. Enter here and in Part I, line 2, above	8	

For Paperwork Reduction Act Notice, see Form 1040 Instructions.
☆U.S. GOVERNMENT PRINTING OFFICE 390 079 1983 (13) (74.815)
Schedule C (Form 1040) 1983

Figure 13-4 Schedule C (Form 1040).

"Election to Postpone Determination." This form states that any hobby-loss determination will be postponed until a later time. In the meantime, you must show a profit in any 2 of the first 5 business years; then you are allowed to deduct losses in any other tax years.

The alternative option, desirable if you are unsure of the success of your business, is to work on consulting on a regular basis, maintain accurate business records and books, and continue the supporting activities

SCHEDULE K-1 (Form 1065) Department of the Treasury Internal Revenue Service	**Partner's Share of Income, Credits, Deductions, etc.** For calendar year 1983 or fiscal year beginning _____, 1983, and ending _____, 19____	OMB No. 1545-0099 19____

Partner's identifying number ▶	Partnership's identifying number ▶
Partner's name, address, and ZIP code	Partnership's name, address, and ZIP code

	(i) Before decrease or termination	(ii) End of year
A Is partner a general partner (see page 3 of Instructions)? ☐ Yes ☐ No **B** Partner's share of liabilities (see page 10 of Instructions): Nonrecourse . . . . $ _____ Other . . . . $ _____ **C** What type of entity is this partner? ▶ _____	**D** Enter partner's percentage of: Profit sharing . . . . _____% Loss sharing . . . . _____% Ownership of capital . . . . _____% **E** IRS Center where partnership filed return ▶ _____	_____% _____% _____%

F Reconciliation of partner's capital account:						
(a) Capital account at beginning of year	(b) Capital contributed during year	(c) Ordinary income (loss) from line 1	(d) Income not included in column (c), plus nontaxable income	(e) Losses not included in column (c), plus unallowable deductions	(f) Withdrawals and distributions	(g) Capital account at end of year

	(a) Distributive share item	(b) Amount	(c) 1040 filers enter the amount in column (b) on:
Income (Loss)	1 Ordinary income (loss)		Sch. E, Part II, col. (d) or (e)
	2 Guaranteed payments		Sch. E, Part II, column (e)
	3 Interest from All-Savers Certificates		Sch. B, Part I, line 4
	4 Dividends qualifying for exclusion		Sch. B, Part II, line 9
	5 Net short-term capital gain (loss)		Sch. D, line 4, col. f. or g.
	6 Net long-term capital gain (loss)		Sch. D, line 12, col. f. or g.
	7 Net gain (loss) from involuntary conversions due to casualty or theft		See attached instructions
	8 Other net gain (loss) under section 1231		Form 4797, line 1
	9 Other (attach schedule)		(Enter on applicable lines of your return)
Deductions	10 Charitable contributions: 50% _____ 30% _____ 20% _____		See Form 1040 instructions
	11 Expense deduction for recovery property (section 179)		Sch. E, Part II, line 28
	12 a Payments for partner to an IRA		See Form 1040 instructions
	b Payments for partner to a Keogh Plan (Type of plan ▶ _____) .		Form 1040, line 26
	c Payments for partner to Simplified Employee Pension (SEP)		Form 1040, line 26
	13 Other (attach schedule)		(Enter on applicable lines of your return)
Credits	14 Jobs credit		Form 5884
	15 Credit for alcohol used as fuel		Form 6478
	16 Credit for income tax withheld		See Form 1040 instructions
	17 Other (attach schedule)		(Enter on applicable lines of your return)
Other	18 a Gross farming or fishing income		See attached instructions
	b Net earnings (loss) from self-employment		Sch. SE, Part I
	c Other (attach schedule)		(Enter on applicable lines of your return)
Tax Preference Items	19 a Accelerated depreciation on nonrecovery real property or 15-year real property.		Form 6251, line 4c
	b Accelerated depreciation on leased personal property or leased recovery property other than 15-year real property.		Form 6251, line 4d
	c Depletion (other than oil and gas)		Form 6251, line 4i
	d (1) Excess intangible drilling costs from oil, gas, or geothermal wells .		See Form 6251 instructions
	(2) Net income from oil, gas, or geothermal wells		
	e Net investment income (loss)		Form 6251, line 2e(2)
	f Other (attach schedule)		See attached instructions

For Paperwork Reduction Act Notice, see Form 1065 Instructions.	Schedule K-1 (Form 1065) 1983

Figure 13-5 Schedule K-1 (Form 1065).

mentioned several paragraphs ago. Rather than file Form 5213, attempt to support your profit motive through these means.

Major Types of Business Deductions

Schedule C (Form 1040) lists several categories of business expenses. Some, such as advertising, office supplies and postage, and insurance, are straightforward; you merely obtain the total amounts from your ledgers and enter the figures onto Schedule C. Others are a bit more complex. Let's take a look.

(a) Distributive share item	(b) Amount	(c) 1040 filers enter the amount in column (b) on:
Investment Interest		
20 a Investment interest expense:		
(1) Indebtedness incurred before 12/17/69		Form 4952, line 1
(2) Indebtedness incurred before 9/11/75, but after 12/16/69		Form 4952, line 15
(3) Indebtedness incurred after 9/10/75		Form 4952, line 5
b Net investment income (loss)		See attached instructions
c Excess expenses from "net lease property"		Form 4952, lines 11 and 19
d Excess of net long-term capital gain over net short-term capital loss from investment property		Form 4952, line 20
Foreign Taxes		
21 a Type of income _____		Form 1116, Checkboxes
b Name of foreign country or U.S. possession _____		Form 1116, Part I
c Total gross income from sources outside the U.S. (attach schedule)		Form 1116, Part I
d Total applicable deductions and losses (attach schedule)		Form 1116, Part I
e Total foreign taxes (check one): ► ☐ Paid ☐ Accrued		Form 1116, Part II
f Reduction in taxes available for credit (attach schedule)		Form 1116, Part III
g Other (attach schedule)		Form 1116, instructions
Property Eligible for Investment Credit		
22 Unadjusted basis of new recovery property **a** 3-Year		See attached instructions
b Other		See attached instructions
Unadjusted basis of used recovery property **c** 3-Year		See attached instructions
d Other		See attached instructions
e Nonrecovery property (see page 15 of Instructions) (attach schedule)		Form 3468, instr., line 2
f New commuter highway vehicle		Form 3468, line 3
g Used commuter highway vehicle		Form 3468, line 4
h Qualified rehabilitation expenditures		Form 3468, line 6a,b,or c

Property Subject to Recapture of Investment Credit		A	B	C
23 Properties:				
a Description of property (state whether recovery or nonrecovery property)				Form 4255, top
b Date placed in service				Form 4255, line 2
c Cost or other basis				Form 4255, line 3
d Class of recovery property or original estimated useful life				Form 4255, line 4
e Date item ceased to be investment credit property				Form 4255, line 8

Figure 13-5 Schedule K-1 (From 1065) (*continued*).

Depreciation and investment tax credits. Depreciation is the method by which the purchase of an asset, such as a computer or printer, is allocated as an expense over several years. For example, the $10,000 computer recorded in our ledger is assumed to have a useful life of 5 years and can be depreciated by one of several methods.

Prior to the Economic Recovery Tax Act of 1981, depreciation took the form of either straight-line, declining-balance, or a similar method (those of you who remember your accounting are undoubtedly familiar with these terms). The above act brought with it the Accelerated Cost Recovery System (ACRS). Most personal property used for your business will be categorized according to one of the following groups:

3-year property: automobile, light-duty trucks, and research and development equipment

5-year property: computers, office equipment, and most everything else you use for your business

15-year property: real estate

You now face several choices. You can use the ACRS tables for calculating your depreciation (for example, 3-year property is depreciated 25 percent in the first year, 38 percent in the second year, and 37 percent in the final year), or you could utilize the old straight-line method over a variety of years (for example, 5-year assets can be depreciated over 5, 12, or 25 years).

Why the variety of options, and which should you choose? If you foresee your income rising substantially over a period of years, you are better off depreciating assets over as long a time as possible. Otherwise, especially if tax rates decrease, you should utilize the ACRS schedules. *Business Tax Deduction Master Guide* discusses these scenarios in more detail.

Another option you have is treating depreciable property as an ordinary expense, up to $7500. This means that a $3000 computer system could be written off in the year of purchase just like your postage stamps and office supplies.

Property costing over $7500 could be partially expensed and partially depreciated. The purchase of a $9500 computer system would allow you to deduct $7500 in the purchase year as well as depreciate $2000 as 5-year property. You still have the options of ACRS or straight-line depreciation.

You do have a bonus if you choose depreciation, however. Any depreciable item is accompanied by an investment tax credit (ITC). A credit, as opposed to a deduction, is a dollar-for-dollar decrease in taxes due *after all deductions have been taken*. That is, you fill out Form 1040 and Schedules A (itemized deductions) and C, computing your taxable income and taxes due. After the calculation is made, your computed tax credits, such as the ITC, reduce the tax liability by the stated amount. The ITC is taken only in the year of purchase and only if the equipment is purchased for business use.

Beginning in 1983, new ITC rules were implemented. Previously, 10 percent of your depreciable amount was the ITC. Currently, you have the choice of either calculating the ITC at 8 percent of the depreciable amount or taking 10 percent of the asset's cost as the ITC but reducing the depreciable amount by half of that ITC amount.

For example, if you purchase a $10,000 computer system, you have the following options available for calculating the ITC and depreciation (assuming ACRS is used):

1. Depreciate the full computer cost and take an 8 percent ITC. A computer is considered 5-year property, so the ACRS deduction in the first year is 15 percent of purchase price. Your first-year tax savings is computed as follows:

Depreciation:	$10,000 × .15 = $1500
Investment tax credit:	$10,000 × .08 = $800

Assuming your taxable income was $20,000 after all other deductions, the $1500 would be subtracted from that amount, giving you $18,500 for total taxable income. After consulting the tax tables (assume single, no dependents), your taxes due are $2956. The $800 is *then* subtracted from the taxes due (thus the dollar-for-dollar credit), giving you a final tax bill of $2156.

2. You can also reduce the depreciable amount by half of the full 10 percent investment tax credit. Your calculations are:

Investment tax credit: $10,000 × .10 = $1000

The $10,000 is reduced by one-half of the ITC ($500) to $9500. Hence:

Depreciation: $9500 × .15 = $1425

Taxable income: $20,000 − 1425 = $18,575

Taxes due on $18,575 are $2970, so:

Final tax bill: $2970 − 1000 = $1970

Note the first-year tax bill is $186 less when using this method than the first one.

3. Finally, you can combine the expensing of the asset up to $7500 with the balance depreciated and considered for an investment tax credit. In this case, your $20,000 taxable income will be reduced by $7875: $7500 as an expense and 15 percent of the $2500 balance ($375). Assuming you use the 8 percent ITC rate, your taxes due will be decreased by $200 ($2500 × .08). Alternatively, you could reduce your depreciable amount by $125 ($2500 × one-half of 10 percent ITC) and then calculate your depreciation.

Unless you foresee your income decreasing, it is always recommended that you depreciate the full amount rather than deduct up to $7500 as an ordinary expense. First, in most cases, your income will probably be rising as your business grows. Second, you can't utilize the investment tax credit with any expensed amount. In most cases, you will come out ahead by utilizing the ACRS schedule.

You should also calculate which ACRS/ITC option (8 percent versus 10 percent with the reduced basis) will provide you with greater tax savings and use that option.

Finally, make sure you examine the current tax rules concerning depreciation and investment tax credits, as these laws change frequently.

Transportation costs.   Your car will be an invaluable asset to your business, as you must travel to meet with your clients, investigate computer systems, and perform business-related tasks. You are not allowed to deduct commuting expenses between your home and place of business, but any business-related travel is tax-deductible.

Assuming that you base your consulting practice in your home, any trips to visit clients or perform business duties are tax-deductible. If you have a separate office, business transportation between your office and those of clients is tax-deductible.

How do you calculate your tax-deductible amount? First you must determine what percentage of your automobile expenses is business-related. A log kept over a certain period of time (such as 1 month) of all miles driven should yield a business percentage. For example, if you drive 1000 miles during the month and 500 are for business use, your business use is 50 percent.

After you have calculated your business use percentage, you must determine if you should use the IRS standard mileage rate (currently 20.5 cents per mile) or take a percentage of the total costs. You should keep a log of all actual expenses (gasoline, oil, repairs, car washes, etc.) and, at the end of the year, apply your business percentage to the total cost.

But wait! You can also depreciate your car *and* take an investment tax credit, just as with other business assets. A car is considered 3-year property, which carries a 6 percent ITC.

Calculate which option, the flat mileage rate or actual expenses, provides you with the largest tax deduction.

Home office. One of the "flags" which allegedly can trigger an IRS audit is the home office deduction. Until a 1983 tax court ruling, a home office could only exist for tax purposes if you had a room dedicated solely as your "primary place of business," a term which invokes great controversy. For a computer consultant, it should be either a place for meeting clients or the place where you do your consulting work (translation: you don't rent any other office space) and have access to needed business facilities.

A 1983 tax court ruling stated that a room could be *partially* used for business and still qualify as a home office. The same rules of "primary place of business" still apply.

In order to establish your home office as a legitimate tax deduction, you should (1) photograph the office, (2) establish phone usage, (3) keep a work activity log, (4) keep a guest book, and (5) receive business mail.[3]

You should calculate whether or not a home office deduction will be of economic benefit. You can deduct a percentage of your utilities and phone (we'll see in a minute how to calculate the percentage) as well as depreciate a portion of your home. If you rent your residence, a portion of your rent is tax-deductible. When you sell your home, the depreciated amount will be "recovered" as a long-term capital gain or ordinary income, depending upon the depreciation method and time frame used.

You calculate your home business percentage as either a percentage of total square feet in the home or as a percentage of the number of rooms. For example, if you own a six-room, 1000-square-foot townhouse and use one room (100 square feet) as a home office, you have a percentage of either 10 percent (based on square feet) or 16.67 percent (based on number of rooms). Check with your accountant to see which figure to use; to avoid raising the tax collector's ire any more than necessary, use a conservative amount (in accounting, conservative means reasonable).

You are also limited to a total home office deduction up to the total income from your home-based business. If you earn $700, that is your limit for that year even if your deduction is calculated at $2500.

Educational expenses.   Educational costs are deductible after you are established in business and must either (1) be taken to maintain or improve the skills required in your profession or (2) be undertaken to meet legal or regulatory requirements to retain your established status or pay. Additionally, the courses *cannot* be part of a program of study to qualify you for a new profession or be required to meet the minimum educational requirements of your current profession.[4]

The above paragraphs presented an overview of the most common types of expenses a consultant is likely to face. For further information about these and other business expenses (such as entertainment and travel), consult the IRS publications and tax references we've reviewed.

Self-employment taxes.   As stated earlier, you must file Form 1040 Schedule SE, "Computation of Social Security Self-Employment Tax." Net earnings of $400 and greater are subject to this tax, currently at a rate of 9.35 percent. If the computed social security tax is added to your primary employment FICA and exceeds the limit (currently $2391.90), you credit the overage against your income taxes due.

State taxes.   Check with your state department of revenue or other taxation agency for their policies regarding business taxes. Most states operate similarly to the IRS for filing requirements and allowable deductions. Be sure to know when and what forms you need to file.

In summary, just as with the deductions mentioned, be sure to consult the listed references for more detailed information about this complicated and often frustrating subject. If further assistance is needed, it's time to check with your accountant (see Help! later in this chapter).

Marketing

The many guidelines presented in Chapter 5 still apply as your business goes from the planning stages to full-scale operation. You should keep a close watch on your advertising budget; just because you are earning more income doesn't mean you should splurge on unnecessary and illogical advertising. You may increase your *Yellow Pages* advertising from a ¼-inch box to a ¼-page display ad, but a $100,000 television advertising budget is probably still a bit extreme.

Always keep your target markets in mind when making any advertising or marketing decisions. Your public relations and word-of-mouth referrals will remain a key factor in your marketing plan; exploit them as best you can.

Insurance

You should determine what type of insurance your business requires. If your office is located at your residence, your homeowner's or renter's insurance should cover fire, theft, and other casualty losses. *Be sure* to notify your insurance company that you will have business equipment (computer, printer, etc.) in your home and that they will be used for business; you may have to pay a small amount more but some companies will not cover business equipment loss or damage under a residential policy.

You may also consider liability insurance (both for you and your "products") to prevent a catastrophic multimillion-dollar suit from devastating your business and personal assets.

If you use your automobile for business, either partially or totally, your policy should include the usual liability, comprehensive, and collision coverages.

You should not have to worry about business interruption insurance, since you probably won't have a retail outlet or factory whose damage could cause temporary or permanent business stoppage. Nor will you need to concern yourself with worker's compensation insurance if you don't have any employees. Once you begin employing workers, however, investigate your state's requirement for this coverage.

There is one major rule with insurance coverage: shop around. Prices vary widely among carriers, and there is no guarantee that an insurer with low automobile coverage will be equally reasonable for liability insurance.

Help!

Throughout this book I've been stressing development of your business and management abilities along with your computer skills. There may come a time, though, when you face a particularly difficult or complex situation that you cannot handle by yourself. When your business was in its infancy, most of the day-to-day business operations could be handled in-house. Now that your practice (and active client list) is growing, these support activities may consume too much of your valuable time, thus stunting your firm's growth.

There are no set rules for when to use outside expertise in these areas. If you have a very strong background in accounting, for example, you may feel comfortable conducting tax planning operations further into your firm's growth cycle than someone with minimal accounting exposure.

Let's take a look at several areas and see how (or if) outside professionals could help your business.

Accounting

Many new consultants prefer to prepare their own tax returns and do their own tax planning, as well as maintain their accounting books. Again, there are no laws etched in granite, but while your business is just starting and revenues are still small, you can manage most accounting functions.

A manual journal and ledger system would be sufficient to post revenues and expenses, and as transaction volume increases, you can use your computer to implement an automated system.

Much of your tax planning can be done using knowledge gained from research. Laws concerning depreciation, investment tax credits, home office deductions, and many other topics can be found in many tax publications and guides.

When should you consider working with an accountant? When your accounting and tax needs and problems outgrow your own expertise and time available for research. For example, during my second year in the consulting profession, I moved from an apartment to a house of which I owned 60 percent, sold one car and bought another, and formed a consulting partnership. While these may seem like simple transactions, when you consider the tax implications of two possible home offices, separate business mileage deductions, and separating sole proprietorship income and expenses from those of the partnership, I was faced with an extremely complex tax planning and return situation. Though revenues were still low, the potential for an auditable error in my tax return and the desire to fully utilize all the tax-saving methods available led me to conclude that professional help (accounting, not psychiatric!) was cost-effective.

Though I probably could have researched all the possible tax consequences and eventually (by April 14) completed my tax forms, I was involved in several consulting projects at the time as well as my writing *and* my full-time Air Force job. It was, therefore, much more cost-effective to give my accountant a summary of business expenses, explain the complicating factors such as a new house and new car, and pick up the completed tax return several weeks later.

Just as we saw with self-publication of commercial software versus contracting with a publishing house, you must consider, in addition to your own expertise, your available time and the opportunity cost of spending that time on program publishing or complicated tax planning or anything else. If you have several other revenue-producing projects that would provide far more income than the amount of money you save by doing your taxes yourself, it makes good economic sense to spend a bit of money (tax-deductible, of course) and devote your time to income-producing (and business-building) projects.

Marketing

Assuming that you have put to work the marketing principles presented in this book and elsewhere, you should have little need for advertising agencies or other marketing assistance while nurturing your business.

You may, however, find yourself suddenly and unexplainedly losing market share and revenue. If, after a thorough analysis, you still don't understand why your business share is dropping, a marketing consultant may be able to provide the answer. Again, consider the costs and benefits of using outside help. If your business revenue from a critical portion of your operations is affected, a marketing consultant may be very cost-effective. However, if the affected area is an experimental or secondary operation that contributes little to total income (and is not expected to in the future), it may be difficult to justify the expense of marketing assistance.

Other marketing services that may be utilized include conducting marketing research. If, for example, you can obtain the mailing labels of all local real estate agents from the local board of realtors, you may be able to design a questionnaire that provides much useful information without assistance. This is especially important during the early years of operation when you are trying to control expenses. A larger firm, however, may wish to use a marketing firm's resources to investigate potential markets, analyze survey results, and recommend a course of action.

Legal

I already mentioned several times before that your contracts should be reviewed (and possibly negotiated) by an attorney experienced in computer and business contracts. The potential for liability and serious problems causes legal assistance to be viewed in the same light as insurance: spend a bit now to save a lot later.

General legal questions, however, may be researched through sources such as Remer's *Legal Care for Your Software,* tax law books, or other sources. You should have an understanding of the problem in question and the alternatives before consulting an attorney.

Financial

If you are considering massive expansion of your business, such as opening offices in several cities or becoming a full-time software house, you may find yourself with the need for additional capital. Your accountant should be the first person you turn to, as he or she can point out the various tax implications of the sought-after financing. You may then be directed to a venture capitalist, Small Business Administration (SBA) lender, underwriter, or other financial source. Unless you yourself are a venture capitalist turned entrepreneur, these financing actions are best left to the professionals. One slip of a contract (which your attorney should review, of course) *could* cost you control of the business to which you have devoted so much time, effort, and money.

Personnel

Unless you are embarking on a massive employment campaign, you should be able to conduct interviews and make hiring decisions without using employment agencies or executive recruiters. A classified newspaper ad should be able to attract enough potential job seekers to allow you to find a qualified person.

Further down the road you may require agency services to attract professionals from other geographic areas or assist you with screening applicants to find that one right person. In these instances, be sure that you can justify the cost of these services by the benefits, both tangible and intangible, provided.

Record Keeping

As much as most people dislike maintaining records, that is as important a function as your bookkeeping, accounting, and other managerial tasks. You should organize your filing system in such a manner that it is easy for you to file and retrieve information. The information you store should include:

Tax returns, financial records, and receipts

Contracts and other legal forms

Proposals

Client project reports

Business correspondence

Important magazine and newspaper clippings

Client information

Be sure that you periodically get rid of out-of-date records and information to prevent your files from becoming too cumbersome.

Using Your Computer

How can you utilize your own computer system to help you manage your own business? We've already discussed several uses in this and previous chapters; these uses and others are listed below.

1. *Word processing:* You will undoubtedly be writing many letters, reports, and proposals and possibly even books and magazine articles. Word processing software will speed up the creation and revision time of these written documents. You can also mass-mail letters to your clients or vendors using a mail-merge facility with your database files (discussed next).

2. *Database management:* You can store lists of everything using a database management system. The most common uses may include (1) client lists, (2) vendor lists, (3) magazine article cross-referencing, and (4) accounting information.

3. *Spreadsheet analysis:* Chapter 4 dealt with cash flow analysis, income statements, and other financial uses of an electronic spreadsheet. You can also perform what-if analysis on various projects, maintain a simple single-entry set of books, and prepare your tax returns (as well as analyze the tax implications of various alternative decisions).

4. *Communications:* You can connect your computer via modem to remote databases to retrieve bibliographic information or access several software databases. For example, a client may be searching for a solution to a particularly difficult problem, and you can access these databases to learn if any software exists that may work in this situation.

5. *Graphics generation:* You can create charts and graphs to be used in your seminars as overhead slides or handouts.

Employee Compensation

When you begin to hire employees for your firm, you need to know what type of compensation to provide. Without adequate and motivating reward, you will have trouble attracting and retaining good employees at all levels, professional and clerical.

You must be able to recognize what motivates people in the computer profession, both financially and in terms of work. Though we will be discussing mostly your professional computer workers, the same basic principles hold true of all employees.

Employee compensation can be broken down into four major categories:[5]

1. *Salary:* The basis of compensation is the salary portion, either as a flat rate or on an hourly basis. The employee's salary is based on job analysis, job level, survey of comparable salaries in other firms, and periodic adjustments. Naturally, a computer programmer with a master's degree will earn more than a secretary with a high school diploma.

2. *Benefits:* Employee benefits can consist of a combination of health care, paid vacations, life and disability insurance, employee services (discounts on company services, for example), survivor benefits, and retirement plans, among others. A recent trend is to allow employees to pick and choose among a set of benefits: a young, unmarried person may not require much (if any) life insurance, while a military retiree would have little need for health insurance.

3. *Perquisites:* Slightly more than benefits, "perks" would include paid vacations at a company ski resort or use of the company car (or company aircraft, if you happen to have one in your inventory!). Perks should be distributed on a somewhat limited basis in order to maintain a reward basis.

4. *Short-term and long-term incentives:* Short-term incentives, such as annual bonuses, and long-term ones, like stock options and discount stock purchase plans, are important factors in motivating and retaining your key employees.

You may also consider plans like deferred compensation, where part of an employee's salary is put off until a later time when his or her tax bracket may be less than at present. You might consider offering employees working on a key project a percentage of that task's profits as an incentive bonus.

How do you decide what type of compensation packages to offer your various employees? You should research the salaries and benefits offered by firms similar to yours, as well as general compensation among employees in other industries. You may also seek assistance from compensation consultants, your accountant, or others who could help you develop a useful package. Be aware of any geographical differences in your surveys, research, and advice; employees in San Francisco or New York City need to earn more than those in Des Moines to maintain a particular standard of living.

Contracts and Fees

Anytime you and your clients enter into an agreement, whether written, spoken, or merely implied, you become parties to a contract. We dealt with contracts briefly in Chapters 10 to 12 in the form of license agreements, nondisclosure agreements, and work-for-hire agreements. This section will deal with contracts in a bit more detail.

Business law, specifically contract law, is a fascinating and complex area. As a consultant, you will be party to many contracts; again, some may be spoken or implied while others are written. It is urged that *all* contracts you enter into be written, even though oral contracts are legally enforceable. By signing written contracts, both you and your clients are somewhat protected against misunderstanding, ambiguity, and deception. Any agreement, even a written letter of agreement, can be considered a contract, so be careful what you sign.

Among the applicable elements of most contracts are:[6]

1. Responsibility of each party
2. Time agreements
3. Financial arrangements
4. Products or services to be delivered
5. Needed cooperation of client during project
6. Establishment of your independent-contractor status rather than employment
7. Establishment of your advisory capacity, as opposed to being a decision maker
8. Client responsibility for review, implementation, and results
9. Your potential work with competitors (nonexclusivity of services)
10. Client's authority to contract for your services
11. Attorney's fee clause
12. Special limitation

Expect to negotiate these terms; your client may desire, for example, to preclude you from working for his or her competitors. If you agree to this, be sure that corresponding terms, such as financial compensation and terms under which the contract may be terminated, provide you with adequate protection.

One of the most important portions is financial arrangements. You should never sign an agreement that doesn't specify *exactly* what you must do or deliver and how much you will be paid (flat fee) or on what basis (hourly or daily rate, for example).[7] Some clients may wish to place you on a retainer (see Chapter 4); be sure that you don't inadvertently lock yourself into an unprofitable situation at the expense of other, better-paying contracts from other clients.

You should also quantify how often you will be paid; you may wish to accept a 30 percent retainer at the start of the project and receive portions of your total fee at various intervals. Your proposal and/or contract should specify what constitutes the end of a contract phase, such as delivery of Report A or implementation of portions 1, 2, and 3 of a client's computer system. Additionally, you should note what payments will be due if the client cancels the project at various stages. Again, be prepared to negotiate.

As I stressed in Chapter 11, the money you spend to have your attorney draft and review contracts to which you will be a party is an investment in the successful operation of your business. If you draft any contracts yourself, skip the "whyforths" and the "party of the third part"; write them in English. Be aware of the consequences of anything you don't explicitly specify (remember "implied warranties" from license agreements?) and know the default conditions.

Ethics and Client Relations

Even though you are not licensed the way an attorney, physician, or accountant is, you are still a professional. A certain code of ethics applies to your client relations. Chief among your responsibilities is confidentiality. You may be tempted to brag about your inside knowledge of XYZ Corporation's expansion plans or your assistance with UVW Company's serious problems. All you do then is invite legal action and destroy your professional and personal credibility. Not too bad, huh?

Since you are an independent consultant, it is extremely likely that at times you will be working with competitors of previous clients. In order to survive in business, you must be considered trustworthy and legal by your present client, but not at the expense of a former one. Anyone who expects you to provide inside information about another one of your clients should be informed that you don't operate your practice in that manner; if they persist, proceed to another client.

Another important subject is conflicts of interest. The previously mentioned confidentiality example is also an instance of potential conflict of interest. If you assist client A with a particular contract, such as providing technical expertise for a government project it seeks, it is unethical to aid client B with the same project even if you have finished consulting with client A—and client B offers you 10 times as much money.

Additionally, you should always check with any client with whom you are under a retainer agreement to see if they intend to pursue a particular project before assisting another client with that job. Depending on your particular retainer agreement, you may find yourself in a precarious position if your main client desires your services and you have already committed yourself to working with another customer.

Another potential conflict of interest was mentioned in Chapter 7. If you cosponsor a seminar with a local computer retailer, you should not be expected to automatically commit your future clients to that store's hardware or software. Each client who pays you deserves the best advice and service you can provide. You shouldn't recommend a $10,000 four-user system when a Kaypro 2 will be sufficient.

You must also honor any contractual time and cost estimates you make, such as a ceiling of hours or guaranteed delivery date. As a professional computer consultant, you are supposed to be enough of an expert that if you estimate a project will be completed in 50 hours and be delivered in 1 month, your actual development time won't be off by much.

Note, though, as we've mentioned several times before, that this is true only if the scope of the project doesn't change. If your client wants to add features to custom software or doesn't provide certain guaranteed support, your obligations to honor your estimates are terminated. To be on the safe side, make sure these conditions are *written in the contract.* A clause such as "additional features beyond those specified will be handled under separate contractual arrangements" is helpful in clarifying and solving any problems that might arise.

You may consider charging separate billing rates depending on the type and amount of services. My personal feeling is that a long-term contract such as custom software development (for example, 80 to 100 hours of work) may call for a slightly lower billing rate per hour because of the "guaranteed" number of hours billed and less idle time. Other consultants charge the same hourly rate for 1-day projects as for 1-year contracts. The important thing is to be honest about your fees and how they are computed. If one client wants to know why another client received your services at a lower rate than you first quoted, explain that the project was of much longer duration with a guaranteed minimum number of hours.

Any agreements at negotiated special rates should contain a clause in the contract stating either a minimum number of hours per day at the negotiated rate with a minimum total fee or number of days or a conditional clause that if the project does not meet a minimum number of hours, you will be paid your standard rate in lieu of the cheaper one.[8]

Finally, you may meet people at parties or other social gatherings who ask you many questions like "What type of computer should I buy?" or "What is the best general-ledger program for the IBM PC?" While you may not mind providing your sister-in-law or college roommate with this free consulting advice, avoid telling casual acquaintances or total strangers too much without a formal agreement. A quick answer such as "There are several good ledger programs; last month's *Popular Computing* featured a special report" would be as far as you should go.

The same is true for current or former clients. If you are installing an inventory system for a fixed fee and your client suddenly wants to add an integrated software package, you may recommend several for him or her to investigate. If your client wants you to install and conduct training for that package, it's time to break out the "separate contractual arrangements" clause of your contract. Be fair with you clients, but make sure they are aware you aren't running a free clinic.

Summary

This chapter covered *a lot* of material. I've attempted to briefly cover most of the major concerns you will face when managing your new consulting practice. Again, this chapter goes beyond the scope of this book's first section, which dealt with your starting concerns. It's hard to squeeze an entire college major such as business management into one chapter, but I hope I've succeeded in providing an overview and checklist of your business operations.

End Notes

1. Bernard Kamoroff, *Small-Time Operator,* Bell Springs Publishing, Layfonville, Calif., 1982, pp. 38–39.

2. Ibid., pp. 42–49.

3. W. Murray Bradford and Ronald V. Reed, *Business Tax Deduction Master Guide,* Prentice-Hall, Englewood Cliffs, N.J., 1982, p. 139.

4. Ibid., p. 142.

5. Soundview Summary of Bruce R. Ellig, *Executive Compensation—A Total Pay Perspective,* Soundview Books, Darien, Conn., 1982, p. 1.

6. Robert E. Kelley, *Consulting: The Complete Guide to a Profitable Career,* Scribner's, New York, 1981, pp. 158–159.

7. Herman Holtz, *How to Succeed as an Independent Consultant,* Wiley, New York, 1983, p. 240.

8. Ibid., p. 245.

CHAPTER 14

How to Stay Current (or How Not to Fall into Computer Oblivion)

Congratulations! Your knowledge of computer and business subjects is so complete that you've made it this far through this book, saying to yourself, "No problem; I know all about marketing, systems design, and how to write commercial software. A bit of research into finance and legal issues, and I can sit back and watch the money roll in." Right? Wrong!

Even if you have followed the guidelines presented in Chapter 2 and selected one or two specialty areas on which to concentrate, your learning days are far from over. I can't count the number of times when I have felt like I was all caught up with the microcomputer industry, with a fairly complete knowledge of the hardware and software commercially available, only to open my mailbox and retrieve several computer magazines, their cover stories screaming, "Five New Portable Computers!" or "Seven New Word Processing Packages for the IBM PC!"

The obvious fact is that the computer industry, especially the microcomputer segment, is so dynamic that a concerted effort is required to keep abreast of new technology and products. This is especially true for computer consultants, who can't afford to not be aware of the latest products, particularly in their specialty areas. As we saw in Chapter 1, you'll never know everything about everything; you just can't stand still and watch the industry streak by.

Here we will discuss how to keep your knowledge as current as possible, both in computer and business subjects. We will look at some of the many periodicals available and discuss their appropriateness to your practice. We'll see some books that will be useful additions to your library. We'll also discuss the role that continuing-education classes, advanced degrees, and seminars play in your acquisition of knowledge. Finally, we'll also look at users' groups, professional organizations, and vendor mailing lists.

Periodicals

About a year ago I wondered why my mailbox hadn't collapsed from the weight of the eleven subscription magazines that arrived at weekly, biweekly, and monthly intervals. Though I felt as if I were weighed down by the amount of information I was trying to absorb, these subscriptions represented but a fraction of the business and computer periodicals available.

How should you decide to which of the many trade and business magazines and newspapers to subscribe? These publications can be roughly

General Microcomputing Microcomputing	Machine-Specific	
Byte	PC Magazine (IBM)	
Interface Age	PC World (IBM)	
Personal Computing	PC Tech Journal (IBM)	
Popular Computing	Softalk (IBM)	
Infoworld	Softalk (Apple)	
Creative Computing	in Cider (Apple)	
Computers and Electronics	Nibble (Apple)	
Microcomputing	MacWorld (Apple Macintosh)	
General Business	**General Computing**	**Small Business**
The Wall Street Journal	Datamation	Inc.
Forbes	Computerworld	Venture
Fortune	Infosystems	
Business Week		

Figure 14-1 Magazine reading list.

divided into five major categories: general microcomputing, machine-specific, general computing, general business, and small business. We'll look at each category separately in a minute.

As an independent consultant, you should regularly read at least one publication from each category to stay as well informed as possible. There is no way for you to read every article in every publication on the market, as much as it may be desirable. You should sample several issues and decide which may be the most useful to your particular consulting practice.

The magazines and newspapers mentioned in the following paragraphs and shown in Figure 14-1 are not meant to comprise an all-encompassing list of recommended publications; rather, they are some that I found useful in establishing and building my own consulting practice. Many more excellent periodicals exist, but limited space precludes a complete listing (which would be out of date by the time this book is published, anyway). Without further ado, then, let's discuss our five categories.

General Microcomputing

For a consultant specializing in microcomputer hardware and software, these are likely to be the most important publications you can read. Magazines such as *BYTE* contain a great deal of technical knowledge (such as discussing how specific operating systems work or the workings of a new microprocessor), while others like *Personal Computing* are aimed toward the managerial end user, who is unlikely to be a technical expert.

Other magazines, such as *Interface Age* and *Popular Computing,* are somewhere in between; they contain some technical information as well as articles intended for the computer novice.

Most magazines are published monthly, while *Infoworld* is a weekly trade journal. Almost all magazines contain sections on new product announcements (both hardware and software), as well as in-depth product reviews. You can use comparison charts, product reviews, and other such articles for much of your preliminary research for your clients.

Subscription prices vary, but, as with most periodicals, the subscription prices are less expensive than buying each issue and paying the cover price. Several trade journals, such as *Micro Marketworld* and *Computer Retail News,* are available free (yes, that's "free" as in "no charge") to qualified resellers of computer products. Since a consultant usually recommends commercial hardware and software, you can receive these weekly or biweekly periodicals at no cost. Though these publications' intended audiences are retail computer outlets, most of the articles and product reviews are just as applicable to computer consultants.

Machine-Specific Magazines

In addition to the product reviews and articles you will find in general publications, you may wish to subscribe to one or two magazines that relate specifically to a machine, such as the IBM PC, Apple IIe, or Apple Macintosh. The articles in these magazines are likely to concentrate on machine-related topics, such as interfacing with the operating system, new products and software for that computer, and special hardware knowledge—all subjects that you should be intimately familiar with as an expert in your specialty machine areas.

These publications include *PC Magazine, PC World,* and *PC Tech Journal* for the (you guessed it) IBM PC, and *Nibble* for the Apple family. As new products reach the market (IBM PCjr and Apple Macintosh, for example), accompanying publications also appear.

Machines other than IBM and Apple have trade magazines, too; check with local retailers or the hardware companies themselves to see if one exists for your specialty machine.

General Computing

As you are undoubtedly aware, there is more to the computer industry than just microcomputers. (The general public may not realize that, though.) To keep abreast of developments in the industry as a whole, as well as new theories in systems design, database management, computer networks, and other subjects, you may wish to refer to some of the general computing periodicals. *Computerworld,* a weekly industry newspaper, discusses the above subjects as well as publishes *Datapro* survey results, company news, and other articles of interest. *Datamation* and *Infosystems,* two monthly magazines, publish articles of interest to information systems executives that are also applicable to consultants.

General Business

Remember the lesson that has been stressed throughout this book: a consultant is also a businessperson. You must stay aware of business subjects that are important to your practice. The following periodicals contain articles discussing and analyzing company strategies and a wide range of financial subjects. There are also periodic advertising supplements that discuss the computer industry, office automation, communication, and other computer-related topics.

Business Week is published weekly, while *Forbes* and *Fortune* are biweekly magazines. For those who desire in-depth daily information, *The Wall Street Journal* is published every business day.

Don't overlook the business section of your local newspapers; you need to be concerned with the business climate, competition, and outlook on a local basis, too.

Small Business Magazines

Since you are starting a consulting practice from the ground up, you can rightfully be called an entrepreneur. Several monthly business magazines deal with subjects that are of special concern to small, growing companies: venture capital and other financing, expanding a business, new product ideas, marketing strategies, and employee compensation strategies, among others. Two such magazines are *Inc.* and *Venture,* both of which are excellent sources of information for the manager of a small, growing business.

Books

In addition to the continuing education provided by periodicals, you should also make use of reference material in the form of books. The number of business and computer books is staggering; short of buying the local library's shelves and restocking them with your personal books, you should purchase only volumes that are applicable to your practice and use them as a reference and learning source.

Don't overlook the availability of books from your local library; many of the books you want will be out of date shortly because of changing technology and laws. Rather than put a substantial investment in several bookshelves worth of volumes, you may wish to utilize your library's collection. Though less expensive, the trade-off of this strategy is the decreased availability of your material.

An alternative strategy is to buy a small contingent (a "critical mass," so to speak) of books that you will find the most useful and use your library for supplemental material when necessary.

As with periodicals, books of interest to an independent computer consultant can be divided into several categories: small business management, finance and taxation, general business, managerial aspects of computing and consulting, and technical reference material.

Small Business Management

These books provide information about the basics of finance, marketing, taxes, and other subjects of concern to the person operating a small business. Much of this material has been used as the basis for this book. For example, *Small-Time Operator,* by Bernard Kamoroff,[1] discusses many of the subjects presented in this book: how to choose a business name, licenses and regulations, accounting and bookkeeping, and business expansion. A good deal of space is devoted to accounting and taxes, probably since Kamoroff is a CPA. Another book, *Up Your Own Organization: A Handbook to Start and Finance a New Business,* by Donald M. Dible,[2] provides an in-depth discussion of business plans (among other topics) and illustrates several sample plans.

Several books are available that deal with small business management for consultants. I have found two particularly useful in establishing my practice. The first is *Consulting: The Complete Guide to a Profitable Career,* by Robert E. Kelley.[3] As I'm sure you've noticed, Kelley has proved an invaluable source in preparing this book. He discusses a wide range of subjects, including marketing, building a practice, writing, and project management. He also includes self-evaluation exercises that help you determine if, as we saw in Chapter 1, you have the personality and background to aid your consulting career.

The second is *How to Succeed as an Independent Consultant,* by Herman Holtz.[4] Holtz, a consultant who specializes in government contracts and marketing, discusses a variety of subjects, such as marketing and the fundamentals of proposal writing; this book has also proved very useful to me.

Finance, Accounting, and Taxation

If you were a business major in college, you may feel comfortable with a textbook source of financial information such as *Managerial Finance* by J. Fred Weston and Eugene F. Brigham[5] or *Principles of Managerial Finance* by Lawrence J. Gitman.[6] Those without an in-depth financial background may prefer Herbert Spiro's *Finance for the Nonfinancial Manager*[7] or a similar tutorial.

The same is true for accounting and taxation; many college texts are available that discuss financial, managerial, and tax accounting, along with books such as *Business Tax Deduction Master Guide* by W. Murray Bradford and Ronald V. Reed.[8] This book discusses taxation strategies especially suited to business and professional people. Chapters include how to correctly utilize tax-deductible entertainment and automobile expenses, depreciation and investment tax credits, and home office deductions. Other subjects are self-employed retirement plans, estimated taxes and penalties, and handling an audit.

A hint about tax information: Don't overlook IRS publications, such as Publication 334, *Tax Guide for Small Business,* and others that deal with depreciation, investment tax credits, business expenses, business use of your home, and employment taxes. These are available free either from your local IRS office or by mail, and it's worth getting the official (and current) information from the source itself.

General Business

There is an almost endless supply of books available about marketing, management, leadership, and other business subjects. Take a look at the business shelves in a nearby bookstore to see what the current popular titles are.

Managerial Aspects of Computing

Unlike the proliferating technical computer books, these would include Daniel Remer's *Legal Care for Your Software* and the *1985 Programmer's Market* (both discussed in Chapter 11). These books provide a computer consultant or consulting manager with reference material for managerial topics such as legal considerations and marketing strategies.

Technical Reference Material

There are many books available that teach you how to program in BASIC or assembler, how to use CP/M or MS-DOS, or how to use your particular personal computer. As a consultant, the type of books you should concentrate on are those that give detailed information and examples about how to interact with operating-system routines (for example, if you write custom or commercial programs, using preprogrammed screen access routines will save you a lot of time) or language and reference manuals that provide *reference* material, as opposed to tutorials that teach a language. Of course, if you don't have much programming background, a less advanced BASIC or assembler tutorial may be appropriate if it provides exercises and many examples.

Other technical reference manuals could include the basics of database management, networks and communications, or structured systems analysis and design. Most of these books double as college texts and are usually technically advanced; others are intended as primers for inexperienced users. If you have been a database programmer for 3 years, be sure to choose reference material appropriate to your level of understanding rather than introductory information you already know.

Education

A major part of your continual learning process is formal education. For those who earned a bachelor's degree and then went on to work and consulting, a master's degree could provide additional knowledge and credibility. If you already have a master's degree, you may wish to earn a doctoral degree; though this undoubtedly will require much time and effort, the additional flexibility to your career may well be worthwhile. You could join the faculty at a major university while continuing your consulting practice.

Though not an inflexible rule, you should consider an advanced degree that complements your undergraduate background but enters new areas of formal learning. If your undergraduate degree is in computer science, a Master of Business Administration (MBA) or other degree from a business college may fill in the gaps in your experience. Similarly, a business major would benefit from graduate computer science courses.

Even if you already have an advanced degree, or don't have the time or resources to pursue a degree program, you can still benefit from educational institution learning by enrolling in continuing education or other classes open to the general public. Many colleges and universities allow nondegree candidates to participate in business and computer classes, among others. You can check with your local community college or a nearby university to see what courses are available to meet your needs.

Seminars and Conferences

Formal classes are not the only educational source to enhance your business and computer knowledge. Seminars and conferences are held constantly, providing an excellent opportunity to spend a day or two concentrating on the latest advances and techniques in a variety of subjects. For example, if you have a need to learn about data communications and networks, an alternative to books and college classes is a specialty seminar. Whatever options you use to enhance your knowledge are up to you; if you have a limited amount of available time a short seminar is an excellent way to acquire knowledge quickly.

Annual conventions, such as Softcon and Comdex, are showcases on new products that are about to reach the commercial market. Some conventions have miniconferences that feature sessions on software marketing, new technologies, and other topics of interest to attendees.

Users' Groups

Groups of people who use common hardware and software are an excellent means to meet with the programmers of specific machines and pick up useful hints to enhance your knowledge. It is also a good way to establish your reputation as a knowledgeable consultant who is willing to work with less experienced users.

Most cities have users' groups for popular computers (IBM, Apple, Kaypro); some organizations emphasize certain applications (for example, Accounting Users of IBM PC's). Many Saturday or Sunday newspapers list active groups, meeting times and locations, and a person to contact for information.

Professional Organizations

Many cities have active chapters of the Association for Computing Machinery (ACM), Data Processing Management Association (DPMA), or similar professional organizations. You may want to join one of these groups, both for the information you can obtain and the professional contacts.

Vendor Mailing Lists

Finally, the more vendor mailing lists you can get on, the more current product information you can obtain. Most hardware and software vendors are more than happy to send consultants new product information and other mailings.

If you specialize in real estate application, for example, you should contact software vendors who market property management, investment analysis, and other systems for information regarding current products and any future software.

Summary

Keeping yourself up to date with developments, techniques, and products in the computer industry is a time-consuming task. Never make the mistake of assuming you know everything necessary to operate successfully for the rest of your career. Periodicals, books, and on-going education play an important role in helping you to maintain your knowledge base and make your business grow. While time dedicated to keeping your information current is not a revenue producer, it is still critical to the continued success of your consulting career.

End Notes

1. Bernard Kamoroff, *Small-Time Operator*, Bell Springs Publishing, Layfonville, Calif., 1982.
2. Donald M. Dible, *Up Your Own Organization: A Handbook to Start and Finance a New Business*, Reston, Reston, Va., 1981.
3. Robert E. Kelley, *Consulting: The Complete Guide to a Profitable Career*, Scribner's, New York, 1981.
4. Herman Holtz, *How to Succeed as an Independent Consultant*, Wiley, New York, 1983.
5. J. Fred Weston and Eugene F. Brigham, *Managerial Finance*, Dryden Press, Hinsdale, Ill., 1981.
6. Lawrence J. Gitman, *Principles of Managerial Finance*, Harper & Row, New York, 1982.
7. Herbert Spiro, *Finance for the Nonfinancial Manager*, Wiley, New York, 1982.
8. W. Murray Bradford and Ronald V. Reed, *Business Tax Deduction Master Guide*, Prentice-Hall, Englewood Cliffs, N.J., 1982.

CHAPTER 15

Expanding Your Consulting Business

So far we've dealt with how to establish a consulting practice, as well as how to manage its operations. In this chapter we'll discuss some of the topics of concern when you are expanding your business. We'll look at factors in partnerships and small business corporations (both briefly dealt with in Chapter 3), additional financing for your firm, expanding your business office space, and personnel issues.

Partnerships

As was mentioned previously a partnership has basically the same structure as a sole proprietorship, except that more than one person is involved in the business. Each partner is legally and financially liable for obligations of the firm. Additionally, each member is liable for the actions of any other partner *when that partner acts on behalf of the partnership.* If Bernie Jordan forms a partnership with two other consultants and one of them contracts to buy a VAX 11/780 for the business, all partners assume financial responsibility for payment.

A partnership must file IRS Form SS-4, "Employer's Federal Identification Number," in order to establish a record of existence with the IRS (see Figure 15-1). Additionally, the partnership files an income tax return, Form 1065. However, the partnership itself does not pay any taxes. The firm's income or loss is allocated to the individual partners via Form 1065, Schedule K, and they forward this amount to their respective 1040s (Schedule E).

How is the income or loss allocated? Each partnership should draw up a *partnership agreement* that states what percentage of income or losses are allocated to each member. Partners may decide upon (1) equal allocations or (2) allotments in proportion to ownership of the firm (assuming all partners do not own an equal share). Whichever method is chosen should be specified in the agreement.

Additionally, each partnership agreement should specify:

1. Mutually agreed-upon business goals
2. Respective contributions of cash, property, and labor
3. Procedures for withdrawal of funds and profit distribution
4. Business continuation if a partner dies or wants to get out of the firm
5. Respective legal and financial powers

The last clause helps protect against the situation Bernie Jordan faced a few paragraphs ago. If a spending limit of, for example, $500 is set

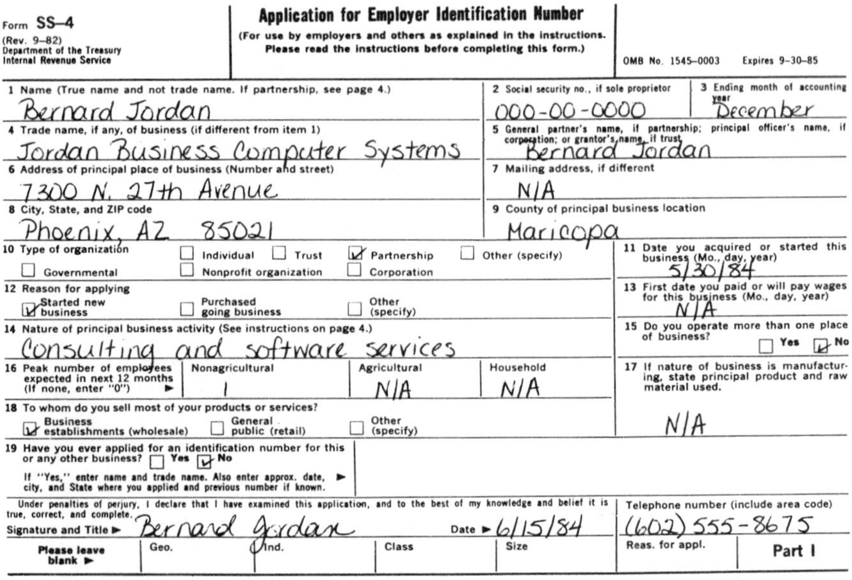

Form SS-4
(Rev. 9-82)
Department of the Treasury
Internal Revenue Service

Application for Employer Identification Number
(For use by employers and others as explained in the instructions.
Please read the instructions before completing this form.)

OMB No. 1545-0003 Expires 9-30-85

1 Name (True name and not trade name. If partnership, see page 4.) Bernard Jordan
2 Social security no., if sole proprietor 000-00-0000
3 Ending month of accounting year December
4 Trade name, if any, of business (if different from item 1) Jordan Business Computer Systems
5 General partner's name, if partnership; principal officer's name, if corporation; or grantor's name, if trust Bernard Jordan
6 Address of principal place of business (Number and street) 7300 N. 27th Avenue
7 Mailing address, if different N/A
8 City, State, and ZIP code Phoenix, AZ 85021
9 County of principal business location Maricopa
10 Type of organization ☐ Individual ☐ Trust ☑ Partnership ☐ Other (specify) ☐ Governmental ☐ Nonprofit organization ☐ Corporation
11 Date you acquired or started this business (Mo., day, year) 5/30/84
12 Reason for applying ☑ Started new business ☐ Purchased going business ☐ Other (specify)
13 First date you paid or will pay wages for this business (Mo., day, year) N/A
14 Nature of principal business activity (See instructions on page 4.) Consulting and software services
15 Do you operate more than one place of business? ☐ Yes ☑ No
16 Peak number of employees expected in next 12 months (If none, enter "0") Nonagricultural 1 Agricultural N/A Household N/A
17 If nature of business is manufacturing, state principal product and raw material used. N/A
18 To whom do you sell most of your products or services? ☑ Business establishments (wholesale) ☐ General public (retail) ☐ Other (specify)
19 Have you ever applied for an identification number for this or any other business? ☐ Yes ☑ No
If "Yes," enter name and trade name. Also enter approx. date, city, and State where you applied and previous number if known.

Under penalties of perjury, I declare that I have examined this application, and to the best of my knowledge and belief it is true, correct, and complete.
Signature and Title Bernard Jordan Date 6/15/84
Telephone number (include area code) (602) 555-8675

Please leave blank Geo. Ind. Class Size Reas. for appl. Part I

Figure 15-1 IRS Form SS-4-

for purchases without majority consent, the other partners may be able to avoid personal financial obligation.

You should be aware that a business partnership among friends and/ or relatives may put great strain on personal relationships. Even the best of friends may have radically different views of how to manage a company.

It is also a good idea to choose partners that complement your own strengths and weaknesses. A top-notch programmer with little business background could probably benefit from the experience of a business information systems graduate, and vice versa.

Any partnership arrangements should be researched thoroughly, and, if necessary, your accountant and your attorney should be consulted. The legal and financial requirements of a partnership are more complex than those of a sole proprietorship, and you should be aware of the consequences of any actions.

Corporations

The primary benefit a corporation offers its owners is limited legal and financial liability. Debts of the corporation cannot be allocated to an owner's personal assets, barring agreements such as pledging one's personal assets against a corporate loan or state-mandated liabilities. It is strongly suggested by small business experts that you check with your attorney for the liability situations of your particular case. In some situations, a corporation's owners can be held responsible for claims against their corporation.

Most likely, if you choose to incorporate, you will become a small business corporation, or subchapter S corporation. Only a firm with 25 or fewer owners (or stockholders) can qualify as a subchapter S corporation.

The two primary advantages a subchapter S corporation has over an ordinary corporation are (1) elimination of double taxation, or the taxation of corporate profits as *both* corporate income and dividends to the owners on their individual tax returns (a corporation, like a partnership, files a separate tax return, but since it is a separate financial entity from its owners, it *does* pay taxes), and (2) the ability to carry losses back against the previous year's business income *or* personal income (if the corporation didn't exist during the previous year).

IRS Publication 589, *Tax Information on Subchapter S Corporations,* lists federal requirements and conditions for this business form. You *must* be aware of the various filing requirements, as stringent tax penalties can result from noncompliance.

Also check with your particular state corporation commission for applicable laws and regulations. Most states allow one person to form a corporation, while others require two or more people. Additionally, you must hold regular meetings with written minutes, elect directors, and have the directors appoint officers.

Usually, you must prepare your Articles of Incorporation, which states your chosen business name, business purpose, names and addresses of owners, office location, and type and amount of stock, among other requirements. Some states also require additional documents or information. Again, check with your corporation commission. More importantly, consult your attorney and discuss the potential financial benefits with your accountant.

Adding to Your Personnel Resources

In Chapter 13 we discussed strategies in employee compensation as a function of your business management. Let's take a step back and decide when it is appropriate (or necessary) to add personnel and, more importantly, in what manner.

As a general guideline, it is time to seek assistance when you find it difficult or impossible to accomplish all that you need to do. This includes both operational tasks (developing commercial software, meeting with clients, conducting seminars, etc.) and business functions (such as bookkeeping, correspondence, and writing reports).

Many people initially feel some resistance to the thought of paying someone else to do what they have done in the past. They may reason, "Why pay a bookkeeper $40 per week when I could devote an extra evening and Saturday afternoon to this task and do it myself?"

There is no actual cast-in-iron rule to cover this decision, but a cost-benefit analysis may provide some guidance. If you can earn $35 per hour consulting for, let's say, each of the 8 hours per week it currently takes to manage your firm's books, it makes sense to hire someone at (for example) $5 per hour to perform this function, freeing you for more profitable ventures. Each hour you can allocate to someone else provides you with a net cash inflow of $30 ($35 − $5).

The key here is regularity of additional income. You may not be able to obtain 8 additional hours of work each week, but if you can regularly gain additional clients (say, at an average of 6 incremental hours per week), you still come out ahead.

The same principle is true of your operational help. If you're currently involved with several projects and a new opportunity presents itself, you could attempt to handle that contract as well. Suppose, though, you are currently working 60 hours per week on existing obligations and, at the risk of your health and sanity, can't effectively conduct the consulting as you should. It makes sense to allocate the job to someone else, pay them $15 per hour from the $35 collected, and you retain the rest.

If you decide, either for reasons of additional opportunities or relieving yourself of certain tasks, to use the services of others, you must decide on what basis the person or people will operate. I strongly encourage that rather than actually hiring employees, either full- or part-time, you *subcontract* work, especially as you just begin to work with others. This is in line with our principle of starting slow and effectively managing growth; just as you shouldn't rush off and lease an office in the first days of your business, neither should you go overboard and hire a programmer, bookkeeper, and secretary the minute you feel your practice is going well. There are three primary reasons for not doing so:

1. Subcontractors can be treated as temporary and sporadic help; if you are particularly busy only at certain times (and not at regular intervals), you can use their help when you need it and not have to worry about keeping someone on the payroll during slow times.

2. You could initially hire people as temporary part-time employees, although there are several problems with this. Most people who seek *employment* rather than subcontract work desire some form of regularity. They may not mind working 30 hours during 1 week and 10 hours the next, but would balk at going 3 to 4 weeks between paychecks when your business is going slowly.

Additionally, all employees, whether full- or part-time, permanent or temporary, require as much as 30 percent cost overhead in the form of benefits, employer's FICA contributions, worker's compensation insurance, unemployment taxes, and other employment expenses. This is to say nothing of the additional paperwork: tax withholding, year-end tax statements (W-2s), and other federal and state requirements. At that rate, you would probably have to hire one additional employee to keep the records of your other employees!

Subcontractors, however, are outside entities. Just as you are not an employee of your clients and therefore manage your own tax withholding, social security payments, and benefits, your subcontractors will also handle these functions for themselves. You merely pay them an agreed-upon amount for services, and you are relieved of these responsibilities.

3. You have some protection in the case of nonperformance or inadequate services. When you sign a contract with a client, it is stated that you will deliver products X, Y, and Z by a given date or you won't be paid (or some other punitive action). A similar relationship should exist with your subcontractors; if they fail to deliver a program by the specified date or misrepresent their capabilities and expertise, you can withhold payment or take some other punitive measure. About all you can do with an employee is fire him or her; you're still liable to pay for work actually done (for example, by number of hours actually worked if an hourly rate was used), regardless of the product's quality.

Note that in the last example, even though you may have protection against incompetent subcontracted work, you still have ultimate responsibility for the project with your client. If you contract with a programmer to produce an inventory management program that doesn't work, your client-consultant contract may still preclude payment. All your client cares about is that you promised to deliver something and failed. Similarly, an administrative assistant who periodically handles your paperwork may forget to mail a federal tax form or submit a proposal. You still lose!

You *must* choose your subcontractors with care. Their actions (or failures) reflect on you and your firm. Again, most clients don't care that your subcontractor didn't produce as expected. You are a businessperson, and that reflects very unfavorably on your ability to manage people and projects.

How do you differentiate a subcontractor from a part-time, temporary employee? The distinguishing characteristic of any employee is employer control of actions—even if flexible hours or other "noncontrol" measures are used. As long as you can say, "Do tasks X, Y, and Z" and provide the tools to perform these tasks, you are an employer.

Alternatively, if you contract with an independent, self-employed programmer for delivery of an inventory management program to be designed, coded, and debugged on his or her own system at his or her own schedule (even if a final delivery date has been specified), you have a contractor-subcontractor relationship.

Admittedly, there is a fine line here between an employee and a subcontractor. When in doubt, consult your attorney for clarification of any working relationships.

Financing Your Growth

Just as most Little Leaguers dream of hitting the game-winning grand slam to win the play-offs, most businesspeople dream of having enough internal cash flow to finance their company's growth. Then, except for an occasional short-term loan from the local bank, they would not have to face dilution of ownership or exorbitant interest charges.

In practice, though, most businesses do require additional capital from at least one source to achieve desired growth. The trick is to determine when and what type of financing is needed.

The cash flow budget introduced in Chapter 4 provides the key to the first item. In addition to monthly cash flow forecasts, your operational plans for the upcoming year can be combined with your strategic plans (updated business plan) to estimate cash flows for the next several years. If you plan to introduce a series of national seminars 2 years from now, you need to calculate what advertising and development costs are necessary; more importantly, you also must determine *when* these expenditures will occur. If you foresee a cash flow problem a year and a half down the road, financing may be necessary.

The method of financing can be chosen from among many alternatives. Two recent books, *Financing the Growing Business*[1] and *Up Front Financing*,[2] deal with the many financing choices available to the entrepreneur. Your choice will be influenced by your business life cycle stage, your willingness to surrender partial ownership of your company, and many environmental factors. Interest rate levels affect the desirability of debt financing, while a weak overall stock market would depress the amount of capital the sale of stock would raise.

Financing can be roughly divided into two major categories: debt and equity. Debt obligations (such as bank loans or long-term bonds) are repaid with interest to the lender over a stated period of time. While you may be required to pledge business or personal assets as collateral for some debt instruments, no partial company ownership is passed to the financier as part of the agreement.

Equity, or ownership, financing carries no fixed repayment schedules since the funding is not a loan but an investment. In exchange for the capital the investors receive partial ownership of the firm (and thus, the same rights to future profits that you have, accompanied by a proportional voice in company strategies and operations).

Some financing methods are a hybrid of debt and equity, such as convertible loans. These are treated as normal debt instruments with provisions to convert the loan into a stated ownership at a certain date and possibly under certain conditions.

Finally, some fund sources, such as grants, are tax shelter fundraising and don't fall neatly into either the debt or equity category. A grant, for example, involves neither ownership dilution nor repayment; the money is given for a specific purpose.

Let's take a look at some of the many methods of financing, with their relative strengths and weaknesses:

1. ***Bank loans:*** Probably the most common source of financing for the small expanding business is a commercial bank loan. This financing can take the form of a line of credit (the right to borrow a stated amount from the bank and pay the money back in installments), loans secured with business or personal assets, or Small Business Administration guaranteed or participating loans (we'll discuss them shortly).

Many banks will require covenants, or pledged agreements to do some things and not do others, to qualify the company. These may be the maintenance of financial ratios (Chapter 4) at certain levels or a minimum amount of working capital. Loans will usually be several percentage points above the prime rate, so periods of historically high interest rates make these loans (like most new debt) expensive and relatively unattractive to the borrower.

You should speak to the bank's loan officer and determine any rules and procedures they have. After meeting with several banks, you should pick the one that you feel most comfortable with (assuming, of course, they'll lend you money) and the best terms.

2. *Small Business Association aid:* The SBA administers two types of financial aid to small businesses: SBA loans (various types) and Small Business Investment Companies (SBICs).

The SBA loan program can take several forms:

a. SBA direct loans.
b. SBA participation loans: part of the funding comes from the SBA, the rest from a commercial bank.
c. SBA guaranteed loans: the SBA guarantees 90 percent of a commercial bank's or other lender's loan.

The SBA-guaranteed loans allow a commercial bank, for example, to make loans in situations that are otherwise too risky if it had the entire loan amount at stake (i.e., the borrower doesn't have any positive earnings or cash flow yet).

There are very stringent requirements to qualify for any SBA loan. A company can't exceed certain industry-specific amounts of earnings and net worth or be a dominant force in its industry. Additionally, SBA loans are unattainable if the needed funding is available elsewhere at a reasonable price.

You must also make personal guarantees to the SBA for the borrowed amount as well as follow covenants as to what the money can be used for. Finally, the application process is long and complicated.

SBICs, on the other hand, are SBA-licensed companies that invest a combination of their owners', investors', and SBA money in small businesses. The funding may take the form of convertible debt, straight debt, or, in some cases, straight stock.

SBICs tend to require current income from their investments, as opposed to other sources willing to wait several years for earnings and positive cash flow. They also include covenants, both positive and negative (such as monthly submittal of financial statements, maintenance of adequate insurance, and some control over subsequent financing and salaries).

MESBICs, or Minority Enterprise Small Business Investment Companies, operate quite similarly to SBICs; "minorities" are currently defined as anyone deprived of economic advantages for a variety of reasons (age, sex, nationality, etc.).

3. *Venture capital:* In recent years newspapers and magazines have been filled with the stories of Apple Computer, Genentech, Tandem Computers, and other companies that grew to huge proportions on the strength of venture capital. The venture capital industry itself has grown remarkably since the early 1970s, with many new funds providing capital to entrepreneurs.

A venture capital fund invests funds of private investors in beginning and growing businesses, usually over a 10-year time frame. The investment ownerships are normally divided 80–20 between the investors and the fund managers, respectively.

As with most other forms of financing, your business plan plays an important role in interesting prospective investors in your business. You should send your plan to at least 20 venture capital funds, and, since many have different investment criteria, research which funds invest in computer-related firms. Chapter 6 discussed several additional rules for business plan submission.

In exchange for the investment capital, you will give up a percentage of your ownership in your firm. What percentage you surrender is a factor of current and projected demand for your business services, the development stage your business and services are in, and current economic conditions, among others. The closer you are to having a marketable product or service when you seek capital, the more likely a venture capital firm will accept a lower ownership percentage owing to their decreased risk.

In addition to private venture capital funds, many large corporations looking for future subsidiaries, new technologies, and parking places for excess cash provide capital to small businesses.

4. *Business development corporations:* Owned by investors, financial institutions, or large corporations, business development corporations (BDCs) make loans to small businesses. The goal of BDCs is to create jobs within their respective states. Currently, over one-half of the states have BDCs, many of which are also SBA lenders or operators of SBICs.

Even states without a formal BDC program have industrial development agencies (IDAs), which also have a goal of creating jobs within their states. They should be consulted if your proposed venture will be creating jobs.

5. *Joint ventures:* We've discussed several types of joint ventures previously: joint seminars with retailers or seminar companies, for example. You may also use joint ventures as a form of permanent financing for business expansion.

Suppose a retail computer store conducts classes and seminars for local customers which concentrate primarily on teaching the use of spreadsheet, database, and word processing software. You also conduct local seminars, dealing primarily with industry-specific end users (realtors and accountants, for example). You may have conducted several joint seminars in the past.

Both of you want to expand your businesses into a neighboring state. You may form a joint venture to conduct regularly scheduled seminars in that state: they will provide capital for advertising, room rental, etc., while you provide the personnel and training expertise. Not much different from local joint seminars, except now you are not contracting for individual offerings, but a long-term partnership.

Another example might be that you develop software to market commercially. Rather than approach a software publisher, the local retailer may have excess capital to invest in your software in exchange for a percentage of revenues. Or, if you develop a real estate package, the local board of realtors or a real estate agency may be interested in a joint commercial effort.

6. *Additional methods:* There are several other financing means, such as forming a limited partnership, taking out loans on your life insurance, and obtaining government grants. The keys to all forms of financing we've discussed, and those we haven't, are applicability, flexibility, and persistence. You must look for the appropriate form of financing given your business and product situation, be flexible among different types of financing and different sources of each type (several banks or venture capital firms, for example), and be persistent in your pursuit of that capital.

Expanding Office Space

Back in Chapter 3 I mentioned that many consultants either work from their homes or rent desk space in a small office. As you begin to take on partners, hire employees, and seek expansion capital, the idea of a centralized office location becomes more attractive.

What should you look for in office space? First, you need room for current *and projected* personnel and equipment. A three-partner firm with two other employees would probably need three individual offices (one for each partner), a work area with desk space for the employees (if one is a receptionist, that may be in a small lobby), and a conference room for group meetings. Naturally, different firms may have different needs (two partners may share one office, for example).

If you expect to hire several new employees, plan for their office space also. If they will be across town in a large city (or in a different metropolitan area), you may rent desk space or a small office for them in an area other than your main office. If they will be based in your main business location, be sure you have enough room for them or that additional space is easily obtainable.

You should choose several alternative locations, comparing each according to lease terms, proximity to employees' homes, applicable building codes (if you are building a new structure), respective property tax rates, and transportation routes, among other factors. If you are contemplating moving your entire business location to another city or state, check cost-of-living figures, housing availability, various tax rates, and general living quality.

An alternative to being stuck with a need for additional office space and not having adjacent or nearby vacancy is to initially lease an extra office and sublet it until needed. This way, you can place new employees nearby when they are hired and not out in Siberia.

Finally, negotiate your lease terms before signing. Not every landlord is willing to adjust terms, but some may, especially if you are already an established company with a good reputation.

Summary

Many consultants will not get past the one-person practice they initially establish, and there is nothing wrong with that; they may earn very comfortable livings from their solo earnings.

In the computer industry, opportunities abound for those with foresight, imagination, and perseverence. If you should discover a niche you feel you can exploit and turn your company into the next IBM or Apple Computer, this chapter provides some basic guidelines to start your expansion.

You don't want to expand too quickly; what is manageable growth for one person or company may result in the downfall of another. You must have the confidence and ability to manage your growth. If you seek investment capital but have never managed a growing company before, your investors may insist on supplying you with a chief executive officer (CEO) and other key employees who have had the experience of taking a product from the idea stage to a finished, marketable item. Every person's situation is different; if these executives could do a much better job at managing certain aspects of your business than you can, by all means consider this alternative.

Even if you retain ownership and managerial control over your company, the "you do everything" guidelines from early in the book no longer exist. It is sometimes difficult to delegate to someone else tasks you previously performed, but unless you want to work 35 hours per day (quite difficult to do, I hear), your executives and employees earn their money by performing many tedious or complicated tasks. Remember that marketing a small one-person consulting firm with a $1000 annual advertising budget is quite different from the same function done for a corporation with $1 million allocated for advertising. Let the experts work for you while you enjoy the rewards of ownership and strategic management rather than day-to-day tasks.

Well, it's time to look at Bernie Jordan's expansion plans. Suddenly deluged by contract programming requests from attorneys who heard of his expertise, Bernie spoke with Sandra Canterman, a recent computer science graduate, about subcontract programming work. After several projects, Bernie was so impressed by Sandra's work that he asked her about joining his consulting firm as a junior partner. Her recent computer science background proved to be very useful to Bernie on several projects in terms of new system design methodologies and other technical knowledge; Sandra had earned a minor in electrical engineering and knew far more about computer hardware than Bernie ever cared to learn.

They drafted a partnership agreement, stating that Sandra would receive 40 percent of total revenues. Bernie would handle all administrative tasks as well as some projects, while Sandra would concentrate on contract programming and commercial software development. The firm's business plan was revised to reflect the current organizational structure as well as the possibility of other future associates and possible incorporation.

While the firm consisted only of two partners, Bernie and Sandra saw no need for moving into an office; they could continue to work from their respective residences. The business plan stated, though, that two more partners were projected for 2 years from now, so Bernie began casually searching for office space, determining appropriate locations and lease prices that were within projected budget.

Bernie's updated business plan illustrated projected cash flow by quarter for the next 3 years, in accordance with projected demand for services and future plans. Because cash flow was sufficient he saw no need for additional financing until a planned major expansion 3 to 5 years from now; at that time, he would investigate the possibilities and alternatives of venture capital investment, debt financing, or other capital sources.

End Notes

1. Thomas J. Martin, *Financing the Growing Business,* Holt, New York, 1980.
2. A. David Silver, *Up Front Financing,* Ronald, New York, 1982.

CHAPTER 16

The Future

Well, you've done it. You've succeeded as an independent computer consultant. Your business skills have enabled you to take a business from the idea stage to a successful consulting operation. Now what?

Why do I ask? Because you have other options available aside from maintaining your business exactly as it is right now. You could continue your practice as a small proprietorship, partnership, or corporation, of course; you could also merge with another consulting firm, sell your practice, or become a software publisher. You could change your target markets or your areas of specialization.

We'll briefly discuss these available options in this final chapter, looking at some of the choices you could make to make your business (and wealth!) grow even more.

The Future of Your Business

We already mentioned that you could simply do nothing—that is, maintain your independence as a local or regional consulting firm specializing in marketing and developing microcomputer-based information systems.

You could, however, expand your operations by merging with another consulting firm. Your partner firm can either be one that is locally operated or one from another geographical area.

Ideally, your partner firm should provide some sort of synergy but be different from yours. For instance, if you specialize in microcomputer real estate applications, a partner who concentrates on defense-related space computer systems may not be the best choice. If you work with accounting systems, however, another firm that deals with other business systems may provide some synergy of operation.

An alternative to merging is to sell your business to another party. You could make an outright sale, of course, divorcing yourself from all aspects of your practice. However, you could sell your firm to a large business (either in the consulting profession or not) and stay on as director of consulting operations or some similar post. Your formerly independent company would then become a consulting-operations arm of a larger organization.

If your product and service mix has drifted primarily toward commercial software development, you may want to investigate entering software publishing full-time, especially if you have self-published some of your programs. Other programmers could submit ideas and finished products to you, and you'll then decide which programs to market. Ideally, you should identify some sort of market niche to exploit rather than be a catch-all for any type of software. You need to concentrate your efforts and resources to effectively reach your market (same old marketing lessons!).

Future Areas of Specialization

You don't have to merge or sell your business to give your practice a facelift. Something as simple as changing target markets for your current product and service line can provide new opportunities. The same seminars, custom software, and consulting could be redirected—for example, away from real estate professionals toward physicians. Naturally, you need to know your new specialty as well as your old one. Alternatively, you may switch your marketing efforts from small businesses to Fortune 500 companies or government agencies.

You could also change the emphasis of your consulting practice. One area of specialization is to provide industry analysis and reports as your primary product. Consulting firms such as The Gartner Group, which produces many of the computer-related special-advertising supplements for *Forbes* and *Business Week,* concentrate on analyzing industry trends and supplying this information to their customers.

Whether you keep your current line of services or expand into industry analysis (or other specialties), you can narrow your services down to a small area of emphasis. Some of these include:

1. *Office automation:* You may specialize in integrating word processing, electronic mail, teleconferencing, facsimile transmission, and other technologies into the "Office of the 1980s" for medium- to large-sized firms.

2. *Communications:* One of the most dynamic areas of the computer industry is communications, both through local networks and long-distance systems. A strong subspecialty in local networks for office technology is likely to be a valuable asset.

3. *Videotext:* Debate exists over the role videotext will play in the automated home of the future. Some analysts predict most homes will be wired for electronic banking, shopping from home, and information retrieval. Others insist that the cost of these technologically feasible systems must come down dramatically before there will be widespread public acceptance. Owing to the various system configurations being proposed, the videotext market offers potential for new products or even in-depth industry analysis.

4. *Government software:* Local, state, and federal government agencies make widespread use of consulting and software services. If you worked for the Air Force on space surveillance computer systems before entering the consulting profession, a massive update of these systems would provide opportunities for contracting agencies to develop specifications, software, and complete systems for the Air Force. Be cautioned, though: government agencies, especially federal ones, have very stringent

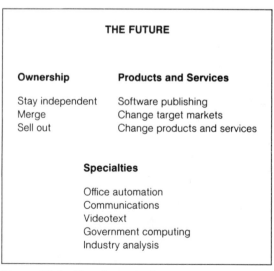

Figure 16-1 Your future options.

contracting requirements. Herman Holtz's book on consulting (Chapter 14) discusses the intricacies of governmental contracting.

Summary

The major emphasis of this chapter is to point out some of the many options available to you in regards to your consulting firm. A brief summary is shown in Figure 16-1. You can continue to own your practice in its present form, attempt to merge with another company, or sell out to another organization. You can also maintain your present target markets or switch to new ones.

Whatever avenues you choose to follow—whether you maintain your practice part-time or embark on a full-time career—keep your goals in mind and have the self-confidence and desire to succeed in your business. And best of luck with your venture!

Index